Prayer Prophetic Verses in the Bible:

From Genesis to Revelation

By Dr. Odion Ojo

Prayer and Prophetic Verses in the Bible:
From Genesis to Revelation

Trilogy Christian Publishers A Wholly Owned Subsidiary of Trinity Broadcasting Network

2442 Michelle Drive Tustin, CA 92780

Rights Department, 2442 Michelle Drive, Tustin, CA 92780.

Trilogy Christian Publishing/TBN and colophon are trademarks of Trinity Broadcasting Network.

Manufactured in the United States of America

10 9 8 7 6 5 4 3 2 1

Library of Congress Cataloging-in-Publication Data is available.

ISBN: 978-1-63769-634-7

E-ISBN: 978-1-63769-635-4

DEDICATION

All Scripture quotations in this project are taken from The Holy Bible, King James Version.

This book is written for the benefit of Christians or anybody for that matter that wants to know how to pray and find prayers and prophetic messages in the Bible easily.

This book is dedicated to my wife, my Soulmate Dr. Bose I. Ojo MD, DC; My four wonderful children and five grandchildren, plus the others on the way. I want to thank my brothers in Christ, Pastor Solomon Akharamen, Pastor Samuel Adeyemi, Brother Ben Akhuemokhan, Evangelist Emeka Muorah, and my spiritual son, Evangelist Nwanchuk-wu Anazodo. Chuck, thanks for being a great son. Thanks for your encouragement and prayers. To Pastor Steve Banning of Braeswood Assembly of GOD, Houston, Texas, my home church.

ACKNOWLEDGEMENTS

I want to acknowledge the Holy Spirit for what HE did by prompting me to start this project. I have read the Holy Bible about five to six times, from Genesis to Revelation, over the years. Each verse that I read, maybe a year or so ago, gives me a deeper meaning another time. Each time you read the Bible, you always get a deeper and different meaning, according to how and what the Holy Spirit wants to tell you. I say the Bible bleeds, and it is alive. With technology and the Bible app, which I didn't like to use initially because I was not comfortable or used to reading without a marker or pen in my hand, I had issues. I then found out that I could use different colors to mark the Bible in the app. Thanks to the Holy Spirit because I was getting exasperated. I continued to read it as usual. Then the Holy Spirit directed me to start all over again in the app because I was already marking promises, prophecies, prayers, and commandment verses in the Bible. I did not know where He was leading me at that time. So I had to go back from Genesis to make sure I marked which was a prayer or a prophecy verse with different colors. I will not forget how He woke me up in the middle of the night one time. I had stopped the writing/ marking for some time, even though I still read my regular paper Bible. That was the day I finally knew this is a project that God wanted me to do.

As you go through this Book, I pray the Holy Spirit will connect you to the throne of Grace in Jesus' name.

TABLE OF CONTENTS

Prayer and Prophetic Verses in the Bible

Table of Contents

Prayer and Prophetic Verses in the Bible

NON-PRAYER BOOKS

For a start, there are 214 (170 in OT and 44 in NT) prayer verses in the Bible from Genesis to the Book of Revelation, a total of 30 books. At the same time, there are 36 books that don't have prayer verses in them. The books that don't have prayers in them are:

Leviticus

Ruth

Esther

Proverbs

Ecclesiastes

Song of Solomon

Hosea

Joel

Obadiah

Micah

Nahum

Zephaniah

Haggai

Zechariah

Malachi

Romans

First Corinthians

Second Corinthians

Galatians

Ephesians

Philippians

Colossians

First Thessalonians

Second Thessalonians

First Timothy

Second Timothy

Titus

Philemon

Hebrews

James

First Peter

Second Peter

First John

Second John

Third John

Jude

PRAYERS IN GENESIS 6

1. Abraham for an heir (Genesis 15:2-3)

*[2] And Abram said, Lord GOD, what wilt thou
give me, seeing I go childless, and the steward of
my house is this Eliezer of Damascus? [3] And
Abram said, Behold, to me thou hast given no
seed: and, lo, one born in my house is mine heir.*

2. Abraham for Ishmael to be his heir (Genesis 17: 17-18)

*[17] Then Abraham fell upon his face, and
laughed, and said in his heart, Shall a child be
born unto him that is an hundred years old? and
shall Sarah, that is ninety years old, bear? [18]
And Abraham said unto God, O that Ishmael
might live before thee!*

3. Abraham for Sodom to be spared if ten persons were
righteous (Genesis 18:23-32)

*[23] And Abraham drew near, and said, Wilt
thou also destroy the righteous with the wicked?
[24] Peradventure there be fifty righteous within the city: wilt thou also destroy and not spare
the place for the fifty righteous that are therein?
[25] That be far from thee to do after this manner, to slay the righteous with the wicked: and
that the righteous should be as the wicked, that
be far from thee: Shall not the Judge of all the*

earth do right? [26] And the Lord said, If I find in Sodom fifty righteous within the city, then I will spare all the place for their sakes. [27] And Abraham answered and said, Behold now, I have taken upon me to speak unto the Lord, which am but dust and ashes: [28] Peradventure there shall lack five of the fifty righteous: wilt thou destroy all the city for lack of five? And he said, If I find there forty and five, I will not destroy it. [29] And he spake unto him yet again, and said, Peradventure there shall be forty found there. And he said, I will not do it for forty' sake . [30] And he said unto him, Oh let not the Lord be angry, and I will speak: Peradventure there shall thirty be found there. And he said, I will not do it, if I find thirty there. [31] And he said, Behold now, I have taken upon me to speak unto the Lord: Peradventure there shall be twenty found there. And he said, I will not destroy it for twenty's sake. [32] And he said, Oh let not the Lord be angry, and I will speak yet but this once: Peradventure ten shall be found there. And he said, I will not destroy it for ten's sake.

4. Eliezer, steward of Abraham, for a bride for Isaac (Genesis 24:12-14)

[12] And he said, O LORD God of my master Abraham, I pray thee, send me good speed this day, and shew kindness unto my master Abra-

ham. [13] Behold, I stand here by the well of water; and the daughters of the men of the city come out to draw water: [14] And let it come to pass, that the damsel to whom I shall say, Let down thy pitcher, I pray thee, that I may drink; and she shall say, Drink, and I will give thy camels drink also: let the same be she that thou hast appointed for thy servant Isaac; and thereby shall I know that thou hast shewed kindness unto my master.

5. Jacob for a blessing (Genesis 28:20-22)

[20] And Jacob vowed a vow, saying, If God will be with me, and will keep me in this way that I go, and will give me bread to eat, and raiment to put on, [21] So that I come again to my father's house in peace; then shall the LORD be my God: [22] And this stone, which I have set for a pillar, shall be God's house: and of all that thou shalt give me I will surely give the tenth unto thee.

6. Jacob for deliverance from Esau (Genesis 32:9-12)

[9] And Jacob said, O God of my father Abraham, and God of my father Isaac, the LORD which saidst unto me, Return unto thy country, and to thy kindred, and I will deal well with thee: [10] I am not worthy of the least of all the mercies, and of all the truth, which thou hast shewed unto thy servant; for with my staff I

passed over this Jordan; and now I am become two bands. [11] Deliver me, I pray thee, from the hand of my brother, from the hand of Esau: for I fear him, lest he will come and smite me, and the mother with the children. [12] And thou saidst, I will surely do thee good, and make thy seed as the sand of the sea, which cannot be numbered for multitude.

PRAYERS IN EXODUS:5

1. Moses for Aaron, his older brother, to go with him (Exodus 4:-13)

> *[13] And he said, O my Lord, send, I pray thee,*
> *by the hand of him whom thou wilt send.*

2. Moses in complaint to JEHOVAH for not delivering the Israelites (Exodus 5:22-23)

> [22] *And Moses returned unto the Lord, and*
> *said, Lord, wherefore hast thou so evil entreated*
> *this people? why is it that thou hast sent me?*
> *[23] For since I came to Pharaoh to speak in thy*
> *name, he hath done evil to this people; neither*
> *hast thou delivered thy people at all.*

3. Moses for forgiveness for the Israelites (Exodus *32:31-32)*

> *[31] And Moses returned unto the LORD, and*
> *said, Oh, this people have sinned a great sin,*
> *and have made them gods of gold. [32] Yet now,*
> *if thou wilt forgive their sin; and if not, blot me, I*
> *pray thee, out of thy book which thou hast writ-*
> *ten.*

4. **Moses f**or JEHOVAH's presence to go with the Israelites to the land of Canaan (Exodus 33:12-13)

[12] And Moses said unto the Lord, See, thou sayest unto me, Bring up this people: and thou hast not let me know whom thou wilt send with me. Yet thou hast said, I know thee by name, and thou hast also found grace in my sight. [13] Now therefore, I pray thee, if I have found grace in thy sight, shew me now thy way, that I may know thee, that I may find grace in thy sight: and consider that this nation is thy people.

Exodus 33:15-16:

[15] And he said unto him, If thy presence go not with me, carry us not up hence. [16] For wherein shall it be known here that I and thy people have found grace in thy sight? is it not in that thou goest with us? so shall we be separated, I and thy people, from all the people that are upon the face of the earth.

5. Moses for wanting to see JEHOVAH (Exodus 33:18)

And he said, I beseech thee, shew me thy glory.

PRAYERS IN NUMBERS: 9

1. Aaron for the blessing of JEHOVAH upon the people (Numbers 6:24-26)

> [24] *The Lord bless thee, and keep thee: [25] The Lord make his face shine upon thee, and be gracious unto thee: [26] The LORD lift up his countenance upon thee, and give thee peace.*

2. Moses for JEHOVAH to bless on the journey (Numbers 10:35-36)

> [35] *And it came to pass, when the ark set forward, that Moses said, Rise up, Lord, and let thine enemies be scattered; and let them that hate thee flee before thee. [36] And when it rested, he said, Return, O LORD, unto the many thousands of Israel.*

3. Moses complaining to JEHOVAH that a load of their problems was too much for him: (Numbers 11:10-15)

> [10] *Then Moses heard the people weep throughout their families, every man in the door of his tent: and the anger of the LORD was kindled greatly; Moses also was displeased.*

[11] And Moses said unto the Lord, Wherefore hast thou afflicted thy servant? and wherefore have I not found favour in thy sight, that thou layest the burden of all this people upon me? [12] Have I conceived all this people? have I begotten them, that thou shouldest say unto me, Carry them in thy bosom, as a nursing father beareth the sucking child, unto the land which thou swarest unto their fathers? [13] Whence should I have flesh to give unto all this people? for they weep unto me, saying, Give us flesh, that we may eat. [14] I am not able to bear all this people alone, because it is too heavy for me. [15] And if thou deal thus with me, kill me, I pray thee, out of hand, if I have found favour in thy sight; and let me not see my wretchedness.

4. Moses for JEHOVAH to show him what to do to give the Israelites flesh (Numbers 11:21-22)

[21] And Moses said, The people, among whom I am, are six hundred thousand footmen; and thou hast said, I will give them flesh, that they may eat a whole month. [22] Shall the flocks and the herds be slain for them, to suffice them? or shall all the fish of the sea be gathered together for them, to suffice them?

5. Moses for the healing of his elder sister, Miriam (Numbers 12:13).

[13] And Moses cried unto the LORD, saying,
Heal her now, O God, I beseech thee.

6. Moses for JEHOVAH to be lenient with the Israelites
and endures his own honor (Numbers 14:13-19)

[13] And Moses said unto the Lord, Then the
Egyptians shall hear it, (for thou broughtest
up this people in thy might from among them;
[14] And they will tell it to the inhabitants of
this land: for they have heard that thou Lord art
among this people, that thou Lord art seen face
to face, and that thy cloud standeth over them,
and that thou goest before them, by day time in a
pillar of a cloud, and in a pillar of fire by night.
[15] Now if thou shalt kill all this people as one
man, then the nations which have heard the fame
of thee will speak, saying, [16] Because the Lord
was not able to bring this people into the land
which he sware unto them, therefore he hath
slain them in the wilderness. [17] And now, I
beseech thee, let the power of my Lord be great,
according as thou hast spoken, saying, [18]
The Lord is longsuffering, and of great mercy,
forgiving iniquity and transgression, and by no
means clearing the guilty, visiting the iniquity of
the fathers upon the children unto the third and
fourth generation. [19] Pardon, I beseech thee,
the iniquity of this people according unto the
greatness of thy mercy, and as thou hast forgiven

this people, from Egypt even until now.

7. Moses for judgment of sin of the sons of Eliab (Numbers 16:15)

> *[15] And Moses was very wroth, and said unto the LORD, Respect not thou their offering: I have not taken one ass from them, neither have I hurt one of them.*

8. Israelites for forgiveness of sin (Numbers 21:7)

> *[7] Therefore the people came to Moses, and said, We have sinned, for we have spoken against the LORD, and against thee; pray unto the LORD, that he take away the serpents from us. And Moses prayed for the people.*

9. Moses for a new leader of Israelites (Numbers 27:16-17)

> *[16] Let the Lord, the God of the spirits of all flesh, set a man over the congregation, [17] Which may go out before them, and which may go in before them, and which may lead them out, and which may bring them in; that the congregation of the LORD be not as sheep which have no shepherd.*

PRAYERS IN DEUTERONOMY: 2

1. Moses asking to go over into Canaan (Deuteronomy 3:24-25)

> *[24] O Lord God, thou hast begun to shew thy servant thy greatness, and thy mighty hand: for what God is there in heaven or in earth, that can do according to thy works, and according to thy might? [25] I pray thee, let me go over, and see the good land that is beyond Jordan, that goodly mountain, and Lebanon.*

2. Moses for Israel to be spared (Deuteronomy 9:26-29)

> *[26] I prayed therefore unto the Lord, and said, O Lord God, destroy not thy people and thine inheritance, which thou hast redeemed through thy greatness, which thou hast brought forth out of Egypt with a mighty hand. [27] Remember thy servants, Abraham, Isaac, and Jacob; look not unto the stubbornness of this people, nor to their wickedness, nor to their sin: [28] Lest the land whence thou broughtest us out say, Because the Lord was not able to bring them into the land which he promised them, and because he hated them, he hath brought them out to slay them in the wilderness. [29] Yet they are thy people and thine inheritance, which thou broughtest out by*

thy mighty power and by thy stretched out arm.

PRAYERS IN JOSHUA: 2

1. Joshua complaining to JEHOVAH for not giving victory (Joshua 7:7-9)

> *[7] And Joshua said, Alas, O Lord God, wherefore hast thou at all brought this people over Jordan, to deliver us into the hand of the Amorites, to destroy us? Would to God we had been content, and dwelt on the other side Jordan! [8] O Lord, what shall I say, when Israel turneth their backs before their enemies! For the Canaanites and all the inhabitants of the land shall hear of it, and shall environ us round, and cut off our name from the earth: and what wilt thou do unto thy great name?*

2. Joshua praying and commanding the sun and the moon to stand still (Joshua 10:12).

> *[12] Then spake Joshua to the LORD in the day when the LORD delivered up the Amorites before the children of Israel, and he said in the sight of Israel, Sun, stand thou still upon Gibeon; and thou, Moon, in the valley of Ajalon.*

PRAYERS IN JUDGES: 9

1. Israel for guidance (Judges 1:1)

> *[1] Now after the death of Joshua it came to pass, that the children of Israel asked the LORD, saying, Who shall go up for us against the Canaanites first, to fight against them?*

2. Gideon for revelation and guidance (Judges 6:13,15,17,18,22)

> *And Gideon said unto him, Oh my Lord, if the LORD be with us, why then is all this befallen us? and where be all his miracles which our fathers told us of, saying, Did not the LORD bring us up from Egypt? but now the LORD hath forsaken us, and delivered us into the hands of the Midianites. [15] And he said unto him, Oh my Lord, wherewith shall I save Israel? behold, my family is poor in Manasseh, and I am the least in my father's house.*
>
> *[17] And he said unto him, If now I have found grace in thy sight, then shew me a sign that thou talkest with me. [18] Depart not hence, I pray thee, until I come unto thee, and bring forth my present, and set it before thee. And he said, I will tarry until thou come again. [22] And when Gideon perceived that he was an angel of the LORD, Gideon said, Alas, O Lord GOD! for*

*because I have seen an angel of the LORD face
to face.*

3. Israel for deliverance and forgiveness of sins (Judges
10:10, 15)

[10] And *the children of Israel cried unto the
LORD, saying, We have sinned against thee,
both because we have forsaken our God, and
also served Baalim. [15] And the children of
Israel said unto the LORD, We have sinned:
do thou unto us whatsoever seemeth good unto
thee; deliver us only, we pray thee, this day.*

4. Jephthah f*or victory* (Judges 11:30-31)

[30] And *Jephthah vowed a vow unto the Lord,
and said, If thou shalt without fail deliver the
children of Ammon into mine hands, [31] Then
it shall be, that whatsoever cometh forth of the
doors of my house to meet me, when I return in
peace from the children of Ammon, shall surely
be the LORD'S, and I will offer it up for a burnt
offering.*

5. Manoah for an Angel to appear and give him direction
(Judges 13:8,11-12,15,17)

*Then Manoah intreated the LORD, and said, O
my Lord, let the man of God which thou didst
send come again unto us, and teach us what we*

shall do unto the child that shall be born. 11-12,15,17*[11] And Manoah arose, , and went after his wife, , and came to the man, , and said unto him, , Art thou the man that spakest unto the woman? And he said, , I am. . [12] And Manoah said, , Now let thy words come to pass. . How shall we order the child, , and how shall we do unto him?[15] And Manoah said unto the angel of the LORD, , I pray thee, , let us detain thee, , until we shall have made ready a kid for thee. [17] And Manoah said unto the angel of the LORD, , What is thy name, , that when thy sayings come to pass we may do thee honour?*

6. Samson for one last victory (Judges 16:28)

[28] And Samson called unto the LORD, and said, O Lord GOD, remember me, I pray thee, and strengthen me, I pray thee, only this once, O God, that I may be at once avenged of the Philistines for my two eyes.

7. Israel for guidance (Judges 20:23)

[23] And the children of Israel went up and wept before the LORD until even, and asked counsel of the LORD, saying, Shall I go up again to battle against the children of Benjamin my brother? And the LORD said, Go up against him.

8. Israel for guidance (Judges 20:28)

[28] And Phinehas, the son of Eleazar, the son of Aaron, stood before it in those days, saying, Shall I yet again go out to battle against the children of Benjamin my brother, or shall I cease? And the LORD said, Go up; for to morrow I will deliver them into thine hand.

9. Israel for Revelation (Judges 21:3)

[3] And said, O LORD God of Israel, why is this come to pass in Israel, that there should be to day one tribe lacking in Israel?

PRAYERS IN 1 SAMUEL: 6

*1 **Hannah** for a son (1 Samuel 1:11)*

[11] And she vowed a vow, and said, O LORD of hosts, if thou wilt indeed look on the affliction of thine handmaid, and remember me, and not forget thine handmaid, but wilt give unto thine handmaid a man child, then I will give him unto the LORD all the days of his life, and there shall no razor come upon his head.

*2. **Hannah** to thank JEHOVAH and appreciate HIM for answered prayer of a son (1 Samuel 2:1-10)*

[1] And Hannah prayed, and said, My heart rejoiceth in the LORD, mine horn is exalted in the LORD: my mouth is enlarged over mine enemies; because I rejoice in thy salvation. [2] There is none holy as the Lord: for there is none beside thee: neither is there any rock like our God. [3] Talk no more so exceeding proudly; let not arrogancy come out of your mouth: for the Lord is a God of knowledge, and by him actions are weighed. [4] The bows of the mighty men are broken, and they that stumbled are girded with strength. [5] They that were full have hired out

themselves for bread; and they that were hungry ceased: so that the barren hath born seven; and she that hath many children is waxed feeble. [6] The Lord killeth, and maketh alive: he bringeth down to the grave, and bringeth up. [7] The Lord maketh poor, and maketh rich: he bringeth low, and lifteth up. [8] He raiseth up the poor out of the dust, and lifteth up the beggar from the dunghill, to set them among princes, and to make them inherit the throne of glory: for the pillars of the earth are the Lord' s, and he hath set the world upon them. [9] He will keep the feet of his saints, and the wicked shall be silent in darkness; for by strength shall no man prevail. [10] The adversaries of the LORD shall be broken to pieces; out of heaven shall he thunder upon them: the LORD shall judge the ends of the earth; and he shall give strength unto his king, and exalt the horn of his anointed.

3. Saul f*or direction* (1 Samuel 14:37)

[37] And *Saul asked counsel of God, Shall I go down after the Philistines? wilt thou deliver them into the hand of Israel? But he answered him not that day.*

4. David for direction (1 Samuel 23:2)

[2] Therefore David enquired of the LORD, saying, Shall I go and smite these Philistines? And the LORD said unto David, Go, and smite the Philistines, and save Keilah.

5. David for divulgence *(1 Samuel 23:10-12)*

[10] Then said David, O Lord God of Israel, thy servant hath certainly heard that Saul seeketh to come to Keilah, to destroy the city for my sake. [11] Will the men of Keilah deliver me up into his hand? will Saul come down, as thy servant hath heard? O LORD God of Israel, I beseech thee, tell thy servant. And the LORD said, He will come down. [12] Then said David, Will the men of Keilah deliver me and my men into the hand of Saul? And the LORD said, They will deliver thee up.

6. David for another divulgence (1 Samuel 30:8)

[8] And David enquired at the LORD, saying, Shall I pursue after this troop? shall I overtake them? And he answered him, Pursue: for thou shalt surely overtake them, and without fail recover all.

PRAYERS IN 2 SAMUEL:4

1. David for divulgence (2 Samuel 2:1)

[1] Shall I go up into any of the cities of Judah? And the LORD said unto him, Go up. And David said, Whither shall I go up? And he said, Unto Hebron.

2. David for divulgence (2 Samuel 5:19)

[19] And David enquired of the LORD, saying, Shall I go up to the Philistines? wilt thou deliver them into mine hand? And the LORD said unto David, Go up: for I will doubtless deliver the Philistines into thine hand.

3. David for realization of his covenant with JEHOVAH (Davidic covenant, 2 Samuel 7:18-29)

[18] Then went king David in, and sat before the Lord, and he said, Who am I, O Lord God? and what is my house, that thou hast brought me hitherto? [19] And this was yet a small thing in thy sight, O Lord God; but thou hast spoken also of thy servant's house for a great while to come. And is this the manner of man, O Lord God? [20] And what can David say more unto thee? for thou, Lord God, knowest thy servant. [21] For thy word's sake, and according to thine own

heart, hast thou done all these great things, to make thy servant know them. [22] Wherefore thou art great, O Lord God: for there is none like thee, neither is there any God beside thee, according to all that we have heard with our ears. [23] And what one nation in the earth is like thy people, even like Israel, whom God went to redeem for a people to himself, and to make him a name, and to do for you great things and terrible, for thy land, before thy people, which thou redeemedst to thee from Egypt, from the nations and their gods? [24] For thou hast confirmed to thyself thy people Israel to be a people unto thee for ever: and thou, Lord, art become their God. [25] And now, O Lord God, the word that thou hast spoken concerning thy servant, and concerning his house, establish it for ever, and do as thou hast said. [26] And let thy name be magnified for ever, saying, The Lord of hosts is the God over Israel: and let the house of thy servant David be established before thee. [27] For thou, O Lord of hosts, God of Israel, hast revealed to thy servant, saying, I will build thee an house: therefore hath thy servant found in his heart to pray this prayer unto thee. [28] And now, O Lord God, thou art that God, and thy words be true, and thou hast promised this goodness unto thy servant: [29] Therefore now let it please thee to bless the house of thy servant, that it may continue for ever before thee: for thou, O Lord GOD, hast spoken it: and with thy blessing let the house of thy servant be blessed for ever.

4. David for forgiveness of sin (2 Samuel 24:10)

[10] And David's heart smote him after that he had numbered the people. And David said unto the LORD, I have sinned greatly in that I have done: and now, I beseech thee, O LORD, take away the iniquity of thy servant; for I have done very foolishly.

PRAYERS IN FIRST KINGS: 5

1. Solomon for knowledge and wisdom (1 Kings 3:6-9)

[6] And Solomon said, Thou hast shewed unto thy servant David my father great mercy, according as he walked before thee in truth, and in righteousness, and in uprightness of heart with thee; and thou hast kept for him this great kindness, that thou hast given him a son to sit on his throne, as it is this day. [7] And now, O Lord my God, thou hast made thy servant king instead of David my father: and I am but a little child: I know not how to go out or come in. [8] And thy servant is in the midst of thy people which thou hast chosen, a great people, that cannot be numbered nor counted for multitude. [9] Give therefore thy servant an understanding heart to judge thy people, that I may discern between good and bad: for who is able to judge this thy so great a people?

2. Solomon dedication of the house of JEHOVAH (1 Kings 8:23-53)

[23] And he said, Lord God of Israel, there is no God like thee, in heaven above, or on earth beneath, who keepest covenant and mercy with thy servants that walk before thee with all their

heart: [24] Who hast kept with thy servant David my father that thou promisedst him: thou spakest also with thy mouth, and hast fulfilled it with thine hand, as it is this day. [25] Therefore now, Lord God of Israel, keep with thy servant David my father that thou promisedst him, saying, There shall not fail thee a man in my sight to sit on the throne of Israel; so that thy children take heed to their way, that they walk before me as thou hast walked before me. [26] And now, O God of Israel, let thy word, I pray thee, be verified, which thou spakest unto thy servant David my father. [27] But will God indeed dwell on the earth? behold, the heaven and heaven of heavens cannot contain thee; how much less this house that I have builded? [28] Yet have thou respect unto the prayer of thy servant, and to his supplication, O Lord my God, to hearken unto the cry and to the prayer, which thy servant prayeth before thee to day: [29] That thine eyes may be open toward this house night and day even toward the place of which thou hast said, My name shall be there: that thou mayest hearken unto the prayer which thy servant shall make toward this place. [30] And hearken thou to the supplication of thy servant, and of thy people Israel, when they shall pray toward this place: and hear thou in heaven thy dwelling place: and when thou hearest, forgive. [31] If any man trespass against his neighbour, and an oath be laid upon him to cause him to swear, and the oath come before thine altar in this house: [32] Then hear thou in heaven, and do, and judge thy servants, condemning the wicked, to bring his way upon his head; and justifying the righteous, to give him according to his righteousness. [33] When thy people Israel be smitten down before the enemy, because they have sinned against thee, and shall turn again to thee, and confess thy name, and pray, and make supplication unto thee in this house: [34] Then hear thou in heaven, and forgive the sin of thy people Israel, and bring them again unto the land which thou gavest unto their fathers. [35] When heaven is shut up, and there is no rain, because they have sinned against thee; if they pray toward this place, and confess thy name, and turn from their sin, when thou afflictest them: [36] Then hear thou in heaven, and forgive the sin of thy servants, and of thy people Israel, that thou teach them the good way wherein they should walk, and give rain upon thy land, which thou hast given to thy people for an inheritance. [37] If there be in the land famine, if there be pestilence, blasting, mildew, locust, or if there be caterpiller; if their enemy besiege them in the land of their cities; whatsoever plague, whatsoever sickness there be; [38] What prayer and supplication soever be made by any man, or by all thy people Israel, which shall know every man the plague of his own heart, and spread forth his hands toward this house: [39] Then hear thou in heaven thy dwelling place, and forgive, and do, and give to every man according to his ways, whose heart thou knowest; (for thou, even thou only, knowest the hearts of all the children of men; [40] That they may fear thee all the days that they live in the land which thou gavest unto our fathers. [41] Moreover concerning a stranger, that is not of thy people Israel, but cometh out of a far country for thy name's sake; [42] For they shall hear of thy great name, and of thy strong hand, and of thy stretched out arm; when he shall come and pray toward this house; [43] Hear thou in heaven thy dwelling place, and do according to all that the stranger calleth to thee for: that all people of the earth may know thy name, to fear thee, as do thy people Israel; and that they may know that this house, which I have builded, is called by thy name. [44] If thy people go out to battle against their enemy, whithersoever thou shalt send them, and shall pray unto the Lord toward the city which thou hast chosen, and toward the house that I have built for thy name: [45] Then hear thou in heaven their prayer and their supplication, and maintain their cause [46] If they sin against thee, (for there is no man that sinneth not,) and thou be angry with them, and deliver them to the enemy, so that they carry them away captives unto the land of the enemy, far or near;

[47] Yet if they shall bethink themselves in the land whither they were carried captives, and repent, and make supplication unto thee in the land of them that carried them captives, saying, We have sinned, and have done perversely, we have committed wickedness; [48] And so return unto thee with all their heart, and with all their soul, in the land of their enemies, which led them away captive, and pray unto thee toward their land, which thou gavest unto their fathers, the city which thou hast chosen, and the house which I have built for thy name: [49] Then hear thou their prayer and their supplication in heaven thy dwelling place, and maintain their cause, [50] And forgive thy people that have sinned against thee, and all their transgressions wherein they have transgressed against thee, and give them compassion before them who carried them captive, that they may have compassion on them: [51] For they be thy people, and thine inheritance, which thou broughtest forth out of Egypt, from the midst of the furnace of iron: [52] That thine eyes may be open unto the supplication of thy servant, and unto the supplication of thy people Israel, to hearken unto them in all that they call for unto thee. [53] For thou didst separate them from among all the people of the earth, to be thine inheritance, as thou spakest by the hand of Moses thy servant, when thou broughtest our fathers out of Egypt, O Lord GOD.

3. Elijah for the resurrection of a dead boy (1 Kings 17:20-21)

> *[20] And he cried unto the Lord, and said, O Lord my God, hast thou also brought evil upon the widow with whom I sojourn, by slaying her son? [21] And he stretched himself upon the child three times, and cried unto the LORD, and said, O LORD my God, I pray thee, let this child' s soul come into him again.*

4. Elijah for heaven to rain fire (1 Kings 18:36-37)

> *[36] And it came to pass at the time of the offering of the evening sacrifice, that Elijah the prophet came near, and said, Lord God of Abraham, Isaac, and of Israel, let it be known this day that thou art God in Israel, and that I am thy servant, and that I have done all these things at thy word. [37] Hear me, O LORD, hear me, that this people may know that thou art the LORD God, and that thou hast turned their heart back again.*

5. Elijah for JEHOVAH to kill him or take him (1 Kings 19:4)

> *[4] But he himself went a day' s journey into the wilderness, and came and sat down under a juniper tree: and he requested for himself that he might die; and said, It is enough; now, O LORD,*

take away my life; for I am not better than my fathers.

PRAYERS IN Second KINGS: 3.

1. Elisha for JEHOVAH to open the eyes of his servant (2 Kings 6:17)

[17] And Elisha prayed, and said, LORD, I pray thee, open his eyes, that he may see. And the LORD opened the eyes of the young man; and he saw: and, behold, the mountain was full of horses and chariots of fire round about Elisha.

2. Hezekiah for deliverance (2 Kings 19:15-19)

[15] And Hezekiah prayed before the Lord, and said, O Lord God of Israel, which dwellest between the cherubims, thou art the God, even thou alone, of all the kingdoms of the earth; thou hast made heaven and earth. [16] Lord, bow down thine ear, and hear: open, Lord, thine eyes, and see: and hear the words of Sennacherib, which hath sent him to reproach the living God. [17] Of a truth, Lord, the kings of Assyria have destroyed the nations and their lands, [18] And have cast their gods into the fire: for they were no gods, but the work of men's hands, wood and stone: therefore they have destroyed them. [19] Now therefore, O LORD our God, I beseech thee, save thou us out of his hand, that all the kingdoms of the earth may know that thou art the

LORD God, even thou only.

3. Hezekiah for JEHOVAH to prolong his life (2 Kings 20:3)

[3] I beseech thee, O LORD, remember now how I have walked before thee in truth and with a perfect heart, and have done that which is good in thy sight. And Hezekiah wept sore.

PRAYERS IN -First CHRONICLES: 2

1. Jabez for his coast to be enlarged (1 Chronicles 4:10)

[10] And Jabez called on the God of Israel, saying, Oh that thou wouldest bless me indeed, and enlarge my coast, and that thine hand might be with me, and that thou wouldest keep me from evil, that it may not grieve me! And God granted him that which he requested.

2. David for Israel and Solomon (1 Chronicles 29:10-19)

[10] Wherefore David blessed the Lord before all the congregation: and David said, Blessed be thou, Lord God of Israel our father, for ever and ever. [11] Thine, O Lord, is the greatness, and the power, and the glory, and the victory, and the majesty: for all that is in the heaven and in the earth is thine; thine is the kingdom, O Lord, and thou art exalted as head above all. [12] Both riches and honour come of thee, and thou reignest over all; and in thine hand is power and might; and in thine hand it is to make great, and to give strength unto all. [13] Now therefore, our God, we thank thee, and praise thy glorious name. [14] But who am I, and what is my people, that we should be able to offer so willingly

after this sort? for all things come of thee, and of thine own have we given thee. [15] For we are strangers before thee, and sojourners, as were all our fathers: our days on the earth are as a shadow, and there is none abiding. [16] O Lord our God, all this store that we have prepared to build thee an house for thine holy name cometh of thine hand, and is all thine own. [17] I know also, my God, that thou triest the heart, and hast pleasure in uprightness. As for me, in the uprightness of mine heart I have willingly offered all these things: and now have I seen with joy thy people, which are present here, to offer willingly unto thee. [18] O Lord God of Abraham, Isaac, and of Israel, our fathers, keep this for ever in the imagination of the thoughts of the heart of thy people, and prepare their heart unto thee: [19] And give unto Solomon my son a perfect heart, to keep thy commandments, thy testimonies, and thy statutes, and to do all these things, and to build the palace, for the which I have made provision.

PRAYERS IN Second CHRONICLES: 2

1. Asa for victory (2 Chronicles 14:11)

[11] And Asa cried unto the LORD his God, and said, LORD, it is nothing with thee to help, whether with many, or with them that have no power: help us, O LORD our God; for we rest on thee, and in thy name we go against this multitude. O LORD, thou art our God; let not man prevail against thee.

2. Jehoshaphat for triumph (2 Chronicles 20:6-12)

[6] And said, O Lord God of our fathers, art not thou God in heaven? and rulest not thou over all the kingdoms of the heathen? and in thine hand is there not power and might, so that none is able to withstand thee? [7] Art not thou our God, who didst drive out the inhabitants of this land before thy people Israel, and gavest it to the seed of Abraham thy friend for ever? [8] And they dwelt therein, and have built thee a sanctuary therein for thy name, saying, [9] If, when evil cometh upon us, as the sword, judgment, or pestilence, or famine, we stand before this house, and in thy presence, for thy name is in this house, and cry unto thee in our affliction, then thou wilt hear and help.

[10] And now, behold, the children of Ammon and Moab and mount Seir, whom thou wouldest not let Israel invade, when they came out of the land of Egypt, but they turned from them, and destroyed them not; [11] Behold, I say, how they reward us, to come to cast us out of thy possession, which thou hast given us to inherit. [12] O our God, wilt thou not judge them? for we have no might against this great company that cometh against us; neither know we what to do: but our eyes are upon thee.

PRAYERS IN EZRA: 2

1. Ezra prayer for thanksgiving (Ezra 7:27-28)

[27] Blessed *be the Lord God of our fathers, which hath put such a thing as this in the king' s heart, to beautify the house of the Lord which is in Jerusalem: [28] And hath extended mercy unto me before the king, and his counsellors, and before all the king' s mighty princes. And I was strengthened as the hand of the LORD my God was upon me, and I gathered together out of Israel chief men to go up with me.*

2. Ezra for assistance and clemency (Ezra 9:5-15)

[5] And at the evening sacrifice I arose up from my heaviness; and having rent my garment and *my mantle, I fell upon my knees, and spread out my hands unto the LORD my God, [6] And said, O my God, I am ashamed and blush to lift up my face to thee, my God: for our iniquities are increased over our head, and our trespass is grown up unto the heavens. [7] Since the days of our fathers have we been in a great trespass unto this day; and for our iniquities have we, our kings, and our priests, been delivered into the hand of the kings of the lands, to the sword, to captivity, and to a spoil, and to confusion of face, as it is this day. [8] And now for a little space grace hath been shewed from the LORD*

our God, to leave us a remnant to escape, and to give us a nail in his holy place, that our God may lighten our eyes, and give us a little reviving in our bondage. [9] For we were bondmen; yet our God hath not forsaken us in our bondage, but hath extended mercy unto us in the sight of the kings of Persia, to give us a reviving, to set up the house of our God, and to repair the desolations thereof, and to give us a wall in Judah and in Jerusalem. [10] And now, O our God, what shall we say after this? for we have forsaken thy commandments, [11] Which thou hast commanded by thy servants the prophets, saying, The land, unto which ye go to possess it, is an unclean land with the filthiness of the people of the lands, with their abominations, which have filled it from one end to another with their uncleanness. [12] Now therefore give not your daughters unto their sons, neither take their daughters unto your sons, nor seek their peace or their wealth for ever: that ye may be strong, and eat the good of the land, and leave it for an inheritance to your children for ever. [13] And after all that is come upon us for our evil deeds, and for our great trespass, seeing that thou our God hast punished us less than our iniquities deserve, and hast given us such deliverance as this; [14] Should we again break thy commandments, and join in affinity with the people of these abominations? wouldest not thou be angry with us till thou hadst consumed us, so that there should be no remnant nor escaping? [15] O LORD God of Israel, thou art righteous: for we remain yet escaped, as it is this day: behold, we are before thee in our trespasses: for we cannot stand before thee because of this.

PRAYERS IN NEHEMIAH: 9

1. Nehemiah for confession of sin and help (Nehemiah 1:5-11)

[5] And *said, I beseech thee, O Lord God of heaven, the great and terrible God, that keepeth covenant and mercy for them that love him and observe his commandments: [6] Let thine ear now be attentive, and thine eyes open, that thou mayest hear the prayer of thy servant, which I pray before thee now, day and night, for the children of Israel thy servants, and confess the sins of the children of Israel, which we have sinned against thee: both I and my father's house have sinned. [7] We have dealt very corruptly against thee, and have not kept the commandments, nor the statutes, nor the judgments, which thou commandedst thy servant Moses. [8] Remember, I beseech thee, the word that thou commandedst thy servant Moses, saying, If ye transgress, I will scatter you abroad among the nations: [9] But if ye turn unto me, and keep my commandments, and do them; though there were of you cast out unto the uttermost part of the heaven, yet will I gather them from thence, and will bring them unto the place that I have chosen to set my name there. [10] Now these are thy servants and thy*

people, whom thou hast redeemed by thy great power, and by thy strong hand. [11] O Lord, I beseech thee, let now thine ear be attentive to the prayer of thy servant, and to the prayer of thy servants, who desire to fear thy name: and prosper, I pray thee, thy servant this day, and grant him mercy in the sight of this man. For I was the king's cupbearer.

2. Nehemiah for judgement (Nehemiah 4:1-5)

[1] But it came to pass, that when Sanballat heard that we builded the wall, he was wroth, and took great indignation, and mocked the Jews. [2] And he spake before his brethren and the army of Samaria, and said, What do these feeble Jews? will they fortify themselves? will they sacrifice? will they make an end in a day? will they revive the stones out of the heaps of the rubbish which are burned? [3] Now Tobiah the Ammonite was by him, and he said, Even that which they build, if a fox go up, he shall even break down their stone wall. [4] Hear, O our God; for we are despised: and turn their reproach upon their own head, and give them for a prey in the land of captivity: [5] And cover not their iniquity, and let not their sin be blotted out from before thee: for they have provoked thee to anger before the builders.

3. Nehemiah for help (Nehemiah 6:9)

[9] For they all made us afraid, saying, Their hands shall be weakened from the work, that it be not done. Now therefore, O God, strengthen my hands.

4. Nehemiah for help (Nehemiah 6:14)

[14] My God, think thou upon Tobiah and San-ballat according to these their works, and on the prophetess Noadiah, and the rest of the prophets, that would have put me in fear.

5. Israel. Confession of their sins (Nehemiah 9:5-38)

[5] Then the Levites, Jeshua, and Kadmiel, Bani, Hashabniah, Sherebiah, Hodijah, Sheba-niah, and Pethahiah, said, Stand up and bless the LORD your God for ever and ever: and blessed be thy glorious name, which is exalted above all blessing and praise. [6] Thou, even thou, art Lord alone; thou hast made heaven, the heaven of heavens, with all their host, the earth, and all things that are therein, the seas, and all that is therein, and thou preservest them all; and the host of heaven worshippeth thee. [7] Thou art the Lord the God, who didst choose Abram, and broughtest him forth out of Ur of the Chaldees, and gavest him the name of Abraham; [8] And foundest his heart faithful before thee, and madest a covenant with him to

*give the land of the Canaanites, the Hittites, the
Amorites, and the Perizzites, and the Jebusites,
and the Girgashites, to give it, I say, to his seed,
and hast performed thy words; for thou art
righteous: [9] And didst see the affliction of our
fathers in Egypt, and heardest their cry by the
Red sea; [10] And shewedst signs and wonders
upon Pharaoh, and on all his servants, and on
all the people of his land: for thou knewest that
they dealt proudly against them. So didst thou
get thee a name, as it is this day. [11] And thou
didst divide the sea before them, so that they
went through the midst of the sea on the dry
land; and their persecutors thou threwest into
the deeps, as a stone into the mighty waters.
[12] Moreover thou leddest them in the day by
a cloudy pillar; and in the night by a pillar of
fire, to give them light in the way wherein they
should go. [13] Thou camest down also upon
mount Sinai, and spakest with them from heav-
en, and gavest them right judgments, and true
laws, good statutes and commandments: [14]
And madest known unto them thy holy sabbath,
and commandedst them precepts, statutes, and
laws, by the hand of Moses thy servant: [15]
And gavest them bread from heaven for their
hunger, and broughtest forth water for them out
of the rock for their thirst, and promisedst them
that they should go in to possess the land which
thou hadst sworn to give them. [16] But they and*

our fathers dealt proudly, and hardened their necks, and hearkened not to thy commandments, [17] And refused to obey, neither were mindful of thy wonders that thou didst among them; but hardened their necks, and in their rebellion appointed a captain to return to their bondage: but thou art a God ready to pardon, gracious and merciful, slow to anger, and of great kindness, and forsookest them not. [18] Yea, when they had made them a molten calf, and said, This is thy God that brought thee up out of Egypt, and had wrought great provocations; [19] Yet thou in thy manifold mercies forsookest them not in the wilderness: the pillar of the cloud departed not from them by day, to lead them in the way; neither the pillar of fire by night, to shew them light, and the way wherein they should go. [20] Thou gavest also thy good spirit to instruct them, and withheldest not thy manna from their mouth, and gavest them water for their thirst. [21] Yea, forty years didst thou sustain them in the wilderness, so that they lacked nothing; their clothes waxed not old, and their feet swelled not. [22] Moreover thou gavest them kingdoms and nations, and didst divide them into corners: so they possessed the land of Sihon, and the land of the king of Heshbon, and the land of Og king of Bashan. [23] Their children also multipliedst thou as the stars of heaven, and broughtest them into the land, concerning which thou hadst promised to

*their fathers, that they should go in to possess it.
[24] So the children went in and possessed the
land, and thou subduedst before them the inhabitants of the land, the Canaanites, and gavest
them into their hands, with their kings, and the
people of the land, that they might do with them
as they would. [25] And they took strong cities,
and a fat land, and possessed houses full of all
goods, wells digged, vineyards, and oliveyards,
and fruit trees in abundance: so they did eat,
and were filled, and became fat, and delighted
themselves in thy great goodness. [26] Nevertheless they were disobedient, and rebelled against
thee, and cast thy law behind their backs, and
slew thy prophets which testified against them to
turn them to thee, and they wrought great provocations. [27] Therefore thou deliveredst them
into the hand of their enemies, who vexed them:
and in the time of their trouble, when they cried
unto thee, thou heardest them from heaven; and
according to thy manifold mercies thou gavest
them saviours, who saved them out of the hand
of their enemies. [28] But after they had rest,
they did evil again before thee: therefore leftest
thou them in the hand of their enemies, so that
they had the dominion over them: yet when they
returned, and cried unto thee, thou heardest
them from heaven; and many times didst thou
deliver them according to thy mercies; [29] And
testifiedst against them, that thou mightest bring*

*them again unto thy law: yet they dealt proud-
ly, and hearkened not unto thy commandments,
but sinned against thy judgments, (which if a
man do, he shall live in them;) and withdrew the
shoulder, and hardened their neck, and would
not hear. [30] Yet many years didst thou forbear them, and testifiedst against them by thy
spirit in thy prophets: yet would they not give
ear: therefore gavest thou them into the hand of
the people of the lands. [31] Nevertheless for
thy great mercies' sake thou didst not utterly
consume them, nor forsake them; for thou art a
gracious and merciful God. [32] Now therefore,
our God, the great, the mighty, and the terrible
God, who keepest covenant and mercy, let not
all the trouble seem little before thee, that hath
come upon us, on our kings, on our princes, and
on our priests, and on our prophets, and on our
fathers, and on all thy people, since the time of
the kings of Assyria unto this day. [33] Howbeit
thou art just in all that is brought upon us; for
thou hast done right, but we have done wickedly:
[34] Neither have our kings, our princes, our
priests, nor our fathers, kept thy law, nor hearkened unto thy commandments and thy testimonies, wherewith thou didst testify against them.
[35] For they have not served thee in their kingdom, and in thy great goodness that thou gavest
them, and in the large and fat land which thou
gavest before them, neither turned they from*

their wicked works. [36] Behold, we are servants this day, and for the land that thou gavest unto our fathers to eat the fruit thereof and the good thereof, behold, we are servants in it: [37] And it yieldeth much increase unto the kings whom thou hast set over us because of our sins: also they have dominion over our bodies, and over our cattle, at their pleasure, and we are in great distress. [38] And because of all this we make a sure covenant, and write it; and our princes, Levites, and priests, seal unto it.

...

6. Nehemiah for blessing (Nehemiah 13:14)

[14] Remember me, O my God, concerning this, and wipe not out my good deeds that I have done for the house of my God, and for the offices thereof.

7. Nehemiah for blessing (Nehemiah 13:22)

[22] And I commanded the Levites that they should cleanse themselves, and that they should come and keep the gates, to sanctify the sabbath day. Remember me, O my God, concerning this also, and spare me according to the greatness of thy mercy.

8. Nehemiah for judgment (Nehemiah 13:29)

[29] Remember them, O my God, because they have defiled the priesthood, and the covenant of

the priesthood, and of the Levites.

9. Nehemiah for blessing (Nehemiah 13:31)

[31] And for the wood offering, at times appointed, and for the firstfruits. Remember me, O my God, for good.

PRAYERS IN JOB: 7

1. Job of thanksgiving and resignation (Job 1:20-22)

[20] Then Job arose, and rent his mantle, and shaved his head, and fell down upon the ground, and worshipped, [21] And said, Naked came I out of my mother's womb, and naked shall I return thither: the Lord gave, and the Lord hath taken away; blessed be the name of the Lord. [22] In all this Job sinned not, nor charged God foolishly.

2. Job asking for relief after expressing displeasure (Job 7:17-21)

[17] What is man, that thou shouldest magnify him? And that thou shouldest set thine heart upon him? [18] And that thou shouldest visit him every morning, and try him every moment? [19] How long wilt thou not depart from me, nor let me alone till I swallow down my spittle? [20] I have sinned; what shall I do unto thee, O thou preserver of men? why hast thou set me as a mark against thee, so that I am a burden to myself? [21] And why dost thou not pardon my transgression, and take away mine iniquity? for now shall I sleep in the dust; and thou shalt seek me in the morning, but I shall not be.

3. Job asking for relief after complaint (Job 9:25-35; 10;1-22)

[25] Now my days are swifter than a post: they flee away, they see no good. [26] They are passed away as the swift ships: as the eagle that hasteth to the prey. [27] If I say, I will forget my complaint, I will leave off my heaviness, and comfort myself: [28] I am afraid of all my sorrows, I know that thou wilt not hold me innocent. [29] If I be wicked, why then labour I in vain? [30] If I wash myself with snow water, and make my hands never so clean; [31] Yet shalt thou plunge me in the ditch, and mine own clothes shall abhor me. [32] For he is not a man, as I am, that I should answer him, and we should come together in judgment. [33] Neither is there any daysman betwixt us, that might lay his hand upon us both. [34] Let him take his rod away from me, and let not his fear terrify me: [35] Then would I speak, and not fear him; but it is not so with me.

10[1] My soul is weary of my life; I will leave my complaint upon myself; I will speak in the bitterness of my soul. [2] I will say unto God, Do not condemn me; shew me wherefore thou contendest with me. [3] Is it good unto thee that thou shouldest oppress, that thou shouldest despise the work of thine hands, and shine upon the counsel of the wicked? [4] Hast thou eyes of

*flesh? or seest thou as man seeth? [5] Are thy
days as the days of man? are thy years as man's
days, [6] That thou enquirest after mine iniquity,
and searchest after my sin? [7] Thou knowest
that I am not wicked; and there is none that
can deliver out of thine hand. [8] Thine hands
have made me and fashioned me together round
about; yet thou dost destroy me. [9] Remember,
I beseech thee, that thou hast made me as the
clay; and wilt thou bring me into dust again?
[10] Hast thou not poured me out as milk, and
curdled me like cheese? [11] Thou hast clothed
me with skin and flesh, and hast fenced me with
bones and sinews. [12] Thou hast granted me
life and favour, and thy visitation hath preserved
my spirit. [13] And these things hast thou hid in
thine heart: I know that this is with thee. [14]
If I sin, then thou markest me, and thou wilt not
acquit me from mine iniquity. [15] If I be wicked,
woe unto me; and if I be righteous, yet will I not
lift up my head. I am full of confusion; therefore
see thou mine affliction; [16] For it increaseth.
Thou huntest me as a fierce lion: and again thou
shewest thyself marvellous upon me. [17] Thou
renewest thy witnesses against me, and increas-
est thine indignation upon me; changes and war
are against me. [18] Wherefore then hast thou
brought me forth out of the womb? Oh that I had
given up the ghost, and no eye had seen me! I
should have been as though I had not been; [19]*

I should have been carried from the womb to the grave. [20] Are not my days few? cease then, and let me alone, that I may take comfort a little, [21] Before I go whence I shall not return, even to the land of darkness and the shadow of death; [22] A land of darkness, as darkness itself; and of the shadow of death, without any order, and where the light is as darkness.

4. Job complaint, for forgiveness and for life (Job 14: 13-22)

[13] O that thou wouldest hide me in the grave, that thou wouldest keep me secret, until thy wrath be past, that thou wouldest appoint me a set time, and remember me! [14] If a man die, shall he live again? all the days of my appointed time will I wait, till my change come. [15] Thou shalt call, and I will answer thee: thou wilt have a desire to the work of thine hands. [16] For now thou numberest my steps: dost thou not watch over my sin? [17] My transgression is sealed up in a bag, and thou sewest up mine iniquity. [18] And surely the mountain falling cometh to nought, and the rock is removed out of his place. [19] The waters wear the stones: thou washest away the things which grow out of the dust of the earth; and thou destroyest the hope of man. [20] Thou prevailest for ever against him, and he passeth: thou changest his countenance, and sendest him away. [21] His sons

*come to honour, and he knoweth it not; and they
are brought low, but he perceiveth it not of them.
[22] But his flesh upon him shall have pain, and
his soul within him shall mourn.*

5. Job for an equitable trial (Job 23:3-5)

*[3] Oh that I knew where I might find him! that
I might come even to his seat! [4] I would order
my cause before him, and fill my mouth with
arguments. [5] I would know the words which
he would answer me, and understand what he
would say unto me.*

6. Job for confession (Job 40:3-5)

*[3] Then Job answered the Lord, and said, [4]
Behold, I am vile; what shall I answer thee? I
will lay mine hand upon my mouth. [5] Once
have I spoken; but I will not answer: yea, twice;
but I will proceed no further.*

7. Job prayer of remorse (Job 42:1-6)

[1] Then *Job answered the LORD, and said, [2] I
know that thou canst do every thing, and that no
thought can be withholden from thee. [3] Who
is he that hideth counsel without knowledge?
therefore have I uttered that I understood not;
things too wonderful for me, which I knew not.
[4] Hear, I beseech thee, and I will speak: I will
demand of thee, and declare thou unto me. [5] I*

have heard of thee by the hearing of the ear: but now mine eye seeth thee. [6] Wherefore I abhor myself, and repent in dust and ashes.

PRAYERS IN PSALMS:64

1. David. To save him (Psalm 3:7)

[7] Arise, O LORD; save me, O my God: for thou hast smitten all mine enemies upon the cheek bone; thou hast broken the teeth of the ungodly.

2. David for JEHOVAH to hear him (Psalm 4:1)

[1] Hear me when I call, O God of my righteousness: thou hast enlarged me when I was in distress; have mercy upon me, and hear my prayer.

3. David for judgement/protection/morning prayer (Psalm 5:1-3;8,10)

[1] Give ear to my words, O LORD, consider my meditation. [2] Hearken unto the voice of my cry, my King, and my God: for unto thee will I pray. [3] My voice shalt thou hear in the morning, O LORD; in the morning will I direct my prayer unto thee, and will look up. [8] Lead me, O LORD, in thy righteousness because of mine enemies; make thy way straight before my face. [10] Destroy thou them, O God; let them fall by their own counsels; cast them out in the multitude of their transgressions; for they have rebelled against thee.

4. David against distress (Psalm 6:1-4)

[1] O LORD, rebuke me not in thine anger, neither chasten me in thy hot displeasure. [2] Have mercy upon me, O Lord; for I am weak: O Lord, heal me; for my bones are vexed. [3] My soul is also sore vexed: but thou, O Lord, how long? [4] Return, O LORD, deliver my soul: oh save me for thy mercies' sake. Let all mine enemies be ashamed and sore vexed: let them return and be ashamed suddenly.

5. David for deliverance/judgement (Psalm 7:1, 6, 8-9)

[1] O LORD my God, in thee do I put my trust: save me from all them that persecute me, and deliver me: [6] Arise, O LORD, in thine anger, lift up thyself because of the rage of mine enemies: and awake for me to the judgment that thou hast commanded. [8] The LORD shall judge the people: judge me, O LORD, according to my righteousness, and according to mine integrity that is in me. [9] Oh let the wickedness of the wicked come to an end; but establish the just: for the righteous God trieth the hearts and reins.

6. David for mercy (Psalm 9:13, 19-2)0)

[13] Have mercy upon me, O LORD; consider my trouble which I suffer of them that hate me, thou that liftest me up from the gates of death [19] Arise, O LORD; let not man prevail: let the heathen be judged in thy sight. [20] Put them in fear, O LORD: that the nations may know themselves to be but men.

7. David for distress (Psalm 12:1)

[1] Help, LORD; for the godly man ceaseth; for the faithful fail from among the children of men.

8. Dvid for consideration (Psalm 13:3-4)

[3] Consider and hear me, O LORD my God: lighten mine eyes, lest I sleep the sleep of death; [4] Lest mine enemy say, I have prevailed against him; and those that trouble me rejoice when I am moved.

9. David. Prayer for the king (Psalm 20:1-4)

[1] The LORD hear thee in the day of trouble; the name of the God of Jacob defend thee; [2] Send thee help from the sanctuary, and strengthen thee out of Zion; [3] Remember all thy offerings, and accept thy burnt sacrifice; Selah. [4] Grant thee according to thine own heart, and fulfil all thy counsel.

10. David of distress and guidance (Psalm 25:2-7)

[2] O my God, I trust in thee: let me not be ashamed, let not mine enemies triumph over me. [3] Yea, let none that wait on thee be ashamed: let them be ashamed which transgress without cause. [4] Shew me thy ways, O Lord; teach me thy paths. [5] Lead me in thy truth, and teach me: for thou art the God of my salvation; on thee do I wait all the day. [6] Remember, O Lord, thy tender mercies and thy lovingkindnesses; for they have been ever of old. [7] Remember not the sins of my youth, nor my

transgressions: according to thy mercy remember thou me for thy goodness' sake, O LORD. [16] Turn thee unto me, and have mercy upon me; for I am desolate and afflicted. [18] Look upon mine affliction and my pain; and forgive all my sins. [20] O keep my soul, and deliver me: let me not be ashamed; for I put my trust in thee. [21] Let integrity and uprightness preserve me; for I wait on thee [22] Redeem Israel, O God, out of all his troubles.

11. David of distress to reverse curse (Psalm 27:7, 9, 11-12)

[7] Hear, O LORD, when I cry with my voice: have mercy also upon me, and answer me. [9] Hide not thy face far from me; put not thy servant away in anger: thou hast been my help; leave me not, neither forsake me, O God of my salvation. [11] Teach me thy way, O LORD, and lead me in a plain path, because of mine enemies. [12] Deliver me not over unto the will of mine enemies: for false witnesses are risen up against me, and such as breathe out cruelty.

12. David. For judgment in trouble times (Psalm 28:2-3)

[2] Hear the voice of my supplications, when I cry unto thee, when I lift up my hands toward thy holy oracle. [3] Draw me not away with the wicked, and with the workers of iniquity, which speak peace to their neighbours, but mischief is in their hearts.

13. David. Of faith in distress (Psalm 31:4-5, 9)

[4] Put me out of the net that they have laid privily for

me: for thou art my strength. [5] Into thine hand I commit my spirit: thou hast redeemed me, O LORD God of truth. [9] Have mercy upon me, O LORD, for I am in trouble: mine eye is consumed with grief, yea, my soul and my belly.

Psalm 31:16-17:

[16] Make thy face to shine upon thy servant: save me for thy mercies' sake. [17] Let me not be ashamed, O LORD; for I have called upon thee: let the wicked be ashamed, and let them be silent in the grave.

14. David. For judgment and help (Psalm 35:1, 22-24)

[1] Plead my cause, O LORD, with them that strive with me: fight against them that fight against me.
[22] This thou hast seen, O LORD: keep not silence: O Lord, be not far from me. [23] Stir up thyself, and awake to my judgment, even unto my cause, my God and my Lord. [24] Judge me, O LORD my God, according to thy righteousness; and let them not rejoice over me.

15. David for him not to speak in anger (Psalm 39:8, 10, 12-13)

[8] Deliver me from all my transgressions: make me not the reproach of the foolish. [10] Remove thy stroke away from me: I am consumed by the blow of thine hand. [12] Hear my prayer, O LORD, and give ear unto my cry; hold not thy peace at my tears: for I am a stranger with thee, and a sojourner, as all my fathers were. [13] O spare me, that I may recover strength, before I go hence, and be no more.

16. David waiting on JEHOVAH for deliverance (Psalm 40:11, 13-16)

> *[11] Withhold not thou thy tender mercies from me, O LORD: let thy lovingkindness and thy truth continually preserve me.*
> *[13] Be pleased, O LORD, to deliver me: O LORD, make haste to help me. [14] Let them be ashamed and confounded together that seek after my soul to destroy it; let them be driven backward and put to shame that wish me evil. [15] Let them be desolate for a reward of their shame that say unto me, Aha, aha. [16] Let all those that seek thee rejoice and be glad in thee: let such as love thy salvation say continually, The LORD be magnified.*

17. David for mercy (Psalm 41:10-11)

> *[10] But thou, O Lord, be merciful unto me, and raise me up, that I may requite them. [11] By this I know that thou favourest me, because mine enemy doth not triumph over me.*

18. David for deliverance (Psalm 43:1-3)

> *[1] Judge me, O God, and plead my cause against an ungodly nation: O deliver me from the deceitful and unjust man. [2] For thou art the God of my strength: why dost thou cast me off? why go I mourning because of the oppression of the enemy? [3] O send out thy light and thy truth: let them lead me; let them bring me unto thy holy hill, and to thy tabernacles.*

19. Sons of Korah for help (Psalm 44:23-26)

[23] Awake, why sleepest thou, O Lord? arise, cast us not off for ever. [24] Wherefore hidest thou thy face, and forgettest our affliction and our oppression? [25] For our soul is bowed down to the dust: our belly cleaveth unto the earth. [26] Arise for our help, and redeem us for thy mercies' sake.

20. David for forgiveness (Psalm 51:1-2:7-12,14,15,18)

[1] Have mercy upon me, O God, according to thy lov-ingkindness: according unto the multitude of thy tender mercies blot out my transgressions. [2] Wash me through-ly from mine iniquity, and cleanse me from my sin. [7] Purge me with hyssop, and I shall be clean: wash me, and I shall be whiter than snow. [8] Make me to hear joy and gladness; that the bones which thou hast broken may rejoice. [9] Hide thy face from my sins, and blot out all mine iniquities. [10] Create in me a clean heart, O God; and renew a right spirit within me. [11] Cast me not away from thy presence; and take not thy Holy Spirit from me. [12] Restore unto me the joy of thy salvation; and uphold me with thy free spirit. [14] Deliver me from bloodguilt-iness, O God, thou God of my salvation: and my tongue shall sing aloud of thy righteousness. [15] O Lord, open thou my lips; and my mouth shall shew forth thy praise. [18] Do good in thy good pleasure unto Zion: build thou the walls of Jerusalem.

21. David for help (Psalm 54:1-3).

[1] Save me, O God, by thy name, and judge me by thy strength. [2] Hear my prayer, O God; give ear to the words of my mouth. [3]
For strangers are risen up against me, and oppressors seek after my soul: they have not set God before them.

22. David about false friends (Psalm 55:1-3, 9.

[1] Give ear to my prayer, O God; and hide not thyself from my supplication. [2] Attend unto me, and hear me: I mourn in my complaint, and make a noise; [3] Because of the voice of the enemy, because of the oppression of the wicked: for they cast iniquity upon me, and in wrath they hate me. [9] Destroy, O Lord, and divide their tongues: for I have seen violence and strife in the city.

23. David for trusting JEHOVAH to help (Psalm 56:1-2)

[1] Be merciful unto me, O God: for man would swallow me up; he fighting daily oppresseth me. [2] Mine enemies would daily swallow me up: for they be many that fight against me, O thou most High.

24. David of trust in a time of distress (Psalm 57:1-2, 5, 9, 11)

[1] Be merciful unto me, O God, be merciful unto me: for my soul trusteth in thee: yea, in the shadow of thy wings will I make my refuge, until these calamities be over past. [2] I will cry unto God most high; unto God that performeth all things for me. [5] Be thou exalted, O God,

*above the heavens; let thy glory be above all the earth.
[9] I will praise thee, O Lord, among the people: I will
sing unto thee among the nations. [11] Be thou exalted,
O God, above the heavens: let thy glory be above all the
earth.*

25. David for judgment (Psalm 58:6-8).

*[6] Break their teeth, O God, in their mouth: break out
the great teeth of the young lions, O LORD. [7] Let them
melt away as waters which run continually: when he
bendeth his bow to shoot his arrows, let them be as cut in
pieces. [8] As a snail which melteth, let every one of them
pass away: like the untimely birth of a woman, that they
may not see the sun.*

26. David for judgment and deliverance from enemies (Psalm
59:1-5, 11, 13)

*[1] Deliver me from mine enemies, O my God: defend me
from them that rise up against me. [2] Deliver me from
the workers of iniquity, and save me from bloody men.
[3] For, lo, they lie in wait for my soul: the mighty are
gathered against me; not for my transgression, nor for my
sin, O Lord. [4] They run and prepare themselves without
my fault: awake to help me, and behold. [5] Thou therefore, O LORD God of hosts, the God of Israel, awake
to visit all the heathen: be not merciful to any wicked
transgressors. [11] Slay them not, lest my people forget:
scatter them by thy power; and bring them down, O Lord
our shield. [13] Consume them in wrath, consume them,*

that they may not be: and let them know that God ruleth in Jacob unto the ends of the earth.

27. David of trust (Psalm 61:1-2).

[1] Hear my cry, O God; attend unto my prayer. [2] From the end of the earth will I cry unto thee, when my heart is overwhelmed: lead me to the rock that is higher than I.

28. David against enemies (Psalm 64:1-2) .

[1] Hear my voice, O God, in my prayer: preserve my life from fear of the enemy. [2] Hide me from the secret counsel of the wicked; from the insurrection of the workers of iniquity.

29. All men for blessings (Psalm 67:1)

[1] God be merciful unto us, and bless us; and cause his face to shine upon us.

30. David against enemies. Moses made the same statements whenever Israelites went out to war (Psalm 68:1-2).

[1] Let God arise, let his enemies be scattered: let them also that hate him flee before him. [2] As smoke is driven away, so drive them away: as wax melteth before the fire, so let the wicked perish at the presence of God.

31. David for help in distress (Psalm 69:1,6,13-18)

[1] Save me, O God; for the waters are come in unto my soul. [6] Let not them that wait on thee, O Lord GOD of hosts, be ashamed for my sake: let not those that seek thee be confounded for my sake, O God of Israel. [13] But as for me, my prayer is unto thee, O Lord, in an acceptable time: O God, in the multitude of thy mercy hear me, in the truth of thy salvation. [14] Deliver me out of the mire, and let me not sink: let me be delivered from them that hate me, and out of the deep waters. [15] Let not the waterflood overflow me, neither let the deep swallow me up, and let not the pit shut her mouth upon me. [16] Hear me, O Lord; for thy lovingkindness is good: turn unto me according to the multitude of thy tender mercies. [17] And hide not thy face from thy servant; for I am in trouble: hear me speedily. [18] Draw nigh unto my soul, and redeem it: deliver me because of mine enemies.

32. David for JEHOVAH to come deliver quickly (Psalm 70:1, 5)

[1] Make haste, O God, to deliver me; make haste to help me, O LORD. . . [5] But I am poor and needy: make haste unto me, O God: thou art my help and my deliverer; O LORD, make no tarrying.

33. David for deliverance (Psalm 71:2-4,9, 12-13, 18)

[2] Deliver me in thy righteousness, and cause me to escape: incline thine ear unto me, and save me. [3] Be thou my strong habitation, whereunto I may continually resort: thou hast given commandment to save me; for thou art my

rock and my fortress. [4] Deliver me, O my God, out of
the hand of the wicked, out of the hand of the unrighteous
and cruel man. [9] Cast me not off in the time of old age;
forsake me not when my strength faileth. [12] O God, be
not far from me: O my God, make haste for my help. [13]
Let them be confounded and consumed that are adver-
saries to my soul; let them be covered with reproach and
dishonour that seek my hurt. [18] Now also when I am
old and grayheaded, O God, forsake me not; until I have
shewed thy strength unto this generation, and thy power
to every one that is to come.

34. Asaph for judgment (Psalm 79:6,8-9,11-12)

[6] Pour out thy wrath upon the heathen that have not
known thee, and upon the kingdoms that have not called
upon thy name. [8] O remember not against us former
iniquities: let thy tender mercies speedily prevent us:
for we are brought very low. [9] Help us, O God of our
salvation, for the glory of thy name: and deliver us, and
purge away our sins, for thy name's sake. [11] Let the
sighing of the prisoner come before thee; according to
the greatness of thy power preserve thou those that are
appointed to die; [12] And render unto our neighbours
sevenfold into their bosom their reproach, wherewith they
have reproached thee, O Lord.

35. Asaph of distress (Psalm 80:1-3 ,7,14-15)

[1] Give ear, O Shepherd of Israel, thou that leadest
Joseph like a flock; thou that dwellest between the cheru-

84

bims, shine forth. [2] Before Ephraim and Benjamin and Manasseh stir up thy strength, and come and save us. [3] Turn us again, O God, and cause thy face to shine; and we shall be saved. [7] Turn us again, O God of hosts, and cause thy face to shine; and we shall be saved. [14] Return, we beseech thee, O God of hosts: look down from heaven, and behold, and visit this vine; [15] And the vineyard which thy right hand hath planted, and the branch that thou madest strong for thyself.

36. Asaph for judgement against enemies (Psalm 83:1, 9, 11, 13, 15-17)

[1] Keep not thou silence, O God: hold not thy peace, and be not still, O God. [9] Do unto them as unto the Midianites; as to Sisera, as to Jabin, at the brook of Kison: [11] Make their nobles like Oreb, and like Zeeb: yea, all their princes as Zebah, and as Zalmunna: [13] O my God, make them like a wheel; as the stubble before the wind. [15] So persecute them with thy tempest, and make them afraid with thy storm. [16] Fill their faces with shame; that they may seek thy name, O Lord. [17] Let them be confounded and troubled for ever; yea, let them be put to shame, and perish.

37. Sons of korah for trust (Psalm 84:8-9).

[8] O Lord God of hosts, hear my prayer: give ear, O God of Jacob. Selah. [9] Behold, O God our shield, and look upon the face of thine anointed.

38. Sons of Korah for mercy and revival (Psalm 85:4-7)

[4] Turn us, O God of our salvation, and cause thine anger toward us to cease. [5] Wilt thou be angry with us for ever? wilt thou draw out thine anger to all generations? [6] Wilt thou not revive us again: that thy people may rejoice in thee? [7] Shew us thy mercy, O LORD, and grant us thy salvation.

39. David of praise and preservation (Psalm 86:1-4,6, 11, 16-17)

[1] Bow down thine ear, O LORD, hear me: for I am poor and needy. [2] Preserve my soul; for I am holy: O thou my God, save thy servant that trusteth in thee. [3] Be merciful unto me, O Lord: for I cry unto thee daily. [4] Rejoice the soul of thy servant: for unto thee, O Lord, do I lift up my soul. [6] Give ear, O LORD, unto my prayer; and attend to the voice of my supplications. [11] Teach me thy way, O LORD; I will walk in thy truth: unite my heart to fear thy name. [16] O turn unto me, and have mercy upon me; give thy strength unto thy servant, and save the son of thine handmaid. [17] Shew me a token for good; that they which hate me may see it, and be ashamed: because thou, LORD, hast holpen me, and comforted me.

40. Moses for mercy (Psalm 90:12-17)

[12] So teach us to number our days, that we may apply our hearts unto wisdom. [13] Return, O LORD, how long? and let it repent thee concerning thy servants. [14]

O satisfy us early with thy mercy; that we may rejoice and be glad all our days. [15] Make us glad according to the days wherein thou hast afflicted us, and the years wherein we have seen evil. [16] Let thy work appear unto thy servants, and thy glory unto their children. [17] And let the beauty of the LORD our God be upon us: and establish thou the work of our hands upon us; yea, the work of our hands establish thou it.

41. A prayer of distress (Psalm 102:1-2 ,13)

[1] Hear my prayer, O LORD, and let my cry come unto thee. [2] Hide not thy face from me in the day when I am in trouble; incline thine ear unto me: in the day when I call answer me speedily. [13] Thou shalt arise, and have mercy upon Zion: for the time to favour her, yea, the set time, is come.

42. Prayer for JEHOVAH to remember (Psalm 106:4-5)

[4] Remember me, O LORD, with the favour that thou bearest unto thy people: O visit me with thy salvation; [5] That I may see the good of thy chosen, that I may rejoice in the gladness of thy nation, that I may glory with thine inheritance. Save us, O LORD our God, and gather us from among the heathen, to give thanks unto thy holy name, and to triumph in thy praise.

43. David of distress against enemies (Psalm 109:1-2 ,21,26,28-29)

[1] Hold not thy peace, O God of my praise; [2] For the mouth of the wicked and the mouth of the deceitful are opened against me: they have spoken against me with a lying tongue. [21] But do thou for me, O GOD the Lord, for thy name's sake: because thy mercy is good, deliver thou me. [26] Help me, O LORD my God: O save me according to thy mercy: [28] Let them curse, but bless thou: when they arise, let them be ashamed; but let thy servant rejoice. [29] Let mine adversaries be clothed with shame, and let them cover themselves with their own confusion, as with a mantle.

44. Messianic prayer for prosperity (Psalm 118:25)

[5] Save now, I beseech thee, O LORD: O LORD, I beseech thee, send now prosperity.

45. David's word of JEHOVAH (PSALM 119:10, 12, 17, 18, 19, 22, 26-29, 33-41,58, 64, 66, 73, 76-80, 86, 88, 107-108, 124, 133-135, 149, 154, 156, 159, 169-170, 173, 175)

[10] With my whole heart have I sought thee: O let me not wander from thy commandments. [12] Blessed art thou, O LORD: teach me thy statutes. [17] Deal bountifully with thy servant, that I may live, and keep thy word. [18] Open thou mine eyes, that I may behold wondrous things out of thy law. [19] I am a stranger in the earth: hide not thy commandments from me. [22] Remove from me reproach and contempt; for I have kept thy testimonies.
[26] I have declared my ways, and thou heardest me:

teach me thy statutes. [27] Make me to understand the way of thy precepts: so shall I talk of thy wondrous works. [28] My soul melteth for heaviness: strengthen thou me according unto thy word. [29] Remove from me the way of lying: and grant me thy law graciously. I have stuck unto thy testimonies: O LORD, put me not to shame. [33] Teach me, O Lord, the way of thy statutes; and I shall keep it unto the end. [34] Give me understanding, and I shall keep thy law; yea, I shall observe it with my whole heart. [35] Make me to go in the path of thy commandments; for therein do I delight. [36] Incline my heart unto thy testimonies, and not to covetousness. [37] Turn away mine eyes from beholding vanity; and quicken thou me in thy way. [38] Stablish thy word unto thy servant, who is devoted to thy fear. [39] Turn away my reproach which I fear: for thy judgments are good. [40] Behold, I have longed after thy precepts: quicken me in thy righteousness. [41] Let thy mercies come also unto me, O LORD, even thy salvation, according to thy word. [58] I intreated thy favour with my whole heart: be merciful unto me according to thy word. [64] The earth, O LORD, is full of thy mercy: teach me thy statutes. [66] Teach me good judgment and knowledge: for I have believed thy commandments. [73] Thy hands have made me and fashioned me: give me understanding, that I may learn thy commandments.

[76] Let, I pray thee, thy merciful kindness be for my comfort, according to thy word unto thy servant. [77] Let thy tender mercies come unto me, that I may live: for thy law is my delight. [78] Let the proud be ashamed; for

they dealt perversely with me without a cause: but I will meditate in thy precepts. [79] Let those that fear thee turn unto me, and those that have known thy testimonies. [80] Let my heart be sound in thy statutes; that I be not ashamed. [86] All thy commandments are faithful: they persecute me wrongfully; help thou me. [88] Quicken me after thy lovingkindness; so shall I keep the testimony of thy mouth.

[107] I am afflicted very much: quicken me, O Lord, according unto thy word. [108] Accept, I beseech thee, the freewill offerings of my mouth, O LORD, and teach me thy judgments. [124] Deal with thy servant according unto thy mercy, and teach me thy statutes.

[133] Order my steps in thy word: and let not any iniquity have dominion over me. [134] Deliver me from the oppression of man: so will I keep thy precepts. [135] Make thy face to shine upon thy servant; and teach me thy statutes. [149] Hear my voice according unto thy lovingkindness: O LORD, quicken me according to thy judgment. [154] Plead my cause, and deliver me: quicken me according to thy word. [156] Great are thy tender mercies, O LORD: quicken me according to thy judgments. [159] Consider how I love thy precepts: quicken me, O LORD, according to thy lovingkindness.

[169] Let my cry come near before thee, O Lord: give me understanding according to thy word. [170] Let my supplication come before thee: deliver me according to thy word. [173] Let thine hand help me; for I have chosen thy precepts.

[175] Let my soul live, and it shall praise thee; and let

thy judgments help me.

46. Unknown. Of distress (Psalm 120:2)

[2] Deliver my soul, O LORD, from lying lips, and from a deceitful tongue.

47. Unknown of distress (Psalm 123:3)

[3] Have mercy upon us, O LORD, have mercy upon us: for we are exceedingly filled with contempt.

48. David for deliverance (Psalm 124:6)

[6 Blessed be the LORD, who hath not given us as a prey to their teeth.

49. Unknown of trust (Psalm 125:4)

[4] Do good, O LORD, unto those that be good, and to them that are upright in their hearts.

50. Unknown. Prayer against Enemies (Psalm 129:5-8)

[5] Let them all be confounded and turned back that hate Zion. [6] Let them be as the grass upon the housetops, which withereth afore it groweth up: [7] Wherewith the mower filleth not his hand; nor he that bindeth sheaves his bosom. [8] Neither do they which go by say, The blessing of the LORD be upon you: we bless you in the name of the LORD.

51. Unknown. Prayer of Distress for mercy (Psalm 130:1-3)

[1] Out of the depths have I cried unto thee, O LORD. [2] Lord, hear my voice: let thine ears be attentive to the voice of my supplications. [3] If thou, LORD, shouldest mark iniquities, O Lord, who shall stand?

52. David of trust in JEHOVAH (Psalm 131:3)

[3] Let Israel hope in the LORD from henceforth and for ever.

53. David of distress and oath (Psalm 132:1, 8-10)

[1] LORD, remember David, and all his afflictions: [8] Arise, O LORD, into thy rest; thou, and the ark of thy strength. [9] Let thy priests be clothed with righteousness; and let thy saints shout for joy. [10] For thy servant David's sake turn not away the face of thine anointed.

54. Unknown Psalm of praise to JEHOVAH (PSALM 135:1-3)

[1] Praise ye the LORD. Praise ye the name of the LORD; praise him, O ye servants of the LORD. [2] Ye that stand in the house of the Lord, in the courts of the house of our God, [3] Praise the LORD; for the LORD is good: sing praises unto his name; for it is pleasant.

Psalm 135:19-21:

[19] Bless the LORD, O house of Israel: bless the LORD, O house of Aaron: [20] Bless the Lord, O house of Levi: ye that fear the Lord, bless the Lord. [21] Blessed be the LORD out of Zion, which dwelleth at Jerusalem. Praise

ye the LORD.

55. Unknown of captivity to Babylon (Psalm137:7)

[7] Remember, O LORD, the children of Edom in the day of Jerusalem; who said, Rase it, rase it, even to the foundation thereof.

56. David of judgment and for protection (Psalm 140:1, 4, 6, 8-11)

[1] Deliver me, O LORD, from the evil man: preserve me from the violent man; [4] Keep me, O LORD, from the hands of the wicked; preserve me from the violent man; who have purposed to overthrow my goings. [6] I said unto the LORD, Thou art my God: hear the voice of my supplications, O LORD.
t [8] Grant not, O LORD, the desires of the wicked: further not his wicked device; lest they exalt themselves. Selah. [9] As for the head of those that compass me about, let the mischief of their own lips cover them. [10] Let burning coals fall upon them: let them be cast into the fire; into deep pits, that they rise not up again. [11] Let not an evil speaker be established in the earth: evil shall hunt the violent man to overthrow him.

57. David of not to sin (Psalm 141:1-4)

[1] LORD, I cry unto thee: make haste unto me; give ear unto my voice, when I cry unto thee.
[2] Let my prayer be set forth before thee as incense; and the lifting up of my hands as the evening sacrifice. [3] Set

a watch, O Lord, before my mouth; keep the door of my lips. [4] Incline not my heart to any evil thing, to practise wicked works with men that work iniquity: and let me not eat of their dainties.

58. David of distress not to be killed (Psalm 143:1, 7-12)

[1] Hear my prayer, O LORD, give ear to my supplications: in thy faithfulness answer me, and in thy righteousness. [7] Hear me speedily, O LORD: my spirit faileth: hide not thy face from me, lest I be like unto them that go down into the pit. [8] Cause me to hear thy lovingkindness in the morning; for in thee do I trust: cause me to know the way wherein I should walk; for I lift up my soul unto thee. [9] Deliver me, O Lord, from mine enemies: I flee unto thee to hide me. [10] Teach me to do thy will; for thou art my God: thy spirit is good; lead me into the land of uprightness. [11] Quicken me, O LORD, for thy name's sake: for thy righteousness' sake bring my soul out of trouble. [12] And of thy mercy cut off mine enemies, and destroy all them that afflict my soul: for I am thy servant.

59. David for victory over enemies (Psalm 144:5-7,11-14)

[5] Bow thy heavens, O LORD, and come down: touch the mountains, and they shall smoke. [6] Cast forth lightning, and scatter them: shoot out thine arrows, and destroy them. [7] Send thine hand from above; rid me, and deliver me out of great waters, from the hand of strange children; [11] Rid me, and deliver me from the hand of strange children, whose mouth speaketh vanity, and their

right hand is a right hand of falsehood: [12] That our sons may be as plants grown up in their youth; that our daughters may be as corner stones, polished after the similitude of a palace: [13] That our garners may be full, affording all manner of store: that our sheep may bring forth thousands and ten thousands in our streets: [14] That our oxen may be strong to labour; that there be no breaking in, nor going out; that there be no complaining in our streets.

60. Unknown of praise (Psalm 146:1)

[1] Praise ye the LORD. Praise the LORD, O my soul.

61. Unknown of praise (Psalm 147:1, 7, 12)

[1] Praise ye the LORD: for it is good to sing praises unto our God; for it is pleasant; and praise is comely. [7] Sing unto the LORD with thanksgiving; sing praise upon the harp unto our God: [12] Praise the LORD, O Jerusalem; praise thy God, O Zion.

62. Unknown. To praise JEHOVAH (Psalm 148:1-5)

[1] Praise ye the LORD. Praise ye the LORD from the heavens: praise him in the heights. [2] Praise ye him, all his angels: praise ye him, all his hosts. [3] Praise ye him, sun and moon: praise him, all ye stars of light. [4] Praise him, ye heavens of heavens, and ye waters that be above the heavens. [5] Let them praise the name of the LORD: for he commanded, and they were created.

63. Unknown. To praise (Psalm 149:1-3,5,6)

[1] Praise ye the LORD. Sing unto the LORD a new song, and his praise in the congregation of saints. [2] Let Israel rejoice in him that made him: let the children of Zion be joyful in their King. [3] Let them praise his name in the dance: let them sing praises unto him with the timbrel and harp. [5] Let the saints be joyful in glory: let them sing aloud upon their beds. [6] Let the high praises of God be in their mouth, and a two-edged sword in their hand;

64. Unknown. To praise JEHOVAH (Psalm 150:1-6)

[1] Praise ye the LORD. Praise God in his sanctuary: praise him in the firmament of his power. [2] Praise him for his mighty acts: praise him according to his excellent greatness. [3] Praise him with the sound of the trumpet: praise him with the psaltery and harp. [4] Praise him with the timbrel and dance: praise him with stringed instruments and organs. [5] Praise him upon the loud cymbals: praise him upon the high sounding cymbals. [6] Let every thing that hath breath praise the LORD. Praise ye the LORD

PRAYERS IN ISAIAH: 3

1. Isaiah for cleansing (Isaiah 6:5)

> *[5] Then said I, Woe is me! for I am undone; because I am a man of unclean lips, and I dwell in the midst of a people of unclean lips: for mine eyes have seen the King, the LORD of hosts.*

2. Hezekiah for deliverance (Isaiah 37:16-20)

> *[16] O Lord of hosts, God of Israel, that dwellest between the cherubims, thou art the God, even thou alone, of all the kingdoms of the earth: thou hast made heaven and earth. [17] Incline thine ear, O Lord, and hear; open thine eyes, O Lord, and see: and hear all the words of Sennacherib, which hath sent to reproach the living God. [18] Of a truth, Lord, the kings of Assyria have laid waste all the nations, and their countries, [19] And have cast their gods into the fire: for they were no gods, but the work of men's hands, wood and stone: therefore they have destroyed them. [20] Now therefore, O LORD our God, save us from his hand, that all the kingdoms of the earth may know that thou art the LORD, even thou only.*

3. Hezekiah for total healing and give him long life (Isaiah 38:3)

> *[3] And said, Remember now, O LORD, I beseech thee,*

how I have walked before thee in truth and with a perfect heart, and have done that which is good in thy sight. And Hezekiah wept sore.

PRAYERS IN JEREMIAH:11

1 Jeremiah because of not obeying JEHOVAH (Jeremiah 1:6)

[6] Then said I, Ah, Lord GOD! behold, I cannot speak: for I am a child.

2. Jeremiah trying to accuse JEHOVAH (Jeremiah 4:10)

[10] Then said I, Ah, Lord GOD! surely thou hast greatly deceived this people and Jerusalem, saying, Ye shall have peace; whereas the sword reacheth unto the soul.

3. Jeremiah asking for judgment (Jeremiah 10:23-25)

[23] O LORD, I know that the way of man is not in himself: it is not in man that walketh to direct his steps. [24] O Lord, correct me, but with judgment; not in thine anger, lest thou bring me to nothing. [25] Pour out thy fury upon the heathen that know thee not, and upon the families that call not on thy name: for they have eaten up Jacob, and devoured him, and consumed him, and have made his habitation desolate.

4 Jeremiah trying to question JEHOVAH (Jeremiah 12:1-4)

[1] Righteous art thou, O LORD, when I plead with thee: yet let me talk with thee of thy judgments: Wherefore doth the way of the wicked prosper? wherefore are all they happy that deal very treacherously? [2] Thou hast plant-

ed them, yea, they have taken root: they grow, yea, they bring forth fruit: thou art near in their mouth, and far from their reins. [3] But thou, O Lord, knowest me: thou hast seen me, and tried mine heart toward thee: pull them out like sheep for the slaughter, and prepare them for the day of slaughter. [4] How long shall the land mourn, and the herbs of every field wither, for the wickedness of them that dwell therein? the beasts are consumed, and the birds; because they said, He shall not see our last end.

5. Jeremiah for JEHOVAH to help Judah (Jeremiah 14:7-9)

[7] O Lord, though our iniquities testify against us, do thou it for thy name's sake: for our backslidings are many; we have sinned against thee. [8] O the hope of Israel, the saviour thereof in time of trouble, why shouldest thou be as a stranger in the land, and as a wayfaring man that turneth aside to tarry for a night? [9] Why shouldest thou be as a man astonied, as a mighty man that cannot save? Yet thou, O LORD, art in the midst of us, and we are called by thy name; leave us not.

6. Jeremiah for JEHOVAH to help (Jeremiah 14:20-22)

[20] We acknowledge, O LORD, our wickedness, and the iniquity of our fathers: for we have sinned against thee. [21] Do not abhor us, for thy name's sake, do not disgrace the throne of thy glory: remember, break not thy covenant with us. [22] Are there any among the vanities of the Gentiles that can cause rain? Or can the heavens give showers? art not thou he, O LORD our God? there-

fore we will wait upon thee: for thou hast made all these things.

7. Jeremiah. For judgment against his mockers (Jeremiah 15:15-18)

[15] O Lord, thou knowest: remember me, and visit me, and revenge me of my persecutors; take me not away in thy longsuffering: know that for thy sake I have suffered rebuke. [16] Thy words were found, and I did eat them; and thy word was unto me the joy and rejoicing of mine heart: for I am called by thy name, O Lord God of hosts. [17] I sat not in the assembly of the mockers, nor rejoiced; I sat alone because of thy hand: for thou hast filled me with indignation. [18] Why is my pain perpetual, and my wound incurable, which refuseth to be healed? wilt thou be altogether unto me as a liar, and as waters that fail?

8. Jeremiah. For judgment against his persecutors (Jeremiah 17:13-18)

[13] O LORD, the hope of Israel, all that forsake thee shall be ashamed, and they that depart from me shall be written in the earth, because they have forsaken the LORD, the fountain of living waters. [14] Heal me, O Lord, and I shall be healed; save me, and I shall be saved: for thou art my praise. [15] Behold, they say unto me, Where is the word of the Lord? let it come now. [16] As for me, I have not hastened from being a pastor to follow thee: neither have I desired the woeful day;

thou knowest: that which came out of my lips was right before thee. [17] Be not a terror unto me: thou art my hope in the day of evil. [18] Let them be confounded that persecute me, but let not me be confounded: let them be dismayed, but let not me be dismayed: bring upon them the day of evil, and destroy them with double destruction.

9. Jeremiah. For judgment against his enemies (Jeremiah 18:19-3)

[19] Give heed to me, O Lord, and hearken to the voice of them that contend with me. [20] Shall evil be recompensed for good? for they have digged a pit for my soul. Remember that I stood before thee to speak good for them, and to turn away thy wrath from them. [21] Therefore deliver up their children to the famine, and pour out their blood by the force of the sword; and let their wives be bereaved of their children, and be widows; and let their men be put to death; let their young men be slain by the sword in battle. [22] Let a cry be heard from their houses, when thou shalt bring a troop suddenly upon them: for they have digged a pit to take me, and hid snares for my feet. [23] Yet, LORD, thou knowest all their counsel against me to slay me: forgive not their iniquity, neither blot out their sin from thy sight, but let them be overthrown before thee; deal thus with them in the time of thine anger.

10. Jeremiah. For judgment against his persecutors (Jeremiah 20:7-12)

[7] O LORD, thou hast deceived me, and I was deceived: thou art stronger than I, and hast prevailed: I am in derision daily, everyone mocketh me. [8] For since I spake, I cried out, I cried violence and spoil; because the word of the LORD was made a reproach unto me, and a derision daily. [9] Then I said, I will not make mention of him, nor speak any more in his name. But his word was in mine heart as a burning fire shut up in my bones, and I was weary with forbearing, and I could not stay. [10] For I heard the defaming of many, fear on every side. Report, say they, and we will report it. All my familiars watched for my halting, saying, Peradventure he will be enticed, and we shall prevail against him, and we shall take our revenge on him. [11] But the Lord is with me as a mighty terrible one: therefore, my persecutors shall stumble, and they shall not prevail: they shall be greatly ashamed; for they shall not prosper: their everlasting confusion shall never be forgotten. [12] But, O LORD of hosts, that triest the righteous, and seest the reins and the heart, let me see thy vengeance on them: for unto thee have I opened my cause.

11. Jeremiah. About Judah being in captivity (Jeremiah 32:17-24)

[17] Ah Lord GOD! behold, thou hast made the heaven and the earth by thy great power and stretched out arm, and there is nothing too hard for thee: [18] Thou shewest lovingkindness unto thousands, and recompensest the iniquity of the fathers into the bosom of their children after them: the Great, the Mighty God, the Lord of hosts, is

his name, [19] Great in counsel, and mighty in work: for thine eyes are open upon all the ways of the sons of men: to give every one according to his ways, and according to the fruit of his doings: [20] Which hast set signs and wonders in the land of Egypt, even unto this day, and in Israel, and among other men; and hast made thee a name, as at this day; [21] And hast brought forth thy people Israel out of the land of Egypt with signs, and with wonders, and with a strong hand, and with a stretched out arm, and with great terror; [22] And hast given them this land, which thou didst swear to their fathers to give them, a land flowing with milk and honey; [23] And they came in, and possessed it; but they obeyed not thy voice, neither walked in thy law; they have done nothing of all that thou commandedst them to do: therefore thou hast caused all this evil to come upon them: [24] Behold the mounts, they are come unto the city to take it; and the city is given into the hand of the Chaldeans, that fight against it, because of the sword, and of the famine, and of the pestilence: and what thou hast spoken is come to pass; and, behold, thou seest it.

PRAYERS IN LAMENTATIONS: 4

1. Jeremiah. For judgement (Lamentations 1:20-22)

[20] Behold, O Lord; for I am in distress: my bowels are troubled; mine heart is turned within me; for I have grievously rebelled: abroad the sword bereaveth, at home there is as death. [21] They have heard that I sigh: there is none to comfort me: all mine enemies have heard of my trouble; they are glad that thou hast done it: thou wilt bring the day that thou hast called, and they shall be like unto me. [22] Let all their wickedness come before thee; and do unto them, as thou hast done unto me for all my transgressions: for my sighs are many, and my heart is faint.

2. Jeremiah. To consider (Lamentations 2:20-22)

[20] Behold, O LORD, and consider to whom thou hast done this. Shall the women eat their fruit, and children of a span long? shall the priest and the prophet be slain in the sanctuary of the Lord? [21] The young and the old lie on the ground in the streets: my virgins and my young men are fallen by the sword; thou hast slain them in the day of thine anger; [22] thou hast killed, and not pitied. Thou hast called as in a solemn day my terrors round about, so that in the day of the LORD'S anger none escaped nor remained: those that I have swaddled and brought up hath mine enemy consumed.

3. Jeremiah. For judgment (Lamentations 3:55-66)

[55] I called upon thy name, O LORD, out of the low dungeon. [56] Thou hast heard my voice: hide not thine ear at my breathing, at my cry. [57] Thou drewest near in the day that I called upon thee: thou saidst, Fear not[58] . O Lord, thou hast pleaded the causes of my soul; thou hast redeemed my life. [59] O Lord, thou hast seen my wrong: judge thou my cause. [60] Thou hast seen all their vengeance and all their imaginations against me. [61] Thou hast heard their reproach, O Lord, and all their imaginations against me; [62] The lips of those that rose up against me, and their device against me all the day. [63] Behold their sitting down, and their rising up; I am their musick. [64 Render unto them a recompence, O Lord, according to the work of their hands. [65] Give them sorrow of heart, thy curse unto them. [66] Persecute and destroy them in anger from under the heavens of the LORD.

4. Jeremiah. For JEHOVAH to consider and behold (Lamentations 5:1-22)

[1] Remember, O LORD, what is come upon us: consider, and behold our reproach. [2] Our inheritance is turned to strangers, our houses to aliens. [3] We are orphans and fatherless, our mothers are as widows. [4] We have drunken our water for money; our wood is sold unto us. [5] Our necks are under persecution: we labour, and have no rest. [6] We have given the hand to the Egyp-

tians, and to the Assyrians, to be satisfied with bread. [7] Our fathers have sinned, and are not; and we have borne their iniquities. [8] Servants have ruled over us: there is none that doth deliver us out of their hand. [9] We gat our bread with the peril of our lives because of the sword of the wilderness. [10] Our skin was black like an oven because of the terrible famine. [11] They ravished the women in Zion, and the maids in the cities of Judah. [12] Princes are hanged up by their hand: the faces of elders were not honoured. [13] They took the young men to grind, and the children fell under the wood. [14] The elders have ceased from the gate, the young men from their musick. [15] The joy of our heart is ceased; our dance is turned into mourning. [16] The crown is fallen from our head: woe unto us, that we have sinned! [17] For this our heart is faint; for these things our eyes are dim. [18] Because of the mountain of Zion, which is desolate, the foxes walk upon it. [19] Thou, O Lord, remainest forever; thy throne from generation to generation. [20] Wherefore dost thou forget us forever, and forsake us so long time? [21] Turn thou us unto thee, O Lord, and we shall be turned; renew our days as of old. [22] But thou hast utterly rejected us; thou art very wroth against us.

PRAYERS IN EZEKIEL: 3

1. Ezekiel. Trying to protest what JEHOVAH wanted him to do (Ezekiel 4:14)

> *[14] Then said I, Ah Lord GOD! behold, my soul hath not been polluted: for from my youth up even till now have I not eaten of that which dieth of itself, or is torn in pieces; neither came there abominable flesh into my mouth.*

2. Ezekiel. For the residents that are left (Ezekiel 9:8)

> *[8] And it came to pass, while they were slaying them, and I was left, that I fell upon my face, and cried, and said, Ah Lord GOD! wilt thou destroy all the residue of Israel in thy pouring out of thy fury upon Jerusalem?*

3. Ezekiel. For the remnant (Ezekiel 11:13)

> *[13] And it came to pass, when I prophesied, that Pelatiah the son of Benaiah died. Then fell I down upon my face, and cried with a loud voice, and said, Ah Lord GOD! wilt thou make a full end of the remnant of Israel?*

PRAYERS IN DANIEL: 2

1. Daniel. For fulfillment of prophecy and forgiveness of sins (Daniel 9:1-19)

[1] In the first year of Darius the son of Ahasuerus, of the seed of the Medes, which was made king over the realm of the Chaldeans; [2] In the first year of his reign I Daniel understood by books the number of the years, whereof the word of the Lord came to Jeremiah the prophet, that he would accomplish seventy years in the desolations of Jerusalem. [3] And I set my face unto the Lord God, to seek by prayer and supplications, with fasting, and sackcloth, and ashes: [4] And I prayed unto the Lord my God, and made my confession, and said, O Lord, the great and dreadful God, keeping the covenant and mercy to them that love him, and to them that keep his commandments; [5] We have sinned, and have committed iniquity, and have done wickedly, and have rebelled, even by departing from thy precepts and from thy judgments: [6] Neither have we hearkened unto thy servants the prophets, which spake in thy name to our kings, our princes, and our fathers, and to all the people of the land. [7] O Lord, righteousness belongeth unto thee, but unto us confusion of faces, as at this day; to the men of Judah, and to the inhabitants of Jerusalem, and unto all Israel, that are near, and that are far off, through all the countries whither thou hast driven them, because of their

trespass that they have trespassed against thee. [8] O Lord, to us belongeth confusion of face, to our kings, to our princes, and to our fathers, because we have sinned against thee. [9] To the Lord our God belong mercies and forgivenesses, though we have rebelled against him; [10] Neither have we obeyed the voice of the LORD our God, to walk in his laws, which he set before us by his servants the prophets. [11] Yea, all Israel have transgressed thy law, even by departing, that they might not obey thy voice; therefore the curse is poured upon us, and the oath that is written in the law of Moses the servant of God, because we have sinned against him. [12] And he hath confirmed his words, which he spake against us, and against our judges that judged us, by bringing upon us a great evil: for under the whole heaven hath not been done as hath been done upon Jerusalem. [13] As it is written in the law of Moses, all this evil is come upon us: yet made we not our prayer before the Lord our God, that we might turn from our iniquities, and understand thy truth. [14] Therefore hath the Lord watched upon the evil, and brought it upon us: for the Lord our God is righteous in all his works which he doeth: for we obeyed not his voice. [15] And now, O Lord our God, that hast brought thy people forth out of the land of Egypt with a mighty hand, and hast gotten thee renown, as at this day; we have sinned, we have done wickedly. [16] O Lord, according to all thy righteousness, I beseech thee, let thine anger and thy fury be turned away from thy city Jerusalem, thy holy mountain: because for our sins, and for the iniquities of our fathers, Jerusalem and thy people are become a reproach to all that are about us. [17] Now therefore, O our God, hear the prayer of thy servant, and his supplications, and cause thy face to shine upon thy sanctuary that is desolate, for the Lord's sake. [18] O my God, incline thine ear, and hear; open thine eyes, and behold our desolations, and the city which is called by thy name: for we do not present our supplications before thee for our righteousnesses, but for thy great mercies. [19] O Lord, hear; O Lord, forgive; O Lord, hearken and do; defer not, for thine own sake, O my God: for thy city and thy people are called by thy name.

2. Daniel. For Revelation (Daniel12:8)

[8] And I heard, but I understood not: then said I, O my Lord, what shall be the end of these things.

PRAYERS IN AMOS: 2

1. Amos. For forgiveness (Amos 7:2)

[2] And it came to pass, that when they had made an end of eating the grass of the land, then I said, O Lord GOD, forgive, I beseech thee: by whom shall Jacob arise? for he is small.

2. Amos. For help to cease (Amos. 7:5)

[5] Then said I, O Lord GOD, cease, I beseech thee: by whom shall Jacob arise? for he is small.

PRAYERS IN JONAH: 3

1. Sailors for mercy (Jonah 1:14)

> *[14] Wherefore they cried unto the LORD, and said, We*
> *beseech thee, O LORD, we beseech thee, let us not perish*
> *for this man's life, and lay not upon us innocent blood:*
> *for thou, O LORD, hast done as it pleased thee.*

2. Jonah. For deliverance from the fish's belly (Jonah 2:1-9)

> *[1] Then Jonah prayed unto the LORD his God out of*
> *the fish's belly, [2] And said, I cried by reason of mine*
> *affliction unto the Lord, and he heard me; out of the belly*
> *of hell cried I, and thou heardest my voice. [3] For thou*
> *hadst cast me into the deep, in the midst of the seas; and*
> *the floods compassed me about: all thy billows and thy*
> *waves passed over me. [4] Then I said, I am cast out of*
> *thy sight; yet I will look again toward thy holy temple.*
> *[5] The waters compassed me about, even to the soul: the*
> *depth closed me round about, the weeds were wrapped*
> *about my head. [6] I went down to the bottoms of the*
> *mountains; the earth with her bars was about me for*
> *ever: yet hast thou brought up my life from corruption,*
> *O Lord my God. [7] When my soul fainted within me I*
> *remembered the Lord: and my prayer came in unto thee,*
> *into thine holy temple. [8] They that observe lying vani-*
> *ties forsake their own mercy. [9] But I will sacrifice unto*
> *thee with the voice of thanksgiving; I will pay that that I*
> *have vowed. Salvation is of the LORD.*

3. Jonah. for death (Jonah 4:2-3)

[2] And he prayed unto the LORD, and said, I pray thee, O LORD, was not this my saying, when I was yet in my country? Therefore I fled before unto Tarshish: for I knew that thou art a gracious God, and merciful, slow to anger, and of great kindness, and repentest thee of the evil. [3] Therefore now, O LORD, take, I beseech thee, my life from me; for it is better for me to die than to live.

PRAYERS IN HABAKKUK: 3

1. Habakkuk. For JEHOVAH to act (Habakkuk 1:1-4).

[1] The burden which Habakkuk the prophet did see. [2] O Lord, how long shall I cry, and thou wilt not hear! even cry out unto thee of violence, and thou wilt not save! [3] Why dost thou shew me iniquity, and cause me to behold grievance? for spoiling and violence are before me: and there are that raise up strife and contention. [4] Therefore the law is slacked, and judgment doth never go forth: for the wicked doth compass about the righteous; therefore wrong judgment proceedeth.

2. Habakkuk for judgement (Habakkuk 1:12-17)

[12] Art thou not from everlasting, O LORD my God, mine Holy One? we shall not die. O LORD, thou hast or-dained them for judgment; and, O mighty God, thou hast established them for correction. [13] Thou art of purer eyes than to behold evil, and canst not look on iniquity: wherefore lookest thou upon them that deal treacherously, and holdest thy tongue when the wicked devoureth the man that is more righteous than he? [14] And makest men as the fishes of the sea, as the creeping things, that have no ruler over them? [15] They take up all of them with the angle, they catch them in their net, and gather them in their drag: therefore they rejoice and are glad. [16] Therefore they sacrifice unto their net, and burn incense

unto their drag; because by them their portion is fat, and their meat plenteous. [17] Shall they therefore empty their net, and not spare continually to slay the nations?

3. Habakkuk for Revival (Habakkuk 3:2-19)

[2] O LORD, I have heard thy speech, and was afraid: O LORD, revive thy work in the midst of the years, in the midst of the years make known; in wrath remember mercy. [3] God came from Teman, and the Holy One from mount Paran. Selah. His glory covered the heavens, and the earth was full of his praise. [4] And his brightness was as the light; he had horns coming out of his hand: and there was the hiding of his power. [5] Before him went the pestilence, and burning coals went forth at his feet. [6] He stood, and measured the earth: he beheld, and drove asunder the nations; and the everlasting mountains were scattered, the perpetual hills did bow: his ways are everlasting. [7] I saw the tents of Cushan in affliction: and the curtains of the land of Midian did tremble. [8] Was the Lord displeased against the rivers? was thine anger against the rivers? was thy wrath against the sea, that thou didst ride upon thine horses and thy chariots of salvation? [9] Thy bow was made quite naked, according to the oaths of the tribes, even thy word. Selah. Thou didst cleave the earth with rivers. [10] The mountains saw thee, and they trembled: the overflowing of the water passed by: the deep uttered his voice, and lifted up his hands on high. [11] The sun and moon stood still in their habitation: at the light of thine arrows they went, and at the shining of thy glittering spear. [12] Thou didst march

through the land in indignation, thou didst thresh the heathen in anger. [13] Thou wentest forth for the salvation of thy people, even for salvation with thine anointed; thou woundedst the head out of the house of the wicked, by discovering the foundation unto the neck. Selah. [14] Thou didst strike through with his staves the head of his villages: they came out as a whirlwind to scatter me: their rejoicing was as to devour the poor secretly. [15] Thou didst walk through the sea with thine horses, through the heap of great waters. [16] When I heard, my belly trembled; my lips quivered at the voice: rottenness entered into my bones, and I trembled in myself, that I might rest in the day of trouble: when he cometh up unto the people, he will invade them with his troops. [17] Although the fig tree shall not blossom, neither shall fruit be in the vines; the labour of the olive shall fail, and the fields shall yield no meat; the flock shall be cut off from the fold, and there shall be no herd in the stalls: [18] Yet I will rejoice in the Lord, I will joy in the God of my salvation. [19] The LORD God is my strength, and he will make my feet like hinds' feet, and he will make me to walk upon mine high places. To the chief singer on my stringed instruments.

PRAYERS IN NEW TESTAMENT

PRAYERS IN MATTHEW: 17

1. JESUS. The Lord' s Prayer (Matthew 6:9-12)

[9] After this manner therefore pray ye: Our Father which art in heaven, Hallowed be thy name. [10] Thy kingdom come. Thy will be done in earth, as it is in heaven. [11] Give us this day our daily bread. [12] And forgive us our debts, as we forgive our debtors. [13] And lead us not into temptation, but deliver us from evil: For thine is the kingdom, and the power, and the glory, for ever. Amen.

2. Leper. For healing (Matthew 8:2)

[2] And, behold, there came a leper and worshipped him, saying, Lord, if thou wilt, thou canst make me clean.

3. The centurion. To heal his mail servant (Matthew 8:6-9)

[6] And saying, Lord, my servant lieth at home sick of the palsy, grievously tormented. [7] And Jesus saith unto him, I will come and heal him. [8] The centurion answered and said, Lord, I am not worthy that thou shouldest come under my roof: but speak the word only, and my servant shall be healed. [9] For I am a man under authority, having soldiers under me: and I say to this man, Go, and he goeth; and to another, Come, and he cometh; and to my servant, Do this, and he doeth it.

4. The disciples. To help from perishing (Matthew 8:25)

[25] And his disciples came to him, and awoke him, saying, Lord, save us: we perish.

5. The demons. To enter herd of swine Matthew 8:29-31)

[29] And, behold, they cried out, saying, What have we to do with thee, Jesus, thou Son of God? art thou come hither to torment us before the time? [30] And there was a good way off from them an herd of many swine feeding. [31] So the devils besought him, saying, If thou cast us out, suffer us to go away into the herd of swine.

6. Certain Ruler. For healing (Matthew 9:18)

[18] While he spake these things unto them, behold, there came a certain ruler, and worshipped him, saying, My daughter is even now dead: but come and lay thy hand upon her, and she shall live.

7. Woman with issue of blood. For healing (Matthew 9:21)

[21] For she said within herself, If I may but touch his garment, I shall be whole.

8. Two blind men. For healing (Matthew 9:27)

[27] And when Jesus departed thence, two blind men followed him, crying, and saying, Thou Son of David, have mercy on us.

9. JESUS. Thanking JEHOVAH (Matthew 11: 25)

[11] At that time Jesus answered and said, I thank thee, O Father, Lord of heaven and earth, because thou hast hid these things from the wise and prudent, and hast revealed them unto babes.

10. Peter. To walk on water (Matthew 14:28)

[28] And Peter answered him and said, Lord, if it be thou, bid me come unto thee on the water.

11. Peter. For help from drowning (Matthew 14:30)

[30] But when he saw the wind boisterous, he was afraid; and beginning to sink, he cried, saying, Lord, save me.

12. Woman. To heal her daughter (Matthew 15:22-27)

[22] And, behold, a woman of Canaan came out of the same coasts, and cried unto him, saying, Have mercy on me, O Lord, thou Son of David; my daughter is grievously vexed with a devil. [23] But he answered her not a word. And his disciples came and besought him, saying, Send her away; for she crieth after us. [24] But he answered and said, I am not sent but unto the lost sheep of the house of Israel. [25] Then came she and worshipped him, saying, Lord, help me. [26] But he answered and said, It is not meet to take the children's bread, and to cast it to dogs. [27] And she said, Truth, Lord: yet the dogs eat of the crumbs which fall from their masters' table.

13. Man. To heal his son (Matthew 17:15-16)

> *[15] Lord, have mercy on my son: for he is lunatick, and sore vexed: for ofttimes he falleth into the fire, and oft into the water. [16] And I brought him to thy disciples, and they could not cure him.*

14. Mother of Zebedee' s sons. To exalt her sons in the kingdom (Matthew 20:21)

> *[21] And he said unto her, What wilt thou? She saith unto him, Grant that these my two sons may sit, the one on thy right hand, and the other on the left, in thy kingdom.*

15. Two blind men. For healing (Matthew 20:30-33)

> *[30] And, behold, two blind men sitting by the way side, when they heard that Jesus passed by, cried out, saying, Have mercy on us, O Lord, thou Son of David. [31] And the multitude rebuked them, because they should hold their peace: but they cried the more, saying, Have mercy on us, O Lord, thou Son of David. [32] And Jesus stood still, and called them, and said, What will ye that I shall do unto you? [33] They say unto him, Lord, that our eyes may be opened.*

16. JESUS. For the cup of death to pass from HIM (Matthew 26:39-44)

> *[39] And he went a little further, and fell on his face, and prayed, saying, O my Father, if it be possible, let this cup pass from me: nevertheless not as I will, but as thou wilt.*

[40] And he cometh unto the disciples, and findeth them asleep, and saith unto Peter, What, could ye not watch with me one hour? [41] Watch and pray, that ye enter not into temptation: the spirit indeed is willing, but the flesh is weak. [42] He went away again the second time, and prayed, saying, O my Father, if this cup may not pass away from me, except I drink it, thy will be done. [43] And he came and found them asleep again: for their eyes were heavy. [44] And he left them, and went away again, and prayed the third time, saying the same words.

17. JESUS. On the cross (Matthew 27:46)

[46] And about the ninth hour Jesus cried with a loud voice, saying, Eli, Eli, lama sabachthani? that is to say, My God, my God, why hast thou forsaken me?

PRAYERS IN MARK: 2

1. Demon for freedom (Mark 1:23-24)

[23] And there was in their synagogue a man with an un-clean spirit; and he cried out, [24] Saying, Let us alone; what have we to do with thee, thou Jesus of Nazareth? art thou come to destroy us? I know thee who thou art, the Holy One of God.

2. JESUS. To heal a deaf and mute man (Matthew 7:34)

[34] And looking up to heaven, he sighed, and saith unto him, Ephphatha, that is, Be opened.

PRAYERS IN LUKE: 7

1. Simeon. When he blessed baby JESUS (Luke 2:29-32)

[29] Lord, now lettest thou thy servant depart in peace, according to thy word: [30] For mine eyes have seen thy salvation, [31] Which thou hast prepared before the face of all people; [32] A light to lighten the Gentiles, and the glory of thy people Israel.

2. The rich man in hell (Luke 16:24-31)

[24] And he cried and said, Father Abraham, have mercy on me, and send Lazarus, that he may dip the tip of his finger in water, and cool my tongue; for I am tormented in this flame. [25] But Abraham said, Son, remember that thou in thy lifetime receivedst thy good things, and likewise Lazarus evil things: but now he is comforted, and thou art tormented. [26] And beside all this, between us and you there is a great gulf fixed: so that they which would pass from hence to you cannot; neither can they pass to us, that would come from thence. [27] Then he said, I pray thee therefore, father, that thou wouldest send him to my father's house: [28] For I have five breth-ren; that he may testify unto them, lest they also come into this place of torment. [29] Abraham saith unto him, They have Moses and the prophets; let them hear them. [30] And he said, Nay, father Abraham: but if one went unto them from the dead, they will repent. [31] And he said unto him, If they hear not Moses and the prophets, neither will they be persuaded, though one rose from the dead.

3. The ten lepers. For healing (Luke 17:13)

> *[13] And they lifted up their voices, and said, Jesus, Master, have mercy on us.*

4. A Pharisee. Pretentious display of being righteous (Luke 18:11)

> *[11] The Pharisee stood and prayed thus with himself, God, I thank thee, that I am not as other men are, extortioners, unjust, adulterers, or even as this publican. I fast twice in the week, I give tithes of all that I possess.*

5. A publican. For JEHOVA to be merciful (Luke 18:13)

> *[13] And the publican, standing afar off, would not lift up so much as his eyes unto heaven, but smote upon his breast, saying, God be merciful to me a sinner.*

6. JESUS CHRIST. On the cross (Luke 23:34)

> *[34] Then said Jesus, Father, forgive them; for they know not what they do. And they parted his raiment, and cast lots.*

7. JESUS CHRIST. On the cross (Luke 23:46)

> *[46] And when Jesus had cried with a loud voice, he said, Father, into thy hands I commend my spirit: and having said thus, he gave up the ghost.*

PRAYERS IN JOHN: 5

1. A Nobleman. For JESUS to heal his child (John 4:49)

[49] The nobleman saith unto him, Sir, come down ere my child die.

2. The crowd. For living bread (John 6:34.

[34] Then said they unto him, Lord, evermore give us this bread.

3. JESUS CHRIST. To bring Lazarus back to life (John 11:41-43

[41] Then they took away the stone from the place where the dead was laid. And Jesus lifted up his eyes, and said, Father, I thank thee that thou hast heard me. {42] And I knew that thou hearest me always: but because of the people which stand by I said it, that they may believe that thou hast sent me. [43] And when he thus had spoken, he cried with a loud voice, Lazarus, come forth.

4. JESUS CHRIST. For JEHOVAH to glorify Himself (John 12:27-28)

[27] Now is my soul troubled; and what shall I say? Father, save me from this hour: but for this cause came I unto this hour. Father, glorify thy name.

5. JESUS CHRIST. For His disciples (John 17:1-26)

[1] Father, the hour is come; glorify thy Son, that thy

Son also may glorify thee: [2] As thou hast given him power over all flesh, that he should give eternal life to as many as thou hast given him. [3] And this is life eternal, that they might know thee the only true God, and Jesus Christ, whom thou hast sent. [4] I have glorified thee on the earth: I have finished the work which thou gavest me to do. [5] And now, O Father, glorify thou me with thine own self with the glory which I had with thee before the world was. [6] I have manifested thy name unto the men which thou gavest me out of the world: thine they were, and thou gavest them me; and they have kept thy word. [7] Now they have known that all things whatsoever thou hast given me are of thee. [8] For I have given unto them the words which thou gavest me; and they have received them, and have known surely that I came out from thee, and they have believed that thou didst send me. [9] I pray for them: I pray not for the world, but for them which thou hast given me; for they are thine. [10] And all mine are thine, and thine are mine; and I am glorified in them. [11] And now I am no more in the world, but these are in the world, and I come to thee. Holy Father, keep through thine own name those whom thou hast given me, that they may be one, as we are. [12] While I was with them in the world, I kept them in thy name: ... those that thou gavest me I have kept, and none of them is lost, but the son of perdition; that the scripture might be fulfilled. [13] And now come I to thee; and these things I speak in the world, that they might have my joy fulfilled in themselves. [14] I have given them thy word; and the world hath hated them, because they are not of the world, even as I am not of the world. [15] I pray not that thou shouldest take them out of the world, but that thou shouldest keep them from the evil. [16] They are not of the world, even as I am not of the world. [17] Sanctify them through thy truth: thy word is truth. [18] As thou hast sent me into the world, even so have I also sent them into the world. [19] And for their sakes I sanctify myself, that they also might be sanctified through the truth. [20] Neither pray I for these alone, but for them also which shall believe on me through their word; [21] That they all may be one; as thou, Father, art in me, and I in thee, that they also may be one in us: that the world may believe that thou hast sent me. [22] And the glory which thou gavest me I have given them; that they may be one, even as we are one: [23] I in them, and thou in me, that they may be made perfect in one; and that the world may know that thou hast sent me, and hast loved them, as thou hast loved me. [24] Father, I will that they also, whom thou hast given me, be with me where I am; that they may behold my glory, which thou hast given me: for thou lovedst me before the foundation of the world. [25] O righteous Father, the world hath not known thee: but I have known thee, and these have known that thou hast sent me. [26] And I have declared unto them thy name, and will declare it: that the love wherewith thou hast loved me may be in them, and I in them.

PRAYERS IN ACTS: 6

1. The disciples. To take the place of Judas (Acts 1:24-25)

[24] And they prayed, and said, Thou, Lord, which knowest the hearts of all men, shew whether of these two thou hast chosen, [25] That he may take part of this ministry and apostleship, from which Judas by transgression fell, that he might go to his own place.

2. Peter. To heal a physically challenged man (Acts 3:6)

[6] Then Peter said, Silver and gold have I none; but such as I have give I thee: In the name of Jesus Christ of Nazareth rise up and walk.

3. The disciples. To be bold and full of power to preach (Acts 4:24-30)

[24] And when they heard that, they lifted up their voice to God with one accord, and said, Lord, thou art God, which hast made heaven, and earth, and the sea, and all that in them is: [25] Who by the mouth of thy servant David hast said, Why did the heathen rage, and the people imagine vain things? [26] The kings of the earth stood up, and the rulers were gathered together against the Lord, and against his Christ. [27] For of a truth against thy holy child Jesus, whom thou hast anointed, both Herod, and Pontius Pilate, with the Gentiles, and the people of Israel, were gathered together, [28] For to do whatsoever thy hand and thy counsel determined before to be done.

[29] And now, Lord, behold their threatenings: and grant unto thy servants, that with all boldness they may speak thy word, [30] By stretching forth thine hand to heal; and that signs and wonders may be done by the name of thy holy child Jesus.

4. Stephen. For the people stoning him (Acts 7:59-60)

[59] And they stoned Stephen, calling upon God, and saying, Lord Jesus, receive my spirit. [60] And he kneeled down, and cried with a loud voice, Lord, lay not this sin to their charge. And when he had said this, he fell asleep.

5. Paul. For guidance (Acts 9:5-6)

[5] And he said, Who art thou, Lord? And the Lord said, I am Jesus whom thou persecutest: it is hard for thee to kick against the pricks. [6] And he trembling and astonished said, Lord, what wilt thou have me to do? And the Lord said unto him, Arise, and go into the city, and it shall be told thee what thou must do.

6. Peter. To bring a girl back to life (Acts 9:40)

[40] But Peter put them all forth, and kneeled down, and prayed; and turning him to the body said, Tabitha, arise. And she opened her eyes: and when she saw Peter, she sat up.

PRAYERS IN REVELATION: 7

1. The twenty-four Elders. Worshiping JEHOVAH (Revelation 4:11)

> *[11] Thou art worthy, O Lord, to receive glory and honour and power: for thou hast created all things, and for thy pleasure they are and were created.*

2. The angels and all creatures. Worshiping JEHOVAH (Revelation 5:12-13)

> *[12] Saying with a loud voice, Worthy is the Lamb that was slain to receive power, and riches, and wisdom, and strength, and honour, and glory, and blessing. [13] And every creature which is in heaven, and on the earth, and under the earth, and such as are in the sea, and all that are in them, heard I saying, Blessing, and honour, and glory, and power, be unto him that sitteth upon the throne, and unto the Lamb for ever and ever.*

3. The people that died for the word. For vengeance (Revelation 6:10)

> *[10] And they cried with a loud voice, saying, How long, O Lord, holy and true, dost thou not judge and avenge our blood on them that dwell on the earth?*

4. The great multitude. In worshiping (Revelation 7:10)

[10] And cried with a loud voice, saying, Salvation to our God which sitteth upon the throne, and unto the Lamb.

5. Angels. In worshiping (Revelation 7:12)

[12] Saying, Amen: Blessing, and glory, and wisdom, and thanksgiving, and honour, and power, and might, be unto our God for ever and ever. Amen.

6. The Saints. In Worship (Revelation 19:1-6)

[1] And after these things I heard a great voice of much people in heaven, saying, Alleluia; Salvation, and glory, and honour, and power, unto the Lord our God: [2] For true and righteous are his judgments: for he hath judged the great whore, which did corrupt the earth with her fornication, and hath avenged the blood of his servants at her hand. [3] And again they said, Alleluia. And her smoke rose up for ever and ever. [4] And the four and twenty elders and the four beasts fell down and worshipped God that sat on the throne, saying, Amen; Alleluia. [5] And a voice came out of the throne, saying, Praise our God, all ye his servants, and ye that fear him, both small and great. [6] And I heard as it were the voice of a great multitude, and as the voice of many waters, and as the voice of mighty thunderings, saying, Alleluia: for the Lord God omnipotent reigneth.

7. John. For the Messiah to come again (Revelation 22:20)

[20] He which testifieth these things saith, Surely I come quickly. Amen. Even so, come, Lord Jesus.

BIBLE PROPHETIC VERSES

from Genesis to Revelation.

Prophecies in Genesis: 48

1. Genesis 3:14-19:

[14] And the Lord God said unto the serpent, Because thou hast done this, thou art cursed above all cattle, and above every beast of the field; upon thy belly shalt thou go, and dust shalt thou eat all the days of thy life: [15] And I will put enmity between thee and the woman, and between thy seed and her seed; it shall bruise thy head, and thou shalt bruise his heel. [16] Unto the woman he said, I will greatly multiply thy sorrow and thy conception; in sorrow thou shalt bring forth children; and thy desire shall be to thy husband, and he shall rule over thee. [17] And unto Adam he said, Because thou hast hearkened unto the voice of thy wife, and hast eaten of the tree, of which I commanded thee, saying, Thou shalt not eat of it: cursed is the ground for thy sake; in sorrow shalt thou eat of it all the days of thy life; [18] Thorns also and thistles shall it bring forth to thee; and thou shalt eat the herb of the field; [19] In the sweat of thy face shalt thou eat bread, till thou return unto the ground; for out of it wast thou taken: for dust thou art, and unto dust shalt thou return.

2. Genesis 6:3:

[3] And the LORD said, My spirit shall not always strive with man, for that he also is flesh: yet his days shall be an

hundred and twenty years.

3. Genesis 6:7:

> *[7] And the LORD said, I will destroy man whom I have created from the face of the earth; both man, and beast, and the creeping thing, and the fowls of the air; for it repenteth me that I have made them.*

4. Genesis 6:13:

> *[13] And God said unto Noah, The end of all flesh is come before me; for the earth is filled with violence through them; and, behold, I will destroy them with the earth.*

5. Genesis 6:17:

> *[17] And, behold, I, even I, do bring a flood of waters upon the earth, to destroy all flesh, wherein is the breath of life, from under heaven; and everything that is in the earth shall die.*

6. Genesis 9:9-10:

> *[9] And I, behold, I establish my covenant with you, and with your seed after you; [10] And with every living creature that is with you, of the fowl, of the cattle, and of every beast of the earth with you; from all that go out of the ark, to every beast of the earth.*

7. Genesis 9:25-27:

> *[25] And he said, Cursed be Canaan; a servant of servants shall he be unto his brethren. [26] And he said, Blessed be the Lord God of Shem; and Canaan shall be his servant. [27] God shall enlarge Japheth, and he shall dwell in the tents of Shem; and Canaan shall be his servant.*

8. Genesis 12:7:

> *[7] And the LORD appeared unto Abram, and said, Unto thy seed will I give this land: and there builded he an altar unto the LORD, who appeared unto him.*

9. Genesis 13:14-16:

> *[14] And the Lord said unto Abram, after that Lot was separated from him, Lift up now thine eyes, and look from the place where thou art northward, and southward, and eastward, and westward: [15] For all the land which thou seest, to thee will I give it, and to thy seed for ever. [16] And I will make thy seed as the dust of the earth: so that if a man can number the dust of the earth, then shall thy seed also be numbered.*

10. Genesis 15:4:

> *[4] And, behold, the word of the LORD came unto him, saying, This shall not be thine heir; but he that shall come forth out of thine own bowels shall be thine heir.*

11. Genesis 15:13-14:

[13] And he said unto Abram, Know of a surety that thy seed shall be a stranger in a land that is not theirs, and shall serve them; and they shall afflict them four hundred years; [14] And also that nation, whom they shall serve, will I judge: and afterward shall they come out with great substance.

12. Genesis 15:18-21:

[18] In the same day the LORD made a covenant with Abram, saying, Unto thy seed have I given this land, from the river of Egypt unto the great river, the river Euphrates: [19] The Kenites, and the Kenizzites, and the Kadmonites, [20] And the Hittites, and the Perizzites, and the Rephaims, [21] And the Amorites, and the Canaanites, and the Girgashites, and the Jebusites.

13. Genesis 16:10-11:

[10] And the angel of the Lord said unto her, I will multiply thy seed exceedingly, that it shall not be numbered for multitude. [11] And the angel of the LORD said unto her, Behold, thou art with child, and shalt bear a son, and shalt call his name Ishmael; because the LORD hath heard thy affliction.

14. Genesis 17:2.

[2] And I will make my covenant between me and thee, and will multiply thee exceedingly.

15. Genesis 17:4:

[4] As for me, behold, my covenant is with thee, and thou shalt be a father of many nations.

16. Genesis 17:15:

[15] And God said unto Abraham, As for Sarai thy wife, thou shalt not call her name Sarai, but Sarah shall her name be.

17. Genesis 17:19:

[19] And God said, Sarah thy wife shall bear thee a son indeed; and thou shalt call his name Isaac: and I will establish my covenant with him for an everlasting covenant, and with his seed after him.

18. Genesis 18:10:

[10] And he said, I will certainly return unto thee according to the time of life; and, lo, Sarah thy wife shall have a son. And Sarah heard it in the tent door, which was behind him.

19. Genesis 18:14:

[14] Is any thing too hard for the LORD? At the time appointed I will return unto thee, according to the time of life, and Sarah shall have a son.

20. Genesis 18:17-18:

[17] And the LORD said, Shall I hide from Abraham that thing which I do; [18] Seeing that Abraham shall surely become a great and mighty nation, and all the nations of the earth shall be blessed in him?

21. Genesis 21:12:

[12] For in Isaac shall thy seed be called.

22. Genesis 21:18:

[18] Arise, lift up the lad, and hold him in thine hand; for I will make him a great nation.

23. Genesis 22:8:

[8] And Abraham said, My son, God will provide himself a lamb for a burnt offering: so they went both of them together.

24. Genesis 22:16:

[16] And said, By myself have I sworn, saith the LORD, for because thou hast done this thing, and hast not withheld thy son, thine only son.

25. Genesis 24:6:

[6] And Abraham said unto him, Beware thou that thou bring not my son thither again.

26. Genesis 24:40-41:

[40] And he said unto me, The Lord, before whom I walk, will send his angel with thee, and prosper thy way; and thou shalt take a wife for my son of my kindred, and of my father's house. [41] Then shalt thou be clear from this my oath, when thou comest to my kindred; and if they give not thee one, thou shalt be clear from my oath.

27. Genesis 25:23:

[23] And the LORD said unto her, Two nations are in thy womb, and two manner of people shall be separated from thy bowels; and the one people shall be stronger than the other people; and the elder shall serve the younger.

28. Genesis 26:2-3:

[2] And the Lord appeared unto him, and said, Go not down into Egypt; dwell in the land which I shall tell thee of: [3] Sojourn in this land, and I will be with thee, and will bless thee.

29. Genesis 26:24:

[24] And the LORD appeared unto him the same night, and said, I am the God of Abraham thy father: fear not, for I am with thee, and will bless thee, and multiply thy seed for my servant Abraham's sake.

30. Genesis 27:28-29:

[28] Therefore God give thee of the dew of heaven, and

the fatness of the earth, and plenty of corn and wine: [29]
Let people serve thee, and nations bow down to thee: be
lord over thy brethren, and let thy mother's sons bow
down to thee: cursed be every one that curseth thee, and
blessed be he that blesseth thee.

31. Genesis 27:37:

[37] And Isaac answered and said unto Esau, Behold, I
have made him thy lord, and all his brethren have I given
to him for servants; and with corn and wine have I sus-
tained him: and what shall I do now unto thee, my son?

32. Genesis 27:39-40:

[39] And Isaac his father answered and said unto him,
Behold, thy dwelling shall be the fatness of the earth, and
of the dew of heaven from above; [40] And by thy sword
shalt thou live, and shalt serve thy brother; and it shall
come to pass when thou shalt have the dominion, that
thou shalt break his yoke from off thy neck.

33. Genesis 28:3-4:

[3] And God Almighty bless thee, and make thee fruitful,
and multiply thee, that thou mayest be a multitude of peo-
ple; [4] And give thee the blessing of Abraham, to thee,
and to thy seed with thee; that thou mayest inherit the
land wherein thou art a stranger, which God gave unto
Abraham.

34. Genesis 28:13-14:

[13] And, behold, the Lord stood above it, and said, I am the Lord God of Abraham thy father, and the God of Isaac: the land whereon thou liest, to thee will I give it, and to thy seed; [14] And thy seed shall be as the dust of the earth, and thou shalt spread abroad to the west, and to the east, and to the north, and to the south: and in thee and in thy seed shall all the families of the earth be blessed.

35. Genesis 30:24:

[24] And she called his name Joseph; and said, The LORD shall add to me another son.

36. Genesis 31:3:

[3] And the LORD said unto Jacob, Return unto the land of thy fathers, and to thy kindred; and I will be with thee.

37. Genesis:32:9:

[9] And Jacob said, O God of my father Abraham, and God of my father Isaac, the LORD which saidst unto me, Return unto thy country, and to thy kindred, and I will deal well with thee: .

38. Genesis 32:12:

[12] And thou saidst, I will surely do thee good, and make thy seed as the sand of the sea, which cannot be numbered for multitude.

39. Genesis 35:11-12:

[11] And God said unto him, I am God Almighty: be fruitful and multiply; a nation and a company of nations shall be of thee, and kings shall come out of thy loins; [12] And the land which I gave Abraham and Isaac, to thee I will give it, and to thy seed after thee will I give the land.

40. Genesis 40:12-13:

[12] And Joseph said unto him, This is the interpretation of it: The three branches are three days: [13] Yet within three days shall Pharaoh lift up thine head, and restore thee unto thy place: and thou shalt deliver Pharaoh's cup into his hand, after the former manner when thou wast his butler.

41. Genesis 40:18-19:

[18] And Joseph answered and said, This is the interpretation thereof: The three baskets are three days: [19] Yet within three days shall Pharaoh lift up thy head from off thee, and shall hang thee on a tree; and the birds shall eat thy flesh from off thee.

42. Genesis 41:26-27:

[26] The seven good kine are seven years; and the seven good ears are seven years: the dream is one. [27] And the seven thin and ill favoured kine that came up after them are seven years; and the seven empty ears blasted with the east wind shall be seven years of famine.

43. Genesis 46:3:

*[3] And he said, I am God, the God of thy father: fear
not to go down into Egypt; for I will there make of thee a
great nation.*

44. Genesis 48:3-4:

*[3] And Jacob said unto Joseph, God Almighty appeared
unto me at Luz in the land of Canaan, and blessed me,
[4] And said unto me, Behold, I will make thee fruitful,
and multiply thee, and I will make of thee a multitude of
people; and will give this land to thy seed after thee for
an everlasting possession.*

45. Genesis 48:15-16:

*[15] And he blessed Joseph, and said, God, before whom
my fathers Abraham and Isaac did walk, the God which
fed me all my life long unto this day, [16] The Angel
which redeemed me from all evil, bless the lads; and let
my name be named on them, and the name of my fathers
Abraham and Isaac; and let them grow into a multitude
in the midst of the earth.*

46. Genesis 48:19-20:

*[19] And his father refused, and said, I know it, my son, I
know it: he also shall become a people, and he also shall
be great: but truly his younger brother shall be greater
than he, and his seed shall become a multitude of nations.
[20] And he blessed them that day, saying, In thee shall*

Israel bless, saying, God make thee as Ephraim and as Manasseh: and he set Ephraim before Manasseh.

47. Genesis 49:3-4:

[3] Reuben, thou art my firstborn, my might, and the beginning of my strength, the excellency of dignity, and the excellency of power: [4] Unstable as water, thou shalt not excel; because thou wentest up to thy father's bed; then defiledst thou it: he went up to my couch.

48. Genesis 50:24:

[24] And Joseph said unto his brethren, I die: and God will surely visit you, and bring you out of this land unto the land which he sware to Abraham, to Isaac, and to Jacob.

PROPHECIES IN EXODUS: 38

1. Exodus 3:8:

[8] And I am come down to deliver them out of the hand of the Egyptians, and to bring them up out of that land unto a good land and a large, unto a land flowing with milk and honey; unto the place of the Canaanites, and the Hittites, and the Amorites, and the Perizzites, and the Hivites, and the Jebusites.

2. Exodus 3:12:

[12] And he said, Certainly I will be with thee; and this shall be a token unto thee, that I have sent thee: When thou hast brought forth the people out of Egypt, ye shall serve God upon this mountain.

3. Exodus 3:17-18:

[17] And I have said, I will bring you up out of the affliction of Egypt unto the land of the Canaanites, and the Hittites, and the Amorites, and the Perizzites, and the Hivites, and the Jebusites, unto a land flowing with milk and honey. [18] And they shall hearken to thy voice: and thou shalt come, thou and the elders of Israel, unto the king of Egypt, and ye shall say unto him, The LORD God

of the Hebrews hath met with us: and now let us go, we beseech thee, three days' journey into the wilderness, that we may sacrifice to the LORD our God.

4. Exodus 4:14:

[14] And the anger of the Lord was kindled against Moses, and he said, Is not Aaron the Levite thy brother? I know that he can speak well. And also, behold, he cometh forth to meet thee: and when he seeth thee, he will be glad in his heart.

5. Exodus 4:21:

[21] And the Lord said unto Moses, When thou goest to return into Egypt, see that thou do all those wonders before Pharaoh, which I have put in thine hand: but I will harden his heart, that he shall not let the people go.

6. Exodus 6:1:

[1] Then the Lord said unto Moses, Now shalt thou see what I will do to Pharaoh: for with a strong hand shall he let them go, and with a strong hand shall he drive them out of his land.

7. Exodus 7:3:

[3] And I will harden Pharaoh's heart, and multiply my signs and my wonders in the land of Egypt.

8. Exodus 7:9:

[9] When Pharaoh shall speak unto you, saying, Shew a miracle for you: then thou shalt say unto Aaron, Take thy rod, and cast it before Pharaoh, and it shall become a serpent.

9. Exodus 7:14:

[14] And the Lord said unto Moses, Pharaoh's heart is hardened, he refuseth to let the people go.

10. Exodus 8:10:

[10] And he said, To morrow. And he said, Be it according to thy word: that thou mayest know that there is none like unto the Lord our God.

11. Exodus 8:16:

[16] And the LORD said unto Moses, Say unto Aaron, Stretch out thy rod, and smite the dust of the land, that it may become lice throughout all the land of Egypt.

12. Exodus 8:20:

[20] And the LORD said unto Moses, Rise up early in the morning, and stand before Pharaoh; lo, he cometh forth to the water; and say unto him, Thus saith the LORD, Let my people go, that they may serve me.

13. Exodus 9:1.

[1] Then the Lord said unto Moses, Go in unto Pharaoh,

*and tell him, Thus saith the Lord God of the Hebrews, Let
my people go, that they may serve me.*

14. Exodus 9:8:

*[8] And the Lord said unto Moses and unto Aaron, Take
to you handfuls of ashes of the furnace, and let Moses
sprinkle it toward the heaven in the sight of Pharaoh.*

15. Exodus 9:13:

*[13] And the Lord said unto Moses, Rise up early in the
morning, and stand before Pharaoh, and say unto him,
Thus saith the Lord God of the Hebrews, Let my people
go, that they may serve me.*

16. Exodus 9:29:

*[29] And Moses said unto him, As soon as I am gone out
of the city, I will spread abroad my hands unto the Lord;
and the thunder shall cease, neither shall there be any
more hail; that thou mayest know how that the earth is
the Lord's.*

17. Exodus 10:2:

*[2] And that thou mayest tell in the ears of thy son, and
of thy son's son, what things I have wrought in Egypt,
and my signs which I have done among them; that ye may
know how that I am the Lord.*

18. Exodus 10:29:

[29] And Moses said, Thou hast spoken well, I will see thy face again no more.

19. Exodus 11:1:

[1] And the Lord said unto Moses, Yet will I bring one plague more upon Pharaoh, and upon Egypt; afterwards he will let you go hence: when he shall let you go, he shall surely thrust you out hence altogether.

20. Exodus 11:4-8:

[4] And Moses said, Thus saith the Lord, About midnight will I go out into the midst of Egypt: [5] And all the firstborn in the land of Egypt shall die, from the firstborn of Pharaoh that sitteth upon his throne, even unto the firstborn of the maidservant that is behind the mill; and all the firstborn of beasts. [6] And there shall be a great cry throughout all the land of Egypt, such as there was none like it, nor shall be like it any more. [7] But against any of the children of Israel shall not a dog move his tongue, against man or beast: that ye may know how that the Lord doth put a difference between the Egyptians and Israel. [8] And all these thy servants shall come down unto me, and bow down themselves unto me, saying, Get thee out, and all the people that follow thee: and after that I will go out. And he went out from Pharaoh in a great anger.

21. Exodus 12:12-1)3

[12] For I will pass through the land of Egypt this night,

and will smite all the firstborn in the land of Egypt, both man and beast; and against all the gods of Egypt I will execute judgment: I am the LORD. [13] And the blood shall be to you for a token upon the houses where ye are: and when I see the blood, I will pass over you, and the plague shall not be upon you to destroy you, when I smite the land of Egypt.

22. Exodus 12:23-25:

[23] For the Lord will pass through to smite the Egyptians; and when he seeth the blood upon the lintel, and on the two side posts, the Lord will pass over the door, and will not suffer the destroyer to come in unto your houses to smite you. [24] And ye shall observe this thing for an ordinance to thee and to thy sons for ever. [25] And it shall come to pass, when ye be come to the land which the LORD will give you, according as he hath promised, that ye shall keep this service.

24. Exodus 13:5:

[5] And it shall be when the Lord shall bring thee into the land of the Canaanites, and the Hittites, and the Amorites, and the Hivites, and the Jebusites, which he sware unto thy fathers to give thee, a land flowing with milk and honey, that thou shalt keep this service in this month.

25. Exodus 13:19:

[19] And Moses took the bones of Joseph with him: for

he had straitly sworn the children of Israel, saying, God will surely visit you; and ye shall carry up my bones away hence with you.

26. Exodus 14:3-4:

[3] For Pharaoh will say of the children of Israel, They are entangled in the land, the wilderness hath shut them in. [4] And I will harden Pharaoh's heart, that he shall follow after them; and I will be honoured upon Pharaoh, and upon all his host; that the Egyptians may know that I am the LORD. And they did so.

27. Exodus 14:13-14:

[13] And Moses said unto the people, Fear ye not, stand still, and see the salvation of the Lord, which he will shew to you to day: for the Egyptians whom ye have seen to day, ye shall see them again no more forever. [14] The LORD shall fight for you, and ye shall hold your peace.

28. Exodus 14:16-18:

[16] But lift thou up thy rod, and stretch out thine hand over the sea, and divide it: and the children of Israel shall go on dry ground through the midst of the sea. [17] And I, behold, I will harden the hearts of the Egyptians, and they shall follow them: and I will get me honour upon Pharaoh, and upon all his host, upon his chariots, and upon his horsemen. [18] And the Egyptians shall know that I am the LORD, when I have gotten me honour upon Pharaoh, upon his chariots, and upon his horsemen.

29. Exodus 16:4-5:

[4] Then said the LORD unto Moses, Behold, I will rain bread from heaven for you; and the people shall go out and gather a certain rate every day, that I may prove them, whether they will walk in my law, or no. [5] And it shall come to pass, that on the sixth day they shall prepare that which they bring in; and it shall be twice as much as they gather daily.

30. Exodus 16:12:

[12] I have heard the murmurings of the children of Israel: speak unto them, saying, At even ye shall eat flesh, and in the morning ye shall be filled with bread; and ye shall know that I am the Lord your God.

31. Exodus 17:5-6:

[5] And the Lord said unto Moses, Go on before the people, and take with thee of the elders of Israel; and thy rod, wherewith thou smotest the river, take in thine hand, and go. [6] Behold, I will stand before thee there upon the rock in Horeb; and thou shalt smite the rock, and there shall come water out of it, that the people may drink. And Moses did so in the sight of the elders of Israel.

32 Exodus 17:14:

[14] And the Lord said unto Moses, Write this for a memorial in a book, and rehearse it in the ears of Joshua: for I will utterly put out the remembrance of Amalek from

under heaven.

33. Exodus 19:9:

[9] And the Lord said unto Moses, Lo, I come unto thee in a thick cloud, that the people may hear when I speak with thee, and believe thee for ever. And Moses told the words of the people unto the Lord.

34. Exodus 23:20:

[20] Behold, I send an Angel before thee, to keep thee in the way, and to bring thee into the place which I have prepared.

35. Exodus 32:34.

[34] Therefore now go, lead the people unto the place of which I have spoken unto thee: behold, mine Angel shall go before thee: nevertheless in the day when I visit I will visit their sin upon them.

36. Exodus 33:1-3:

[1] And the Lord said unto Moses, Depart, and go up hence, thou and the people which thou hast brought up out of the land of Egypt, unto the land which I sware unto Abraham, to Isaac, and to Jacob, saying, Unto thy seed will I give it: [2] And I will send an angel before thee; and I will drive out the Canaanite, the Amorite, and the Hittite, and the Perizzite, the Hivite, and the Jebusite: [3] Unto a land flowing with milk and honey: for I will not go

*up in the midst of thee; for thou art a stiffnecked people:
lest I consume thee in the way.*

37. Exodus 34:10:

*[10] And he said, Behold, I make a covenant: before all
thy people I will do marvels, such as have not been done
in all the earth, nor in any nation: and all the people
among which thou art shall see the work of the Lord: for
it is a terrible thing that I will do with thee.*

38. Exodus 34:24:

*[24] For I will cast out the nations before thee, and en-
large thy borders: neither shall any man desire thy land,
when thou shalt go up to appear before the Lord thy God
thrice in the year.*

PROPHECIES IN LEVITICUS: 6

1. Leviticus 9:4:

[4] Also a bullock and a ram for peace offerings, to sacrifice before the Lord; and a meat offering mingled with oil: for to day the Lord will appear unto you.

2. Leviticus 9:6:

[6] And Moses said, This is the thing which the Lord commanded that ye should do: and the glory of the Lord shall appear unto you.

3. Leviticus 18:24-25:

[24] Defile not ye yourselves in any of these things: for in all these the nations are defiled which I cast out before you: [25] And the land is defiled: therefore I do visit the iniquity thereof upon it, and the land itself vomiteth out her inhabitants.

4. Leviticus 20:22:

[22] Ye shall therefore keep all my statutes, and all my judgments, and do them: that the land, whither I bring you to dwell therein, spue you not out.

5. Leviticus 25:18:

[18] Wherefore ye shall do my statutes, and keep my

judgments, and do them; and ye shall dwell in the land in safety.

6. Leviticus 26:3-4:

[3] If ye walk in my statutes, and keep my commandments, and do them; [4] Then I will give you rain in due season, and the land shall yield her increase.

PROPHECIES IN NUMBERS: 16

1. Numbers 11:17:

[17] And I will come down and talk with thee there: and I will take of the spirit which is upon thee, and will put it upon them; and they shall bear the burden of the people with thee, that thou bear it not thyself alone.

2. Numbers 14:21:

[21] But as truly as I live, all the earth shall be filled with the glory of the Lord.

3. Numbers 14:28-31:

[28] Say unto them, As truly as I live, saith the Lord, as ye have spoken in mine ears, so will I do to you: [29] Your carcases shall fall in this wilderness; and all that were numbered of you, according to your whole number, from twenty years old and upward, which have murmured against me, [30] Doubtless ye shall not come into the land, concerning which I sware to make you dwell therein, save Caleb the son of Jephunneh, and Joshua the son of Nun. [31] But your little ones, which ye said should be a prey, them will I bring in, and they shall know the land which ye have despised.

4. Numbers 16:5:

> *[5] And he spake unto Korah and unto all his company, saying, Even to morrow the Lord will shew who are his, and who is holy; and will cause him to come near unto him: even him whom he hath chosen will he cause to come near unto him.*

5. Numbers 16:28-30:

> *[28] And Moses said, Hereby ye shall know that the Lord hath sent me to do all these works; for I have not done them of mine own mind. [29] If these men die the common death of all men, or if they be visited after the visitation of all men; then the Lord hath not sent me. [30] But if the Lord make a new thing, and the earth open her mouth, and swallow them up, with all that appertain unto them, and they go down quick into the pit; then ye shall understand that these men have provoked the Lord.*

6. Numbers 17:5:

> *[5] And it shall come to pass, that the man's rod, whom I shall choose, shall blossom: and I will make to cease from me the murmurings of the children of Israel, whereby they murmur against you.*

7. Numbers 20:12:

> *[12] And the Lord spake unto Moses and Aaron, Because ye believed me not, to sanctify me in the eyes of the children of Israel, therefore ye shall not bring this congrega-*

tion into the land which I have given them.

8. Numbers 20:24:

[24] Aaron shall be gathered unto his people: for he shall not enter into the land which I have given unto the children of Israel, because ye rebelled against my word at the water of Meribah.

9. Numbers 21:16:

[16] And from thence they went to Beer: that is the well whereof the Lord spake unto Moses, Gather the people together, and I will give them water.

10. Numbers 21:34:

[34] And the Lord said unto Moses, Fear him not: for I have delivered him into thy hand, and all his people, and his land; and thou shalt do to him as thou didst unto Sihon king of the Amorites, which dwelt at Heshbon.

11. Numbers 23:7-10:

[7] And he took up his parable, and said, Balak the king of Moab hath brought me from Aram, out of the mountains of the east, saying, Come, curse me Jacob, and come, defy Israel. [8] How shall I curse, whom God hath not cursed? or how shall I defy, whom the Lord hath not defied? [9] For from the top of the rocks I see him, and from the hills I behold him: lo, the people shall dwell alone, and shall not be reckoned among the nations. [10]

Who can count the dust of Jacob, and the number of the fourth part of Israel? Let me die the death of the righteous, and let my last end be like his!

12. Numbers 23:18-24:

[18] And he took up his parable, and said, Rise up, Balak, and hear; hearken unto me, thou son of Zippor: [19] God is not a man, that he should lie; neither the son of man, that he should repent: hath he said, and shall he not do it? Or hath he spoken, and shall he not make it good? [20] Behold, I have received commandment to bless: and he hath blessed; and I cannot reverse it. [21] He hath not beheld iniquity in Jacob, neither hath he seen perverseness in Israel: the Lord his God is with him, and the shout of a king is among them. [22] God brought them out of Egypt; he hath as it were the strength of an unicorn. [23] Surely there is no enchantment against Jacob, neither is there any divination against Israel: according to this time it shall be said of Jacob and of Israel, What hath God wrought! [24] Behold, the people shall rise up as a great lion, and lift up himself as a young lion: he shall not lie down until he eat of the prey, and drink the blood of the slain.

13. Numbers 24:3-5:

[3] And he took up his parable, and said, Balaam the son of Beor hath said, and the man whose eyes are open hath said: [4] He hath said, which heard the words of

God, which saw the vision of the Almighty, falling into a trance, but having his eyes open: [5] How goodly are thy tents, O Jacob, and thy tabernacles, O Israel!

14. Numbers 24:15-20:

[15] And he took up his parable, and said, Balaam the son of Beor hath said, and the man whose eyes are open hath said: [16] He hath said, which heard the words of God, and knew the knowledge of the most High, which saw the vision of the Almighty, falling into a trance, but having his eyes open: [17] I shall see him, but not now: I shall behold him, but not nigh: there shall come a Star out of Jacob, and a Sceptre shall rise out of Israel, and shall smite the corners of Moab, and destroy all the children of Sheth. [18] And Edom shall be a possession, Seir also shall be a possession for his enemies; and Israel shall do valiantly. [19] Out of Jacob shall come he that shall have dominion, and shall destroy him that remaineth of the city. [20] And when he looked on Amalek, he took up his parable, and said, Amalek was the first of the nations; but his latter end shall be that he perish for ever.

15. Numbers 24:21-24:

[21] And he looked on the Kenites, and took up his parable, and said, Strong is thy dwelling place, and thou puttest thy nest in a rock. [22] Nevertheless the Kenite shall be wasted, until Asshur shall carry thee away captive. [23] And he took up his parable, and said, Alas, who

shall live when God doeth this! [24] And ships shall come from the coast of Chittim, and shall afflict Asshur, and shall afflict Eber, and he also shall perish for ever.

16. Numbers 33:55:

[55] But if ye will not drive out the inhabitants of the land from before you; then it shall come to pass, that those which ye let remain of them shall be pricks in your eyes, and thorns in your sides, and shall vex you in the land wherein ye dwell. Moreover it shall come to pass, that I shall do unto you, as I thought to do unto them.

PROPHECIES IN DEUTERONOMY: 26

1 Deuteronomy 1:35-36:

[35] Surely there shall not one of these men of this evil generation see that good land, which I sware to give unto your fathers, [36] Save Caleb the son of Jephunneh; he shall see it, and to him will I give the land that he hath trodden upon, and to his children, because he hath wholly followed the Lord.

2. Deuteronomy 2:24:

[24] Rise ye up, take your journey, and pass over the river Arnon: behold, I have given into thine hand Sihon the Amorite, king of Heshbon, and his land: begin to possess it, and contend with him in battle.

3. Deuteronomy 3:2:

[2] And the Lord said unto me, Fear him not: for I will deliver him, and all his people, and his land, into thy hand; and thou shalt do unto him as thou didst unto Sihon king of the Amorites, which dwelt at Heshbon.

4. Deuteronomy 3:21:

[21] And I commanded Joshua at that time, saying, Thine eyes have seen all that the Lord your God hath done unto these two kings: so shall the Lord do unto all the kingdoms whither thou passest.

5. Deuteronomy 3:27:

[27] Get thee up into the top of Pisgah, and lift up thine eyes westward, and northward, and southward, and eastward, and behold it with thine eyes: for thou shalt not go over this Jordan.

6. Deuteronomy 4:21-22:

[21] Furthermore the Lord was angry with me for your sakes, and sware that I should not go over Jordan, and that I should not go in unto that good land, which the Lord thy God giveth thee for an inheritance: [22] But I must die in this land, I must not go over Jordan: but ye shall go over, and possess that good land.

7. Deuteronomy 4:25-2)6

[25] When thou shalt beget children, and children's children, and ye shall have remained long in the land, and shall corrupt yourselves, and make a graven image, or the likeness of anything, and shall do evil in the sight of the Lord thy God, to provoke him to anger: [26] I call heaven and earth to witness against you this day, that ye shall soon utterly perish from off the land whereunto ye go over Jordan to possess it; ye shall not prolong your days upon it, but shall utterly be destroyed.

8. Deuteronomy 6:10-11:

[10] And it shall be, when the Lord thy God shall have brought thee into the land which he sware unto thy

fathers, to Abraham, to Isaac, and to Jacob, to give thee great and goodly cities, which thou buildedst not, [11] And houses full of all good things, which thou filledst not, and wells digged, which thou diggedst not, vineyards and olive trees, which thou plantedst not; when thou shalt have eaten and be full.

9. Deuteronomy 8:7-9:

[7] For the Lord thy God bringeth thee into a good land, a land of brooks of water, of fountains and depths that spring out of valleys and hills; [8] A land of wheat, and barley, and vines, and fig trees, and pomegranates; a land of oil olive, and honey; [9] A land wherein thou shalt eat bread without scarceness, thou shalt not lack any thing in it; a land whose stones are iron, and out of whose hills thou mayest dig brass.

10. Deuteronomy 9:3:

[3] Understand therefore this day, that the Lord thy God is he which goeth over before thee; as a consuming fire he shall destroy them, and he shall bring them down before thy face: so shalt thou drive them out, and destroy them quickly, as the Lord hath said unto thee.

11. Deuteronomy 11:13:

[13] And it shall come to pass, if ye shall hearken dili-gently unto my commandments which I command you this day, to love the Lord your God, and to serve him with all your heart and with all your soul.

12. Deuteronomy 17:14:

[14] When thou art come unto the land which the Lord thy God giveth thee, and shalt possess it, and shalt dwell therein, and shalt say, I will set a king over me, like as all the nations that are about me.

13. Deuteronomy 18:15.

[15] The Lord thy God will raise up unto thee a Prophet from the midst of thee, of thy brethren, like unto me; unto him ye shall hearken.

14. Deuteronomy 18:18:

[18] I will raise them up a Prophet from among their brethren, like unto thee, and will put my words in his mouth; and he shall speak unto them all that I shall command him.

15. Deuteronomy 25:19:

[25] Therefore it shall be, when the Lord thy God hath given thee rest from all thine enemies round about, in the land which the Lord thy God giveth thee for an inheritance to possess it, that thou shalt blot out the remembrance of Amalek from under heaven; thou shalt not forget it.

16. Deuteronomy 28:1:

[1] And it shall come to pass, if thou shalt hearken diligently unto the voice of the Lord thy God, to observe and

to do all his commandments which I command thee this day, that the Lord thy God will set thee on high above all nations of the earth.

17. Deuteronomy 29:18:

[18] Lest there should be among you man, or woman, or family, or tribe, whose heart turneth away this day from the Lord our God, to go and serve the gods of these nations; lest there should be among you a root that beareth gall and wormwood.

18. Deuteronomy 30:1:

[1] And it shall come to pass, when all these things are come upon thee, the blessing and the curse, which I have set before thee, and thou shalt call them to mind among all the nations, whither the Lord thy God hath driven thee.

19. Deuteronomy 30:15-16:

[15] See, I have set before thee this day life and good, and death and evil; [16] In that I command thee this day to love the Lord thy God, to walk in his ways, and to keep his commandments and his statutes and his judgments, that thou mayest live and multiply: and the Lord thy God shall bless thee in the land whither thou goest to possess it.

20. Deuteronomy 31:2:

[2] And he said unto them, I am an hundred and twenty

*years old this day; I can no more go out and come in:
also the Lord hath said unto me, Thou shalt not go over
this Jordan.*

21. Deuteronomy 31:16:

*[16] And the Lord said unto Moses, Behold, thou shalt
sleep with thy fathers; and this people will rise up, and
go a whoring after the gods of the strangers of the land,
whither they go to be among them, and will forsake me,
and break my covenant which I have made with them.*

22. Deuteronomy 31:23:

*[23] And he gave Joshua the son of Nun a charge, and
said, Be strong and of a good courage: for thou shalt
bring the children of Israel into the land which I sware
unto them: and I will be with thee.*

23. Deuteronomy 31:27:

*[27] For I know thy rebellion, and thy stiff neck: be-
hold, while I am yet alive with you this day, ye have been
rebellious against the Lord; and how much more after my
death?*

24. Deuteronomy 32:19:

*[19] And when the Lord saw it, he abhorred them, be-
cause of the provoking of his sons, and of his daughters.*

25. Deuteronomy 33:6:

[6] Let Reuben live, and not die; and let not his men be few.

26. Deuteronomy 34:4:

[4] And the Lord said unto him, This is the land which I sware unto Abraham, unto Isaac, and unto Jacob, saying, I will give it unto thy seed: I have caused thee to see it with thine eyes, but thou shalt not go over thither.

PROPHECIES IN JOSHUA: 14

1. Joshua 1:11:

[11] Pass through the host, and command the people, saying, Prepare you victuals; for within three days ye shall pass over this Jordan, to go in to possess the land, which the Lord your God giveth you to possess it.

2. Joshua 3:5:

[5] And Joshua said unto the people, Sanctify yourselves: for to morrow the Lord will do wonders among you.

3. Joshua 3:7:

[7] And the Lord said unto Joshua, This day will I begin to magnify thee in the sight of all Israel, that they may know that, as I was with Moses, so I will be with thee.

4. Joshua 3:10:

[10] And Joshua said, Hereby ye shall know that the living God is among you, and that he will without fail drive out from before you the Canaanites, and the Hittites, and the Hivites, and the Perizzites, and the Girgashites, and the Amorites, and the Jebusites.

5. Joshua 6:2:

[2] And the Lord said unto Joshua, See, I have given into

thine hand Jericho, and the king thereof, and the mighty men of valour.

6. Joshua 6:26.

[26] And Joshua adjured them at that time, saying, Cursed be the man before the Lord, that riseth up and buildeth this city Jericho: he shall lay the foundation thereof in his firstborn, and in his youngest son shall he set up the gates of it.

7. Joshua 8:1-2:

[1] And the Lord said unto Joshua, Fear not, neither be thou dismayed: take all the people of war with thee, and arise, go up to Ai: see, I have given into thy hand the king of Ai, and his people, and his city, and his land: [2] And thou shalt do to Ai and her king as thou didst unto Jericho and her king: only the spoil thereof, and the cattle thereof, shall ye take for a prey unto yourselves: lay thee an ambush for the city behind it.

8. Joshua 8:18:

[18] And the Lord said unto Joshua, Stretch out the spear that is in thy hand toward Ai; for I will give it into thine hand. And Joshua stretched out the spear that he had in his hand toward the city.

9. Joshua 10:8:

[8] And the Lord said unto Joshua, Fear them not: for

I have delivered them into thine hand; there shall not a man of them stand before thee.

10. Joshua 10:25:

[25] And Joshua said unto them, Fear not, nor be dismayed, be strong and of good courage: for thus shall the Lord do to all your enemies against whom ye fight.

11. Joshua 11:6:

[6] And the Lord said unto Joshua, Be not afraid because of them: for to morrow about this time will I deliver them up all slain before Israel: thou shalt hough their horses, and burn their chariots with fire.

12. Joshua 13:6:

[6] All the inhabitants of the hill country from Lebanon unto Misrephoth-maim, and all the Sidonians, them will I drive out from before the children of Israel: only divide thou it by lot unto the Israelites for an inheritance, as I have commanded thee.

13. Joshua 14:9:

[9] And Moses sware on that day, saying, Surely the land whereon thy feet have trodden shall be thine inheritance, and thy children's for ever, because thou hast wholly followed the Lord my God.

14. Joshua 23:5:

[5] And the Lord your God, he shall expel them from before you, and drive them from out of your sight; and ye shall possess their land, as the Lord your God hath promised unto you.

PROPHECIES IN JUDGES:14

1. Judges 1:2:

[2] And the Lord said, Judah shall go up: behold, I have delivered the land into his hand.

2. Judges 4:6:

[6] And she sent and called Barak the son of Abinoam out of Kedesh-naphtali, and said unto him, Hath not the Lord God of Israel commanded, saying, Go and draw toward mount Tabor, and take with thee ten thousand men of the children of Naphtali and of the children of Zebulun?

3. Judges 4:9:

[9] And she said, I will surely go with thee: notwithstanding the journey that thou takest shall not be for thine honour; for the Lord shall sell Sisera into the hand of a woman. And Deborah arose, and went with Barak to Kedesh.

4. Judges 4:14:

[14] And Deborah said unto Barak, Up; for this is the day in which the Lord hath delivered Sisera into thine hand: is not the Lord gone out before thee? So Barak went down from mount Tabor, and ten thousand men after him.

5. Judges 6:14:

[14] And the Lord looked upon him, and said, Go in this thy might, and thou shalt save Israel from the hand of the Midianites: have not I sent thee?

6. Judges 6:16.

[16] And the Lord said unto him, Surely I will be with thee, and thou shalt smite the Midianites as one man.

7. Judges 7:7:

[7] And the Lord said unto Gideon, By the three hundred men that lapped will I save you, and deliver the Midianites into thine hand: and let all the other people go every man unto his place.

8. Judges 7:9:

[9] And it came to pass the same night, that the Lord said unto him, Arise, get thee down unto the host; for I have delivered it into thine hand.

9. Judges 7:13:

[13] And when Gideon was come, behold, there was a man that told a dream unto his fellow, and said, Behold, I dreamed a dream, and, lo, a cake of barley bread tumbled into the host of Midian, and came unto a tent, and smote it that it fell, and overturned it, that the tent lay along.

10. Judges 8:7:

[7] And Gideon said, Therefore when the Lord hath de-livered Zebah and Zalmunna into mine hand, then I will tear your flesh with the thorns of the wilderness and with briers.

11. Judges 8:9:

[9] And he spake also unto the men of Penuel, saying, When I come again in peace, I will break down this tower.

12. Judges 9:8-9:

[8] The trees went forth on a time to anoint a king over them; and they said unto the olive tree, Reign thou over us. [9] But the olive tree said unto them, Should I leave my fatness, wherewith by me they honour God and man, and go to be promoted over the trees?

13. Judges 13:3:

[3] And the angel of the Lord appeared unto the woman, and said unto her, Behold now, thou art barren, and bear-est not: but thou shalt conceive, and bear a son.

14. Judges 20:28.

[28] And Phinehas, the son of Eleazar, the son of Aaron, stood before it in those days,) saying, Shall I yet again go out to battle against the children of Benjamin my brother, or shall I cease? And the Lord said, Go up; for to morrow I will deliver them into thine hand.

PROPHECIES IN FIRST SAMUEL: 12

1. 1 Samuel 2:1:

[1] And Hannah prayed, and said, My heart rejoiceth in the Lord, mine horn is exalted in the Lord: my mouth is enlarged over mine enemies; because I rejoice in thy salvation.

2. 1 Samuel 2:27-36:

[27] And there came a man of God unto Eli, and said unto him, Thus saith the Lord, Did I plainly appear unto the house of thy father, when they were in Egypt in Pharaoh's house? [28] And did I choose him out of all the tribes of Israel to be my priest, to offer upon mine altar, to burn incense, to wear an ephod before me? and did I give unto the house of thy father all the offerings made by fire of the children of Israel? [29] Wherefore kick ye at my sacrifice and at mine offering, which I have commanded in my habitation; and honourest thy sons above me, to make yourselves fat with the chiefest of all the offerings of Israel my people? [30] Wherefore the Lord God of Israel saith, I said indeed that thy house, and the house of thy father, should walk before me for ever: but now the Lord saith, Be it far from me; for them that honour me I will honour, and they that despise me shall be lightly esteemed.
[31] Behold, the days come, that I will cut off thine arm,

*and the arm of thy father's house, that there shall not
be an old man in thine house. [32] And thou shalt see an
enemy in my habitation, in all the wealth which God shall
give Israel: and there shall not be an old man in thine
house for ever[33] . And the man of thine, whom I shall
not cut off from mine altar, shall be to consume thine
eyes, and to grieve thine heart: and all the increase of
thine house shall die in the flower of their age. [34] And
this shall be a sign unto thee, that shall come upon thy
two sons, on Hophni and Phinehas; in one day they shall
die both of them. [35] And I will raise me up a faithful
priest, that shall do according to that which is in mine
heart and in my mind: and I will build him a sure house;
and he shall walk before mine anointed for ever. [36] And
it shall come to pass, that every one that is left in thine
house shall come and crouch to him for a piece of silver
and a morsel of bread, and shall say, Put me, I pray thee,
into one of the priests' offices, that I may eat a piece of
bread.*

3. 1 Samuel 3:11-14:

*[11] And the Lord said to Samuel, Behold, I will do a
thing in Israel, at which both the ears of every one that
heareth it shall tingle.
[12] In that day I will perform against Eli all things
which I have spoken concerning his house: when I begin,
I will also make an end. [13] For I have told him that
I will judge his house for ever for the iniquity which he
knoweth; because his sons made themselves vile, and he
restrained them not. [14] And therefore I have sworn unto*

the house of Eli, that the iniquity of Eli's house shall not be purged with sacrifice nor offering for ever.

4. 1 Samuel 9:19:

[19] And Samuel answered Saul, and said, I am the seer: go up before me unto the high place; for ye shall eat with me to day, and to morrow I will let thee go, and will tell thee all that is in thine heart.

5. 1 Samuel 10:2-8:

[2] When thou art departed from me to day, then thou shalt find two men by Rachel's sepulchre in the border of Benjamin at Zelzah; and they will say unto thee, The asses which thou wentest to seek are found: and, lo, thy father hath left the care of the asses, and sorroweth for you, saying, What shall I do for my son? [3] Then shalt thou go on forward from thence, and thou shalt come to the plain of Tabor, and there shall meet thee three men going up to God to Beth-el, one carrying three kids, and another carrying three loaves of bread, and another carrying a bottle of wine: [4] And they will salute thee, and give thee two loaves of bread; which thou shalt receive of their hands. [5] After that thou shalt come to the hill of God, where is the garrison of the Philistines: and it shall come to pass, when thou art come thither to the city, that thou shalt meet a company of prophets coming down from the high place with a psaltery, and a tabret, and a pipe, and a harp, before them; and they shall prophesy: [6] And the Spirit of the Lord will come upon thee, and thou

shalt prophesy with them, and shalt be turned into another man. [7] And let it be, when these signs are come unto thee, that thou do as occasion serve thee; for God is with thee. [8] And thou shalt go down before me to Gilgal; and, behold, I will come down unto thee, to offer burnt offerings, and to sacrifice sacrifices of peace offerings: seven days shalt thou tarry, till I come to thee, and shew thee what thou shalt do.

6. 1 Samuel 12:14:

[14] If ye will fear the Lord, and serve him, and obey his voice, and not rebel against the commandment of the Lord, then shall both ye and also the king that reigneth over you continue following the Lord your God.

7. 1 Samuel 12:24-25:

[24] Only fear the Lord, and serve him in truth with all your heart: for consider how great things he hath done for you. [25] But if ye shall still do wickedly, ye shall be consumed, both ye and your king.

8. 1 Samuel 13:13-14:

[13] And Samuel said to Saul, Thou hast done foolishly: thou hast not kept the commandment of the Lord thy God, which he commanded thee: for now would the Lord have established thy kingdom upon Israel for ever. [14] But now thy kingdom shall not continue: the Lord hath sought

him a man after his own heart, and the Lord hath com-manded him to be captain over his people, because thou hast not kept that which the Lord commanded thee.

9. 1 Samuel 17:46.

[46] This day will the Lord deliver thee into mine hand; and I will smite thee, and take thine head from thee; and I will give the carcases of the host of the Philistines this day unto the fowls of the air, and to the wild beasts of the earth; that all the earth may know that there is a God in Israel.

10. 1 Samuel 23:11:

[11] Will the men of Keilah deliver me up into his hand? will Saul come down, as thy servant hath heard? O Lord God of Israel, I beseech thee, tell thy servant. And the Lord said, He will come down.

11. 1 Samuel 26:10:

[10] David said furthermore, As the Lord liveth, the Lord shall smite him; or his day shall come to die; or he shall descend into battle, and perish.

12. 1 Samuel 30:8:

[8] And David enquired at the Lord, saying, Shall I pursue after this troop? shall I overtake them? And he an-swered him, Pursue: for thou shalt surely overtake them, and without fail recover all.

PROPHECIES IN SECOND SAMUEL: 5

1. 2 Samuel 5:19:

[19] And David enquired of the Lord, saying, Shall I go up to the Philistines? Wilt thou deliver them into mine hand? And the Lord said unto David, Go up: for I will doubtless deliver the Philistines into thine hand.

2. 2 Samuel 5:23-24.

[23] And when David enquired of the Lord, he said, Thou shalt not go up; but fetch a compass behind them, and come upon them over against the mulberry trees. [24] And let it be, when thou hearest the sound of a going in the tops of the mulberry trees, that then thou shalt bestir thyself: for then shall the Lord go out before thee, to smite the host of the Philistines.

3. 2 Samuel 7:10-11:

[10] Moreover I will appoint a place for my people Israel, and will plant them, that they may dwell in a place of their own, and move no more; neither shall the children of wickedness afflict them any more, as beforetime, [11] And as since the time that I commanded judges to be over my people Israel, and have caused thee to rest from all thine enemies. Also the Lord telleth thee that he will make thee an house.

4. 2 Samuel 12:10-12:

[10] Now therefore the sword shall never depart from thine house; because thou hast despised me, and hast taken the wife of Uriah the Hittite to be thy wife. [11] Thus saith the Lord, Behold, I will raise up evil against thee out of thine own house, and I will take thy wives before thine eyes, and give them unto thy neighbour, and he shall lie with thy wives in the sight of this sun. [12] For thou didst it secretly: but I will do this thing before all Israel, and before the sun.

5. 2 Samuel 22:51:

[51] He is the tower of salvation for his king: and sheweth mercy to his anointed, unto David, and to his seed for evermore.

PROPHECIES IN FIRST KINGS: 28

1. 1 Kings 2:4:

[4] That the Lord may continue his word which he spake concerning me, saying, If thy children take heed to their way, to walk before me in truth with all their heart and with all their soul, there shall not fail thee (said he) a man on the throne of Israel.

2. 1 Kings 3:11:

[11] And God said unto him, Because thou hast asked this thing, and hast not asked for thyself long life; neither hast asked riches for thyself, nor hast asked the life of thine enemies; but hast asked for thyself understanding to discern judgment.

3. 1 Kings 5:5:

[5] And, behold, I purpose to build an house unto the name of the Lord my God, as the Lord spake unto David my father, saying, Thy son, whom I will set upon thy throne in thy room, he shall build an house unto my name.

4. 1 Kings 8:19:

[19] Nevertheless thou shalt not build the house; but thy son that shall come forth out of thy loins, he shall build the house unto my name.

5. 1 Kings 8:25:

[25] Therefore now, Lord God of Israel, keep with thy servant David my father that thou promisedst him, saying, There shall not fail thee a man in my sight to sit on the throne of Israel; so that thy children take heed to their way, that they walk before me as thou hast walked before me.

6. 1 Kings 9:3:

[3] And the Lord said unto him, I have heard thy prayer and thy supplication, that thou hast made before me: I have hallowed this house, which thou hast built, to put my name there for ever; and mine eyes and mine heart shall be there perpetually.

7. 1 Kings 11:11-13:

[11] Wherefore the Lord said unto Solomon, Forasmuch as this is done of thee, and thou hast not kept my covenant and my statutes, which I have commanded thee, I will surely rend the kingdom from thee, and will give it to thy servant. [12] Notwithstanding in thy days I will not do it for David thy father's sake: but I will rend it out of the hand of thy son. [13] Howbeit I will not rend away all the kingdom; but will give one tribe to thy son for David my servant's sake, and for Jerusalem's sake which I have chosen.

8. 1 Kings 11:30-33:

[30] And Ahijah caught the new garment that was on him, and rent it in twelve pieces: [31] And he said to

Jeroboam, Take thee ten pieces: for thus saith the Lord, the God of Israel, Behold, I will rend the kingdom out of the hand of Solomon, and will give ten tribes to thee. [32] But he shall have one tribe for my servant David's sake, and for Jerusalem's sake, the city which I have chosen out of all the tribes of Israel. [33] Because that they have forsaken me, and have worshipped Ashtoreth the goddess of the Zidonians, Chemosh the god of the Moabites, and Milcom the god of the children of Ammon, and have not walked in my ways, to do that which is right in mine eyes, and to keep my statutes and my judgments, as did David his father.

9. 1 Kings 13:2:

[2] And he cried against the altar in the word of the Lord, and said, O altar, altar, thus saith the Lord; Behold, a child shall be born unto the house of David, Josiah by name; and upon thee shall he offer the priests of the high places that burn incense upon thee, and men's bones shall be burnt upon thee.

10. 1 Kings 13:21-22:

[21] And he cried unto the man of God that came from Judah, saying, Thus saith the Lord, Forasmuch as thou hast disobeyed the mouth of the Lord, and hast not kept the commandment which the Lord thy God commanded thee, [22] But camest back, and hast eaten bread and drunk water in the place, of the which the Lord did say to thee, Eat no bread, and drink no water; thy carcase shall

not come unto the sepulchre of thy fathers.

11. 1 Kings 14:7-10

[7] Go, tell Jeroboam, Thus saith the Lord God of Israel,
Forasmuch as I exalted thee from among the people, and
made thee prince over my people Israel, [8] And rent the
kingdom away from the house of David, and gave it thee:
and yet thou hast not been as my servant David, who
kept my commandments, and who followed me with all
his heart, to do that only which was right in mine eyes;
[9] But hast done evil above all that were before thee:
for thou hast gone and made thee other gods, and molten
images, to provoke me to anger, and hast cast me behind
thy back: [10] Therefore, behold, I will bring evil upon
the house of Jeroboam, and will cut off from Jeroboam
him that pisseth against the wall, and him that is shut up
and left in Israel, and will take away the remnant of the
house of Jeroboam, as a man taketh away dung, till it be
all gone.

12. 1 Kings 16:1-3:

[1] Then the word of the Lord came to Jehu the son of
Hanani against Baasha, saying, [2] Forasmuch as I
exalted thee out of the dust, and made thee prince over
my people Israel; and thou hast walked in the way of
Jeroboam, and hast made my people Israel to sin, to
provoke me to anger with their sins; [3] Behold, I will
take away the posterity of Baasha, and the posterity of
his house; and will make thy house like the house of Je-

roboam the son of Nebat.

13. 1 Kings 17:1:

[1] And Elijah the Tishbite, who was of the inhabitants of Gilead, said unto Ahab, As the Lord God of Israel liveth, before whom I stand, there shall not be dew nor rain these years, but according to my word.

14. 1 Kings 17:3:

[3] Get thee hence, and turn thee eastward, and hide thyself by the brook Cherith, that is before Jordan.

15. 1 Kings 17:9:

[9] Arise, get thee to Zarephath, which belongeth to Zi-don, and dwell there: behold, I have commanded a widow woman there to sustain thee.

16. 1 Kings 17:13-14:

[13] And Elijah said unto her, Fear not; go and do as thou hast said: but make me thereof a little cake first, and bring it unto me, and after make for thee and for thy son. [14] For thus saith the Lord God of Israel, The barrel of meal shall not waste, neither shall the cruse of oil fail, until the day that the Lord sendeth rain upon the earth.

17. 1 Kings 18:1:

[18] And it came to pass after many days, that the word

of the Lord came to Elijah in the third year, saying, Go, shew thyself unto Ahab; and I will send rain upon the earth.

18. 1 Kings 20:13:

[13] And, behold, there came a prophet unto Ahab king of Israel, saying, Thus saith the Lord, Hast thou seen all this great multitude? behold, I will deliver it into thine hand this day; and thou shalt know that I am the Lord.

19. 1 Kings 19:17:

[17] And it shall come to pass, that him that escapeth the sword of Hazael shall Jehu slay: and him that escapeth from the sword of Jehu shall Elisha slay.

20. 1 Kings 20:22:

[22] And the prophet came to the king of Israel, and said unto him, Go, strengthen thyself, and mark, and see what thou doest: for at the return of the year the king of Syria will come up against thee.

21. 1 Kings 20:28:

[28] And there came a man of God, and spake unto the king of Israel, and said, Thus saith the Lord, Because the Syrians have said, The Lord is God of the hills, but he is not God of the valleys, therefore will I deliver all this great multitude into thine hand, and ye shall know that I am the Lord.

22. 1 Kings 20:36:

[36] Then said he unto him, Because thou hast not obeyed the voice of the Lord, behold, as soon as thou art departed from me, a lion shall slay thee. And as soon as he was departed from him, a lion found him, and slew him.

23. 1 Kings 21: 19:

[19] And thou shalt speak unto him, saying, Thus saith the Lord, Hast thou killed, and also taken possession? And thou shalt speak unto him, saying, Thus saith the Lord, In the place where dogs licked the blood of Naboth shall dogs lick thy blood, even thine.

24. 1 Kings 21:21-22:

[21] Behold, I will bring evil upon thee, and will take away thy posterity, and will cut off from Ahab him that pisseth against the wall, and him that is shut up and left in Israel, [22] And will make thine house like the house of Jeroboam the son of Nebat, and like the house of Baasha the son of Ahijah, for the provocation wherewith thou hast provoked me to anger, and made Israel to sin.

25. 1 Kings 21:29:

[29] Seest thou how Ahab humbleth himself before me? because he humbleth himself before me, I will not bring the evil in his days: but in his son's days will I bring the evil upon his house.

26. 1 Kings 22:17:

[17] And he said, I saw all Israel scattered upon the hills, as sheep that have not a shepherd: and the Lord said, These have no master: let them return every man to his house in peace.

27. 1 Kings 22:25:

[25] And Micaiah said, Behold, thou shalt see in that day, when thou shalt go into an inner chamber to hide thyself.

28. 1 Kings 22:28:

[28] And Micaiah said, If thou return at all in peace, the Lord hath not spoken by me. And he said, Hearken, O people, every one of you.

PROPHECIES IN SECOND KINGS: 21

1. 2 Kings 1:4:

   [4] Now therefore thus saith the Lord, Thou shalt not come down from that bed on which thou art gone up, but shalt surely die. And Elijah departed.

2. 2 Kings 1:6:

   [6] And they said unto him, There came a man up to meet us, and said unto us, Go, turn again unto the king that sent you, and say unto him, Thus saith the Lord, Is it not because there is not a God in Israel, that thou sendest to enquire of Baal-zebub the god of Ekron? Therefore thou shalt not come down from that bed on which thou art gone up, but shalt surely die.

3. 2 Kings 1:16:

   [16] And he said unto him, Thus saith the Lord, Forasmuch as thou hast sent messengers to enquire of Baal-zebub the god of Ekron, is it not because there is no God in Israel to enquire of his word? Therefore thou shalt not come down off that bed on which thou art gone up, but shalt surely die.

4. 2 Kings 3:16-17:

   [16] And he said, Thus saith the Lord, Make this valley

full of ditches. [17] For thus saith the Lord, Ye shall not see wind, neither shall ye see rain; yet that valley shall be filled with water, that ye may drink, both ye, and your cattle, and your beasts.

5. 2 Kings 4:16:

[16] And he said, About this season, according to the time of life, thou shalt embrace a son. And she said, Nay, my lord, thou man of God, do not lie unto thine handmaid.

6. 2 Kings 5:10:

[10] And Elisha sent a messenger unto him, saying, Go and wash in Jordan seven times, and thy flesh shall come again to thee, and thou shalt be clean.

7. 2 Kings 5:27:

[27] The leprosy therefore of Naaman shall cleave unto thee, and unto thy seed for ever. And he went out from his presence a leper as white as snow.

8. 2 Kings 7:1:

[1] Then Elisha said, Hear ye the word of the Lord; Thus saith the Lord, To morrow about this time shall a measure of fine flour be sold for a shekel, and two measures of barley for a shekel, in the gate of Samaria.

9. 2 Kings 8:1:

[1] Then spake Elisha unto the woman, whose son he

had restored to life, saying, Arise, and go thou and thine household, and sojourn wheresoever thou canst sojourn: for the Lord hath called for a famine; and it shall also come upon the land seven years.

10. 2 Kings 8:10:

[10] And Elisha said unto him, Go, say unto him, Thou mayest certainly recover: howbeit the Lord hath shewed me that he shall surely die.

11. 2 Kings 8:12:

[12] And Hazael said, Why weepeth my lord? And he answered, Because I know the evil that thou wilt do unto the children of Israel: their strong holds wilt thou set on fire, and their young men wilt thou slay with the sword, and wilt dash their children, and rip up their women with child.

12. 2 Kings 9:6:

[6] And he arose, and went into the house; and he poured the oil on his head, and said unto him, Thus saith the Lord God of Israel, I have anointed thee king over the people of the Lord, even over Israel.

13. 2 Kings:10:30:

[30] And the Lord said unto Jehu, Because thou hast done well in executing that which is right in mine eyes, and hast done unto the house of Ahab according to all

*that was in mine heart, thy children of the fourth genera-
tion shall sit on the throne of Israel.*

14. 2 Kings 20:1.

*[1] In those days was Hezekiah sick unto death. And the
prophet Isaiah the son of Amoz came to him, and said
unto him, Thus saith the Lord, Set thine house in order;
for thou shalt die, and not live.*

15. 2 Kings 20:5:

*[5] Turn again, and tell Hezekiah the captain of my
people, Thus saith the Lord, the God of David thy father,
I have heard thy prayer, I have seen thy tears: behold, I
will heal thee: on the third day thou shalt go up unto the
house of the Lord.*

16. 2 Kings 20:9:

*[9] And Isaiah said, This sign shalt thou have of the
Lord, that the Lord will do the thing that he hath spoken:
shall the shadow go forward ten degrees, or go back ten
degrees?*

17. 2 Kings 20:16-18:

*[16] And Isaiah said unto Hezekiah, Hear the word of
the Lord. [17] Behold, the days come, that all that is in
thine house, and that which thy fathers have laid up in
store unto this day, shall be carried into Babylon: nothing shall be left, saith the Lord. [18] And of thy sons that*

shall issue from thee, which thou shalt beget, shall they take away; and they shall be eunuchs in the palace of the king of Babylon.

18. 2 Kings 21:7-8:

[7] And he set a graven image of the grove that he had made in the house, of which the Lord said to David, and to Solomon his son, In this house, and in Jerusalem, which I have chosen out of all tribes of Israel, will I put my name for ever:
[8] Neither will I make the feet of Israel move any more out of the land which I gave their fathers; only if they will observe to do according to all that I have commanded them, and according to all the law that my servant Moses commanded them.

19. 2 Kings 21:10-14:

[10] And the Lord spake by his servants the prophets, saying, [11] Because Manasseh king of Judah hath done these abominations, and hath done wickedly above all that the Amorites did, which were before him, and hath made Judah also to sin with his idols: [12] Therefore thus saith the Lord God of Israel, Behold, I am bringing such evil upon Jerusalem and Judah, that whosoever heareth of it, both his ears shall tingle. [13] And I will stretch over Jerusalem the line of Samaria, and the plummet of the house of Ahab: and I will wipe Jerusalem as a man wipeth a dish, wiping it, and turning it upside down. [14] And I will forsake the remnant of mine inheritance, and

deliver them into the hand of their enemies; and they
shall become a prey and a spoil to all their enemies.

20. 2 Kings 22:16-17:

[16] Thus saith the Lord, Behold, I will bring evil upon
this place, and upon the inhabitants thereof, even all the
words of the book which the king of Judah hath read:
[17] Because they have forsaken me, and have burned
incense unto other gods, that they might provoke me to
anger with all the works of their hands; therefore my
wrath shall be kindled against this place, and shall not be
quenched.

21. 2 Kings 23:27:

[27] And the Lord said, I will remove Judah also out of
my sight, as I have removed Israel, and will cast off this
city Jerusalem which I have chosen, and the house of
which I said, My name shall be there.

PROPHECIES IN FIRST CHRONICLES: 6

1. 1 Chronicles 11:2:

   [2] And moreover in time past, even when Saul was king, thou wast he that leddest out and broughtest in Israel: and the Lord thy God said unto thee, Thou shalt feed my people Israel, and thou shalt be ruler over my people Israel.

2. 1 Chronicles 14:10:

   [10] And David enquired of God, saying, Shall I go up against the Philistines? And wilt thou deliver them into mine hand? And the Lord said unto him, Go up; for I will deliver them into thine hand.

3. 1 Chronicles 14:15:

   [15] And it shall be, when thou shalt hear a sound of going in the tops of the mulberry trees, that then thou shalt go out to battle: for God is gone forth before thee to smite the host of the Philistines.

4. 1 Chronicles 17:9-10:

   [9] Also I will ordain a place for my people Israel, and will plant them, and they shall dwell in their place, and shall be moved no more; neither shall the children of wickedness waste them any more, as at the beginning,

[10] And since the time that I commanded judges to be over my people Israel. Moreover I will subdue all thine enemies. Furthermore I tell thee that the Lord will build thee an house.

5. 1 Chronicles 22:9:

[9] Behold, a son shall be born to thee, who shall be a man of rest; and I will give him rest from all his enemies round about: for his name shall be Solomon, and I will give peace and quietness unto Israel in his days. He shall build an house for my name; and he shall be my son, and I will be his father; and I will establish the throne of his kingdom over Israel for ever.

6. 1 Chronicles 28:6-7:

[6] And he said unto me, Solomon thy son, he shall build my house and my courts: for I have chosen him to be my son, and I will be his father. [7] Moreover I will establish his kingdom for ever, if he be constant to do my commandments and my judgments, as at this day.

PROPHECIES IN SECOND CHRONICLES: 18

1._2 Chronicles 1:12:

[12] Wisdom and knowledge is granted unto thee; and I will give thee riches, and wealth, and honour, such as none of the kings have had that have been before thee, neither shall there any after thee have the like.

2. 2 Chronicles 6:9:

[9] Notwithstanding thou shalt not build the house; but thy son which shall come forth out of thy loins, he shall build the house for my name.

3. 2 Chronicles 6:16:

[16] Now therefore, O Lord God of Israel, keep with thy servant David my father that which thou hast promised him, saying, There shall not fail thee a man in my sight to sit upon the throne of Israel; yet so that thy children take heed to their way to walk in my law, as thou hast walked before me.

4. 2 Chronicles 7:13-14:

[13] If I shut up heaven that there be no rain, or if I command the locusts to devour the land, or if I send pesti-

lence among my people; [14] If my people, which are called by my name, shall humble themselves, and pray, and seek my face, and turn from their wicked ways; then will I hear from heaven, and will forgive their sin, and will heal their land.

5. 2 Chronicles 12:7:

[7] And when the Lord saw that they humbled themselves, the word of the Lord came to Shemaiah, saying, They have humbled themselves; therefore I will not destroy them, but I will grant them some deliverance; and my wrath shall not be poured out upon Jerusalem by the hand of Shishak.

6. 2 Chronicles 16:9:

[9] For the eyes of the Lord run to and fro throughout the whole earth, to shew himself strong in the behalf of them whose heart is perfect toward him. Herein thou hast done foolishly: therefore from henceforth thou shalt have wars.

7. 2 Chronicles 18:16.

[16] Then he said, I did see all Israel scattered upon the mountains, as sheep that have no shepherd: and the Lord said, These have no master; let them return therefore every man to his house in peace.

8. 2 Chronicles 18:24:

[24] And Micaiah said, Behold, thou shalt see on that

day when thou shalt go into an inner chamber to hide thyself.

9. 2 Chronicles 18:27:

[27] And Micaiah said, If thou certainly return in peace, then hath not the Lord spoken by me. And he said, Hearken, all ye people.

10. 2 Chronicles 19:2:

[2] And Jehu the son of Hanani the seer went out to meet him, and said to king Jehoshaphat, Shouldest thou help the ungodly, and love them that hate the Lord ? therefore is wrath upon thee from before the Lord.

11. 2 Chronicles 20:15-17:

[15] And he said, Hearken ye, all Judah, and ye inhabitants of Jerusalem, and thou king Jehoshaphat, Thus saith the Lord unto you, Be not afraid nor dismayed by reason of this great multitude; for the battle is not yours, but God's. [16] To morrow go ye down against them: behold, they come up by the cliff of Ziz; and ye shall find them at the end of the brook, before the wilderness of Jeruel. [17] Ye shall not need to fight in this battle: set yourselves, stand ye still, and see the salvation of the Lord with you, O Judah and Jerusalem: fear not, nor be dismayed; to morrow go out against them: for the Lord will be with you.

12. 2 Chronicles 20:37:

[37] Then Eliezer the son of Dodavah of Mareshah prophesied against Jehoshaphat, saying, Because thou hast joined thyself with Ahaziah, the Lord hath broken thy works. And the ships were broken, that they were not able to go to Tarshish.

13. 2 Chronicles 21:12-15

[12] And there came a writing to him from Elijah the prophet, saying, Thus saith the Lord God of David thy father, Because thou hast not walked in the ways of Jehoshaphat thy father, nor in the ways of Asa king of Judah, [13] But hast walked in the way of the kings of Israel, and hast made Judah and the inhabitants of Jerusalem to go a whoring, like to the whoredoms of the house of Ahab, and also hast slain thy brethren of thy father's house, which were better than thyself: [14] Behold, with a great plague will the Lord smite thy people, and thy children, and thy wives, and all thy goods: [15] And thou shalt have great sickness by disease of thy bowels, until thy bowels fall out by reason of the sickness day by day.

14. 2 Chronicles 24:20:

[20] And the Spirit of God came upon Zechariah the son of Jehoiada the priest, which stood above the people, and said unto them, Thus saith God, Why transgress ye the commandments of the Lord, that ye cannot prosper? because ye have forsaken the Lord, he hath also forsaken you.

15. 2 Chronicles 25:16:

[16] And it came to pass, as he talked with him, that the king said unto him, Art thou made of the king's counsel? forbear; why shouldest thou be smitten? Then the prophet forbare, and said, I know that God hath determined to destroy thee, because thou hast done this, and hast not hearkened unto my counsel.

16. 2 Chronicles 33:4:

[3] Also he built altars in the house of the Lord, whereof the Lord had said, In Jerusalem shall my name be for ever.

17. 2 Chronicles 33:7-8:

[7] And he set a carved image, the idol which he had made, in the house of God, of which God had said to David and to Solomon his son, In this house, and in Jerusalem, which I have chosen before all the tribes of Israel, will I put my name for ever: [8] Neither will I any more remove the foot of Israel from out of the land which I have appointed for your fathers; so that they will take heed to do all that I have commanded them, according to the whole law and the statutes and the ordinances by the hand of Moses.

18. 2 Chronicles 34:24-25:

[24] Thus saith the Lord, Behold, I will bring evil upon this place, and upon the inhabitants thereof, even all the

curses that are written in the book which they have read before the king of Judah: [25] Because they have for-saken me, and have burned incense unto other gods, that they might provoke me to anger with all the works of their hands; therefore my wrath shall be poured out upon this place, and shall not be quenched.

PROPHECIES IN NEHEMIAH: 2

1. Nehemiah 1:8-9:

[8] Remember, I beseech thee, the word that thou commandedst thy servant Moses, saying, If ye transgress, I will scatter you abroad among the nations: [9] But if ye turn unto me, and keep my commandments, and do them; though there were of you cast out unto the uttermost part of the heaven, yet will I gather them from thence, and will bring them unto the place that I have chosen to set my name there.

2. Nehemiah 2:20:

[20] Then answered I them, and said unto them, The God of heaven, he will prosper us; therefore we his servants will arise and build: but ye have no portion, nor right, nor memorial, in Jerusalem.

PROPHECIES IN ESTHER: 1

Esther 6:13:

[13] And Haman told Zeresh his wife and all his friends every thing that had befallen him. Then said his wise men and Zeresh his wife unto him, If Mordecai be of the seed of the Jews, before whom thou hast begun to fall, thou shalt not prevail against him, but shalt surely fall before him.

PROPHECIES IN JOB: 2

1. Job 19:25-27:

[25] For I know that my redeemer liveth, and that he shall stand at the latter day upon the earth: [26] And though after my skin worms destroy this body, yet in my flesh shall I see God: [27] Whom I shall see for myself, and mine eyes shall behold, and not another; though my reins be consumed within me.

2. Job 23:10:

[10] But he knoweth the way that I take: when he hath tried me, I shall come forth as gold.

PROPHECIES IN PSALMS: 70

1. Psalm 8:2:

   [2] Out of the mouth of babes and sucklings hast thou ordained strength because of thine enemies, that thou mightest still the enemy and the avenger.

2. Psalm 9:7:

   [7] But the Lord shall endure for ever: he hath prepared his throne for judgment.

3. Psalm 9:17-18:

   [17] The wicked shall be turned into hell, and all the nations that forget God. [18] For the needy shall not I be forgotten: the expectation of the poor shall not perish for ever.

4. Psalm 10:15:

   [15] Break thou the arm of the wicked and the evil man: seek out his wickedness till thou find none.

5. Psalm 11:6:

   [6] Upon the wicked he shall rain snares, fire and brimstone, and an horrible tempest: this shall be the portion of their cup.

6. Psalm 12:3:

[3] The Lord shall cut off all flattering lips, and the tongue that speaketh proud things:

7. Psalm 12:7:

[7] Thou shalt keep them, O Lord, thou shalt preserve them from this generation for ever.

8. Psalm 14:7:

[7] Oh that the salvation of Israel were come out of Zion! When the Lord bringeth back the captivity of his people, Jacob shall rejoice, and Israel shall be glad.

9. Psalm 15:2-3:

[2] He that walketh uprightly, and worketh righteousness, and speaketh the truth in his heart. [3] He that backbiteth not with his tongue, nor doeth evil to his neighbour, nor taketh up a reproach against his neighbour.

10. Psalm 17:15:

[15] As for me, I will behold thy face in righteousness: I shall be satisfied, when I awake, with thy likeness.

11. Psalm 18:50:

[50] Great deliverance giveth he to his king; and sheweth mercy to his anointed, to David, and to his seed for evermore.

12. Psalm 21:1:

[1] The king shall joy in thy strength, O Lord; and in thy salvation how greatly shall he rejoice!

13. Psalm 22:1:

[1] My God, my God, why hast thou forsaken me? Why art thou so far from helping me, and from the words of my roaring?

14. Psalm 22:6:

[6] But I am a worm, and no man; a reproach of men, and despised of the people.

15. Psalm 23:6:

[6] Surely goodness and mercy shall follow me all the days of my life: and I will dwell in the house of the Lord for ever.

16. Psalm 24:1:

[1] The earth is the Lord's, and the fulness thereof; the world, and they that dwell therein.

17. Psalm 27:2:

[2] When the wicked, even mine enemies and my foes, came upon me to eat up my flesh, they stumbled and fell.

18. Psalm 34:19:

> *[19] Many are the afflictions of the righteous: but the Lord delivereth him out of them all.*

19. Psalm 35:15:

> *[15] But in mine adversity they rejoiced, and gathered themselves together: yea, the abjects gathered themselves together against me, and I knew it not; they did tear me, and ceased not.*

20. Psalm 36:8:

> *[8] They shall be abundantly satisfied with the fatness of thy house; and thou shalt make them drink of the river of thy pleasures.*

21. Psalm 37:2:

> *[2] For they shall soon be cut down like the grass, and wither as the green herb.*

22. Psalm 37:9:

> *[9] For evildoers shall be cut off: but those that wait upon the Lord, they shall inherit the earth.*

23. Psalm 37:13:

> *[13] The Lord shall laugh at him: for he seeth that his day is coming.*

24. Psalm 37:17:

[17] For the arms of the wicked shall be broken: but the Lord upholdeth the righteous.

25. Psalm 37:22:

[22] For such as be blessed of him shall inherit the earth; and they that be cursed of him shall be cut off.

26. Psalm 37:27:

[27] Depart from evil, and do good; and dwell for evermore.

28. Psalm 37:37:

[37] Mark the perfect man, and behold the upright: for the end of that man is peace.

29. Psalm 40:6.

[6] Sacrifice and offering thou didst not desire; mine ears hast thou opened: burnt offering and sin offering hast thou not required.

30. Psalm 41:9:

[9] Yea, mine own familiar friend, in whom I trusted, which did eat of my bread, hath lifted up his heel against me.

31. Psalm 45:17:

[17] I will make thy name to be remembered in all generations: therefore shall the people praise thee for ever and ever.

32. Psalm 46:4:

[4] There is a river, the streams whereof shall make glad the city of God, the holy place of the tabernacles of the most High.

33. Psalm 48:1:

[1] Great is the Lord, and greatly to be praised in the city of our God, in the mountain of his holiness.

34. Psalm 48:14:

[14] For this God is our God for ever and ever: he will be our guide even unto death.

35. Psalm 49:14:

[14] Like sheep they are laid in the grave; death shall feed on them; and the upright shall have dominion over them in the morning; and their beauty shall consume in the grave from their dwelling.

36. Psalm 52:5:

[5] God shall likewise destroy thee for ever, he shall take thee away, and pluck thee out of thy dwelling place, and

root thee out of the land of the living. Selah.

37. Psalm 53:6:

[6] Oh that the salvation of Israel were come out of Zion! When God bringeth back the captivity of his people, Jacob shall rejoice, and Israel shall be glad.

38. Psalm 55:12:

[12] For it was not an enemy that reproached me; then I could have borne it: neither was it he that hated me that did magnify himself against me; then I would have hid myself from him.

39. Psalm 57:3:

[3] He shall send from heaven, and save me from the reproach of him that would swallow me up. Selah. God shall send forth his mercy and his truth.

40. Psalm 58:9:

[9] Before your pots can feel the thorns, he shall take them away as with a whirlwind, both living, and in his wrath.

41 Psalm 59:8:

[8] But thou, O Lord, shalt laugh at them; thou shalt have all the heathen in derision.

42. Psalm 59:10:

> *[10] The God of my mercy shall prevent me: God shall let me see my desire upon mine enemies.*

43. Psalm 60:6:

> *[6] God hath spoken in his holiness; I will rejoice, I will divide Shechem, and mete out the valley of Succoth.*

44. Psalm 67:6:

> *[6] Then shall the earth yield her increase; and God, even our own God, shall bless us.*

45. Psalm 68:13:

> *[13] Though ye have lien among the pots, yet shall ye be as the wings of a dove covered with silver, and her feathers with yellow gold.*

46. Psalm 68:18:

> *[18] Thou hast ascended on high, thou hast led captivity captive: thou hast received gifts for men; yea, for the rebellious also, that the Lord God might dwell among them.*

47. Psalm 68:21:

> *[21] But God shall wound the head of his enemies, and the hairy scalp of such an one as goeth on still in his trespasses.*

48. Psalm 69:4:

> *[4] They that hate me without a cause are more than the hairs of mine head: they that would destroy me, being mine enemies wrongfully, are mighty: then I restored that which I took not away.*

49. Psalm 69:22:

> *[22] Let their table become a snare before them: and that which should have been for their welfare, let it become a trap.*

50. Psalm 71:20:

> *[20] Thou, which hast shewed me great and sore troubles, shalt quicken me again, and shalt bring me up again from the depths of the earth.*

51. Psalm 72:2:

> *[2] He shall judge thy people with righteousness, and thy poor with judgment.*

52. Psalm 73:24:

> *[24] Thou shalt guide me with thy counsel, and afterward receive me to glory.*

53. Psalm 75:2:

> *[2] When I shall receive the congregation, I will judge*

uprightly.

54 Psalm 75:8:

[8] For in the hand of the Lord there is a cup, and the wine is red; it is full of mixture; and he poureth out of the same: but the dregs thereof, all the wicked of the earth shall wring them out, and drink them.

55. Psalm 76:10:

[10] Surely the wrath of man shall praise thee: the remainder of wrath shalt thou restrain.

56. Psalm 82:6-7:

[6] I have said, Ye are gods; and all of you are children of the most High. [7] But ye shall die like men, and fall like one of the princes.

57. Psalm 86:9:

[9] All nations whom thou hast made shall come and worship before thee, O Lord; and shall glorify thy name.

58. Psalm 89:4:

[4] Thy seed will I establish for ever, and build up thy throne to all generations. Selah.

59. Psalm 89:14-16:

> *[14] Justice and judgment are the habitation of thy throne: mercy and truth shall go before thy face. [15] Blessed is the people that know the joyful sound: they shall walk, O Lord, in the light of thy countenance. [16] In thy name shall they rejoice all the day: and in thy righteousness shall they be exalted.*

60. Psalm 98:9:

> *[9] Before the Lord; for he cometh to judge the earth: with righteousness shall he judge the world, and the people with equity.*

61. Psalm 102:12:

> *[12] But thou, O Lord, shalt endure for ever; and thy remembrance unto all generations.*

62 Psalm 102:18:

> *[18] This shall be written for the generation to come: and the people which shall be created shall praise the Lord.*

63. Psalm 108:7:

> *[7] God hath spoken in his holiness; I will rejoice, I will divide Shechem, and mete out the valley of Succoth.*

64. Psalm 109:1-2:

[1] Hold not thy peace, O God of my praise; [2] For the mouth of the wicked and the mouth of the deceitful are opened against me: they have spoken against me with a lying tongue.

65. Psalm 110:1:

[1] The Lord said unto my Lord, Sit thou at my right hand, until I make thine enemies thy footstool.

66. Psalm 118:22:

[22] The stone which the builders refused is become the head stone of the corner.

67. Psalm 118:26:

[26] Blessed be he that cometh in the name of the Lord: we have blessed you out of the house of the Lord.

68. Psalm 132:11:

[11] The Lord hath sworn in truth unto David; he will not turn from it; Of the fruit of thy body will I set upon thy throne.

69. Psalm 138:4:

[4] All the kings of the earth shall praise thee, O Lord, when they hear the words of thy mouth.

70. Psalm 139:19:

> *[19] Surely thou wilt slay the wicked, O God: depart from me therefore, ye bloody men.*

PROPHECIES IN PROVERBS: 10

1. Proverbs 2:21-22:

> *[21] For the upright shall dwell in the land, and the perfect shall remain in it. [22] But the wicked shall be cut off from the earth, and the transgressors shall be rooted out of it.*

2. Proverbs 3:35:

> *[35] The wise shall inherit glory: but shame shall be the promotion of fools.*

3. Proverbs 4:18-19:

> *[18] But the path of the just is as the shining light, that shineth more and more unto the perfect day. [19] The way of the wicked is as darkness: they know not at what they stumble.*

4. Proverbs 5:22-23:

> *[22] His own iniquities shall take the wicked himself, and he shall be holden with the cords of his sins. [23] He shall die without instruction; and in the greatness of his folly he shall go astray.*

5. Proverbs 10:30:

[30] The righteous shall never be removed: but the wicked shall not inhabit the earth.

6. Proverbs 12:19:

[19] The lip of truth shall be established for ever: but a lying tongue is but for a moment.

7. Proverbs 13:9:

[9] The light of the righteous rejoiceth: but the lamp of the wicked shall be put out.

8. Proverbs 13:13:

[13] Whoso despiseth the word shall be destroyed: but he that feareth the commandment shall be rewarded.

9. Proverbs 14:11:

[11] The house of the wicked shall be overthrown: but the tabernacle of the upright shall flourish.

10. Proverbs 21:16:

[16] The man that wandereth out of the way of understanding shall remain in the congregation of the dead.

PROPHECIES IN ISAIAH: 45

1. Isaiah 1:24-26:

[24] Therefore saith the Lord, the Lord of hosts, the mighty One of Israel, Ah, I will ease me of mine adversaries, and avenge me of mine enemies: [25] And I will turn my hand upon thee, and purely purge away thy dross, and take away all thy tin: [26] And I will restore thy judges as at the first, and thy counsellors as at the beginning: afterward thou shalt be called, The city of righteousness, the faithful city.

2. Isaiah 2:2-4:

[2] And it shall come to pass in the last days, that the mountain of the Lord's house shall be established in the top of the mountains, and shall be exalted above the hills; and all nations shall flow unto it. [3] And many people shall go and say, Come ye, and let us go up to the mountain of the Lord, to the house of the God of Jacob; and he will teach us of his ways, and we will walk in his paths: for out of Zion shall go forth the law, and the word of the Lord from Jerusalem. [4] And he shall judge among the nations, and shall rebuke many people: and they shall beat their swords into plowshares, and their spears into pruninghooks: nation shall not lift up sword against nation, neither shall they learn war any more.

Prayer and Prophetic Verses in the Bible

3. Isaiah 3:1-3:

[1] For, behold, the Lord, the Lord of hosts, doth take away from Jerusalem and from Judah the stay and the staff, the whole stay of bread, and the whole stay of water, [2] The mighty man, and the man of war, the judge, and the prophet, and the prudent, and the ancient, [3] The captain of fifty, and the honourable man, and the counsellor, and the cunning artificer, and the eloquent orator.

4. Isaiah 3:16-24:

[16] Moreover the Lord saith, Because the daughters of Zion are haughty, and walk with stretched forth necks and wanton eyes, walking and mincing as they go, and making a tinkling with their feet: [17] Therefore the Lord will smite with a scab the crown of the head of the daughters of Zion, and the Lord will discover their secret parts. [18] In that day the Lord will take away the bravery of their tinkling ornaments about their feet, and their cauls, and their round tires like the moon, [19] The chains, and the bracelets, and the mufflers, [20] The bonnets, and the ornaments of the legs, and the headbands, and the tablets, and the earrings, [21] The rings, and nose jewels, [22] The changeable suits of apparel, and the mantles, and the wimples, and the crisping pins, [23] The glasses, and the fine linen, and the hoods, and the vails. [24] And it shall come to pass, that instead of sweet smell there shall be stink; and instead of a girdle a rent; and instead of well set hair baldness; and instead of a stomacher a girding of sackcloth; and burning instead of beauty.

5. Isaiah 8:6-8:

[6] Forasmuch as this people refuseth the waters of Shiloah that go softly, and rejoice in Rezin and Remaliah's son; [7] Now therefore, behold, the Lord bringeth up upon them the waters of the river, strong and many, even the king of Assyria, and all his glory: and he shall come up over all his channels, and go over all his banks: [8] And he shall pass through Judah; he shall overflow and go over, he shall reach even to the neck; and the stretching out of his wings shall fill the breadth of thy land, O Immanuel.

6. Isaiah 9:6-8:

[6] For unto us a child is born, unto us a son is given: and the government shall be upon his shoulder: and his name shall be called Wonderful, Counsellor, The mighty God, The everlasting Father, The Prince of Peace. [7] Of the increase of his government and peace there shall be no end, upon the throne of David, and upon his kingdom, to order it, and to establish it with judgment and with justice from henceforth even for ever. The zeal of the Lord of hosts will perform this. [8] The Lord sent a word into Jacob, and it hath lighted upon Israel.

7. Isaiah 10:20:

[20] And it shall come to pass in that day, that the remnant of Israel, and such as are escaped of the house of Jacob, shall no more again stay upon him that smote

them; but shall stay upon the Lord, the Holy One of Israel, in truth.

8. Isaiah 11:1-6:

[1] And there shall come forth a rod out of the stem of Jesse, and a Branch shall grow out of his roots: [2] And the spirit of the Lord shall rest upon him, the spirit of wisdom and understanding, the spirit of counsel and might, the spirit of knowledge and of the fear of the Lord; [3] And shall make him of quick understanding in the fear of the Lord: and he shall not judge after the sight of his eyes, neither reprove after the hearing of his ears: [4] But with righteousness shall he judge the poor, and reprove with equity for the meek of the earth: and he shall smite the earth with the rod of his mouth, and with the breath of his lips shall he slay the wicked. [5] And righteousness shall be the girdle of his loins, and faithfulness the girdle of his reins. [6] The wolf also shall dwell with the lamb, and the leopard shall lie down with the kid; and the calf and the young lion and the fatling together; and a little child shall lead them.

9. Isaiah 13:17-19:

[17] Behold, I will stir up the Medes against them, which shall not regard silver; and as for gold, they shall not delight in it. [18] Their bows also shall dash the young men to pieces; and they shall have no pity on the fruit of the womb; their eye shall not spare children. [19] And Babylon, the glory of kingdoms, the beauty of the Chaldees'

excellency, shall be as when God overthrew Sodom and Gomorrah.

10. Isaiah 16:13-14:

[13] This is the word that the Lord hath spoken concerning Moab since that time. [14] But now the Lord hath spoken, saying, Within three years, as the years of an hireling, and the glory of Moab shall be contemned, with all that great multitude; and the remnant shall be very small and feeble.

11. Isaiah 17:1:

[1] The burden of Damascus. Behold, Damascus is taken away from being a city, and it shall be a ruinous heap.

12. Isaiah 18:1-2:

[1] Woe to the land shadowing with wings, which is beyond the rivers of Ethiopia: [2] That sendeth ambassadors by the sea, even in vessels of bulrushes upon the waters, saying, Go, ye swift messengers, to a nation scattered and peeled, to a people terrible from their beginning hitherto; a nation meted out and trodden down, whose land the rivers have spoiled!

13. Isaiah 19:1:

[1] The burden of Egypt. Behold, the Lord rideth upon a swift cloud, and shall come into Egypt: and the idols of Egypt shall be moved at his presence, and the heart of

Egypt shall melt in the midst of it.

14. Isaiah 21:13:

[13] The burden upon Arabia. In the forest in Arabia shall ye lodge, O ye travelling companies of Dedanim.

15. Isaiah 23:18.

[18] And her merchandise and her hire shall be holiness to the Lord: it shall not be treasured nor laid up; for her merchandise shall be for them that dwell before the Lord, to eat sufficiently, and for durable clothing.

16. Isaiah 24:1-2:

[1] Behold, the Lord maketh the earth empty, and maketh it waste, and turneth it upside down, and scattereth abroad the inhabitants thereof. [2] And it shall be, as with the people, so with the priest; as with the servant, so with his master; as with the maid, so with her mistress; as with the buyer, so with the seller; as with the lender, so with the borrower; as with the taker of usury, so with the giver of usury to him.

17. Isaiah 28:1:

[1] Woe to the crown of pride, to the drunkards of Ephraim, whose glorious beauty is a fading flower, which are on the head of the fat valleys of them that are overcome with wine!

18. Isaiah 30:1-2:

[1] Woe to the rebellious children, saith the Lord, that take counsel, but not of me; and that cover with a covering, but not of my spirit, that they may add sin to sin: [2] That walk to go down into Egypt, and have not asked at my mouth; to strengthen themselves in the strength of Pharaoh, and to trust in the shadow of Egypt!

19. Isaiah 30:18-19:

[18] And therefore will the Lord wait, that he may be gracious unto you, and therefore will he be exalted, that he may have mercy upon you: for the Lord is a God of judgment: blessed are all they that wait for him. [19] For the people shall dwell in Zion at Jerusalem: thou shalt weep no more: he will be very gracious unto thee at the voice of thy cry; when he shall hear it, he will answer thee.

20. Isaiah 31:1:

[1] Woe to them that go down to Egypt for help; and stay on horses, and trust in chariots, because they are many; and in horsemen, because they are very strong; but they look not unto the Holy One of Israel, neither seek the Lord!

21. Isaiah 31:3:

[3] Now the Egyptians are men, and not God; and their horses flesh, and not spirit. When the Lord shall stretch out his hand, both he that helpeth shall fall, and he that is holpen shall fall down, and they all shall fail together.

22. Isaiah 32:1-5:

[1] Behold, a king shall reign in righteousness, and princes shall rule in judgment. [2] And a man shall be as an hiding place from the wind, and a covert from the tempest; as rivers of water in a dry place, as the shadow of a great rock in a weary land. [3] And the eyes of them that see shall not be dim, and the ears of them that hear shall hearken. [4] The heart also of the rash shall understand knowledge, and the tongue of the stammerers shall be ready to speak plainly. [5] The vile person shall be no more called liberal, nor the churl said to be bountiful.

23. Isaiah 35:1-2:

[1] The wilderness and the solitary place shall be glad for them; and the desert shall rejoice, and blossom as the rose[2] . It shall blossom abundantly, and rejoice even with joy and singing: the glory of Lebanon shall be given unto it, the excellency of Carmel and Sharon, they shall see the glory of the Lord, and the excellency of our God.

24. Isaiah 37:6-7:

[6] And Isaiah said unto them, Thus shall ye say unto your master, Thus saith the Lord, Be not afraid of the words that thou hast heard, wherewith the servants of the king of Assyria have blasphemed me. [7] Behold, I will send a blast upon him, and he shall hear a rumour, and return to his own land; and I will cause him to fall by the sword in his own land.

25. Isaiah 37:21:

[21] Then Isaiah the son of Amoz sent unto Hezekiah, saying, Thus saith the Lord God of Israel, Whereas thou hast prayed to me against Sennacherib king of Assyria.

26. Isaiah 38:1:

[1] In those days was Hezekiah sick unto death. And Isaiah the prophet the son of Amoz came unto him, and said unto him, Thus saith the Lord, Set thine house in order: for thou shalt die, and not live.

27. Isaiah 38:5:

[5] Go, and say to Hezekiah, Thus saith the Lord, the God of David thy father, I have heard thy prayer, I have seen thy tears: behold, I will add unto thy days fifteen years.

28. Isaiah 39:5-6:

[5] Then said Isaiah to Hezekiah, Hear the word of the Lord of hosts: [6] Behold, the days come, that all that is in thine house, and that which thy fathers have laid up in store until this day, shall be carried to Babylon: nothing shall be left, saith the Lord.

29. Isaiah 40:3-5:

[3] The voice of him that crieth in the wilderness, Prepare ye the way of the Lord, make straight in the desert a highway for our God. [4] Every valley shall be exalted,

and every mountain and hill shall be made low: and the crooked shall be made straight, and the rough places plain: [5] And the glory of the Lord shall be revealed, and all flesh shall see it together: for the mouth of the Lord hath spoken it.

30. Isaiah 41:10:

[10] Fear thou not; for I am with thee: be not dismayed; for I am thy God: I will strengthen thee; yea, I will help thee; yea, I will uphold thee with the right hand of my righteousness.

31. Isaiah 41:25:

[25] I have raised up one from the north, and he shall come: from the rising of the sun shall he call upon my name: and he shall come upon princes as upon morter, and as the potter treadeth clay.

32. Isaiah 41:27:

[27] The first shall say to Zion, Behold, behold them: and I will give to Jerusalem one that bringeth good tidings.

33. Isaiah 42:1:

[1] Behold my servant, whom I uphold; mine elect, in whom my soul delighteth; I have put my spirit upon him: he shall bring forth judgment to the Gentiles.

34. Isaiah 43:1-2:

[1] But now thus saith the Lord that created thee, O Jacob, and he that formed thee, O Israel, Fear not: for I have redeemed thee, I have called thee by thy name; thou art mine. [2] When thou passest through the waters, I will be with thee; and through the rivers, they shall not over-flow thee: when thou walkest through the fire, thou shalt not be burned; neither shall the flame kindle upon thee.

35. Isaiah 44:21:

[21] Remember these, O Jacob and Israel; for thou art my servant: I have formed thee; thou art my servant: O Israel, thou shalt not be forgotten of me.

36. Isaiah 44:26-28:

[26] That confirmeth the word of his servant, and performeth the counsel of his messengers; that saith to Jerusalem, Thou shalt be inhabited; and to the cities of Judah, Ye shall be built, and I will raise up the decayed places thereof: [27] That saith to the deep, Be dry, and I will dry up thy rivers: [28] That saith of Cyrus, He is my shepherd, and shall perform all my pleasure: even saying to Jerusalem, Thou shalt be built; and to the temple, Thy foundation shall be laid.

37. Isaiah 45:8:

[8] Drop down, ye heavens, from above, and let the skies

pour down righteousness: let the earth open, and let them bring forth salvation, and let righteousness spring up together; I the Lord have created it.

38. Isaiah 45:13:

[13] I have raised him up in righteousness, and I will direct all his ways: he shall build my city, and he shall let go my captives, not for price nor reward, saith the Lord of hosts.

39. Isaiah 45:23:

[23] I have sworn by myself, the word is gone out of my mouth in righteousness, and shall not return, That unto me every knee shall bow, every tongue shall swear.

40. Isaiah 46:10-13:

[10] Declaring the end from the beginning, and from ancient times the things that are not yet done, saying, My counsel shall stand, and I will do all my pleasure: [11] Calling a ravenous bird from the east, the man that executeth my counsel from a far country: yea, I have spoken it, I will also bring it to pass; I have purposed it, I will also do it. [12] Hearken unto me, ye stouthearted, that are far from righteousness: [13] I bring near my righteousness; it shall not be far off, and my salvation shall not tarry: and I will place salvation in Zion for Israel my glory.

41. Isaiah 48:14:

[14] All ye, assemble yourselves, and hear; which among them hath declared these things ? The Lord hath loved him: he will do his pleasure on Babylon, and his arm shall be on the Chaldeans.

42. Isaiah 49:7:

[7] Thus saith the Lord, the Redeemer of Israel, and his Holy One, to him whom man despiseth, to him whom the nation abhorreth, to a servant of rulers, Kings shall see and arise, princes also shall worship, because of the Lord that is faithful, and the Holy One of Israel, and he shall choose thee.

43. Isaiah 55:10:

[10] For as the rain cometh down, and the snow from heaven, and returneth not thither, but watereth the earth, and maketh it bring forth and bud, that it may give seed to the sower, and bread to the eater.

44. Isaiah 56:1:

[1] Thus saith the Lord, Keep ye judgment, and do justice: for my salvation is near to come, and my righteousness to be revealed.

45. Isaiah 61:1-3:

[1] The Spirit of the Lord God is upon me; because the

*Lord hath anointed me to preach good tidings unto the
meek; he hath sent me to bind up the brokenhearted,
to proclaim liberty to the captives, and the opening of
the prison to them that are bound; [2] To proclaim the
acceptable year of the Lord, and the day of vengeance of
our God; to comfort all that mourn; [3] To appoint unto
them that mourn in Zion, to give unto them beauty for
ashes, the oil of joy for mourning, the garment of praise
for the spirit of heaviness; that they might be called trees
of righteousness, the planting of the Lord, that he might
be glorified.*

46. Isaiah 62:1:

*[1] For Zion's sake will I not hold my peace, and for
Jerusalem's sake I will not rest, until the righteousness
thereof go forth as brightness, and the salvation thereof
as a lamp that burneth.*

47. Isaiah 65:6-7:

*[6] Behold, it is written before me: I will not keep silence,
but will recompense, even recompense into their bosom,
[7] Your iniquities, and the iniquities of your fathers
together, saith the Lord, which have burned incense upon
the mountains, and blasphemed me upon the hills: therefore will I measure their former work into their bosom.*

PROPHECIES IN JEREMIAH: 96

1. Jeremiah 1:4-8:

[4] Then the word of the Lord came unto me, saying, [5] Before I formed thee in the belly I knew thee; and before thou camest forth out of the womb I sanctified thee, and I ordained thee a prophet unto the nations. [6] Then said I, Ah, Lord God! behold, I cannot speak: for I am a child. [7] But the Lord said unto me, Say not, I am a child: for thou shalt go to all that I shall send thee, and whatsoever I command thee thou shalt speak. [8] Be not afraid of their faces: for I am with thee to deliver thee, saith the Lord.

2. Jeremiah 1:13-16:

[13] And the word of the Lord came unto me the second time, saying, What seest thou? And I said, I see a seething pot; and the face thereof is toward the north. [14] Then the Lord said unto me, Out of the north an evil shall break forth upon all the inhabitants of the land. [15] For, lo, I will call all the families of the kingdoms of the north, saith the Lord; and they shall come, and they shall set every one his throne at the entering of the gates of Jerusalem, and against all the walls thereof round about, and against all the cities of Judah. [16] And I will utter my judgments against them touching all their wickedness, who have forsaken me, and have burned incense unto

other gods, and worshipped the works of their own hands.

3. Jeremiah 2:1-2:

> *[1] Moreover the word of the Lord came to me, saying,*
> *[2] Go and cry in the ears of Jerusalem, saying, Thus*
> *saith the Lord; I remember thee, the kindness of thy*
> *youth, the love of thine espousals, when thou wentest*
> *after me in the wilderness, in a land that was not sown.*

4. Jeremiah 2:9:

> *[9] Wherefore I will yet plead with you, saith the Lord,*
> *and with your children's children will I plead.*

5. Jeremiah 2:14-15:

> *[14] Is Israel a servant? is he a homeborn slave? why*
> *is he spoiled? [15] The young lions roared upon him,*
> *and yelled, and they made his land waste: his cities are*
> *burned without inhabitant.*

6. Jeremiah 2:26-27:

> *[26] As the thief is ashamed when he is found, so is the*
> *house of Israel ashamed; they, their kings, their princ-*
> *es, and their priests, and their prophets, [27] Saying to*
> *a stock, Thou art my father; and to a stone, Thou hast*
> *brought me forth: for they have turned their back unto*
> *me, and not their face: but in the time of their trouble they*
> *will say, Arise, and save us.*

7. Jeremiah 2:35-37:

[35] Yet thou sayest, Because I am innocent, surely his anger shall turn from me. Behold, I will plead with thee, because thou sayest, I have not sinned. [36] Why gaddest thou about so much to change thy way? thou also shalt be ashamed of Egypt, as thou wast ashamed of Assyria. [37] Yea, thou shalt go forth from him, and thine hands upon thine head: for the Lord hath rejected thy confidences, and thou shalt not prosper in them.

8. Jeremiah 3:14-18:

[14] Turn, O backsliding children, saith the Lord; for I am married unto you: and I will take you one of a city, and two of a family, and I will bring you to Zion: [15] And I will give you pastors according to mine heart, which shall feed you with knowledge and understanding. [16] And it shall come to pass, when ye be multiplied and increased in the land, in those days, saith the Lord, they shall say no more, The ark of the covenant of the Lord: neither shall it come to mind: neither shall they remember it; neither shall they visit it; neither shall that be done any more. [17] At that time they shall call Jerusalem the throne of the Lord; and all the nations shall be gathered unto it, to the name of the Lord, to Jerusalem: neither shall they walk any more after the imagination of their evil heart. [18] In those days the house of Judah shall walk with the house of Israel, and they shall come together out of the land of the north to the land that I have given for an inheritance unto your fathers.

9 Jeremiah 4:9:

[9] And it shall come to pass at that day, saith the Lord, that the heart of the king shall perish, and the heart of the princes; and the priests shall be astonished, and the prophets shall wonder.

10. Jeremiah 5:6:

[6] Wherefore a lion out of the forest shall slay them, and a wolf of the evenings shall spoil them, a leopard shall watch over their cities: every one that goeth out thence shall be torn in pieces: because their transgressions are many, and their backslidings are increased.

11. Jeremiah 5:13-15:

[13] And the prophets shall become wind, and the word is not in them: thus shall it be done unto them. [14] Wherefore thus saith the Lord God of hosts, Because ye speak this word, behold, I will make my words in thy mouth fire, and this people wood, and it shall devour them. [15] Lo, I will bring a nation upon you from far, O house of Israel, saith the Lord: it is a mighty nation, it is an ancient nation, a nation whose language thou knowest not, neither understandest what they say.

12. Jeremiah 5:17-19:

[17] And they shall eat up thine harvest, and thy bread, which thy sons and thy daughters should eat: they shall eat up thy flocks and thine herds: they shall eat up thy

vines and thy fig trees: they shall impoverish thy fenced cities, wherein thou trustedst, with the sword. [18] Nevertheless in those days, saith the Lord, I will not make a full end with you. [19] And it shall come to pass, when ye shall say, Wherefore doeth the Lord our God all these things unto us? then shalt thou answer them, Like as ye have forsaken me, and served strange gods in your land, so shall ye serve strangers in a land that is not yours.

13. Jeremiah 6:1:

[1] O ye children of Benjamin, gather yourselves to flee out of the midst of Jerusalem, and blow the trumpet in Tekoa, and set up a sign of fire in Beth-haccerem: for evil appeareth out of the north, and great destruction.

14. Jeremiah 7:13-15:

[13] And now, because ye have done all these works, saith the Lord, and I spake unto you, rising up early and speaking, but ye heard not; and I called you, but ye answered not; [14] Therefore will I do unto this house, which is called by my name, wherein ye trust, and unto the place which I gave to you and to your fathers, as I have done to Shiloh. [15] And I will cast you out of my sight, as I have cast out all your brethren, even the whole seed of Ephraim.

15. Jeremiah 7:20:

[20] Therefore thus saith the Lord God; Behold, mine

anger and my fury shall be poured out upon this place, upon man, and upon beast, and upon the trees of the field, and upon the fruit of the ground; and it shall burn, and shall not be quenched.

16. Jeremiah 7:27:

[27] Therefore thou shalt speak all these words unto them; but they will not hearken to thee: thou shalt also call unto them; but they will not answer thee.

17. Jeremiah 7:32:

[32] Therefore, behold, the days come, saith the Lord, that it shall no more be called Tophet, nor the valley of the son of Hinnom, but the valley of slaughter: for they shall bury in Tophet, till there be no place.

18. Jeremiah 8:10:

[10] Therefore will I give their wives unto others, and their fields to them that shall inherit them: for every one from the least even unto the greatest is given to covetousness, from the prophet even unto the priest every one dealeth falsely.

19. Jeremiah 8:12-13:

[12] Were they ashamed when they had committed abomination? nay, they were not at all ashamed, neither could they blush: therefore shall they fall among them that fall:

in the time of their visitation they shall be cast down, saith the Lord. [13] I will surely consume them, saith the Lord: there shall be no grapes on the vine, nor figs on the fig tree, and the leaf shall fade; and the things that I have given them shall pass away from them.

20. Jeremiah 9:7:

[7] Therefore thus saith the Lord of hosts, Behold, I will melt them, and try them; for how shall I do for the daughter of my people?

21. Jeremiah 9:15-16:

[15] Therefore thus saith the Lord of hosts, the God of Israel; Behold, I will feed them, even this people, with wormwood, and give them water of gall to drink. [16] I will scatter them also among the heathen, whom neither they nor their fathers have known: and I will send a sword after them, till I have consumed them.

22. Jeremiah 11:21-23:

[21] Therefore thus saith the Lord of the men of Anathoth, that seek thy life, saying, Prophesy not in the name of the Lord, that thou die not by our hand: [22] Therefore thus saith the Lord of hosts, Behold, I will punish them: the young men shall die by the sword; their sons and their daughters shall die by famine: [23] And there shall be no remnant of them: for I will bring evil upon the men of Anathoth, even the year of their visitation.

23. Jeremiah 12:5-6:

*[5] If thou hast run with the footmen, and they have
wearied thee, then how canst thou contend with horses?
and if in the land of peace, wherein thou trustedst, they
wearied thee, then how wilt thou do in the swelling of
Jordan? [6] For even thy brethren, and the house of thy
father, even they have dealt treacherously with thee; yea,
they have called a multitude after thee: believe them not,
though they speak fair words unto thee.*

24. Jeremiah 13:1:

*[1] Thus saith the Lord unto me, Go and get thee a linen
girdle, and put it upon thy loins, and put it not in water.*

25. Jeremiah 13:9:

*[9] Thus saith the Lord, After this manner will I mar the
pride of Judah, and the great pride of Jerusalem.*

26. Jeremiah 14:1-6:

*[1] The word of the Lord that came to Jeremiah concern-
ing the dearth. [2] Judah mourneth, and the gates thereof
languish; they are black unto the ground; and the cry of
Jerusalem is gone up. [3] And their nobles have sent their
little ones to the waters: they came to the pits, and found
no water; they returned with their vessels empty; they
were ashamed and confounded, and covered their heads.
[4] Because the ground is chapt, for there was no rain
in the earth, the plowmen were ashamed, they covered*

their heads. [5] Yea, the hind also calved in the field, and forsook it, because there was no grass. [6] And the wild asses did stand in the high places, they snuffed up the wind like dragons; their eyes did fail, because there was no grass.

27. Jeremiah 14:10:

[10] Thus saith the Lord unto this people, Thus have they loved to wander, they have not refrained their feet, therefore the Lord doth not accept them; he will now remember their iniquity, and visit their sins.

28. Jeremiah 14:12:

[12] When they fast, I will not hear their cry; and when they offer burnt offering and an oblation, I will not accept them: but I will consume them by the sword, and by the famine, and by the pestilence.

29. Jeremiah 14:15-16:

[15] Therefore thus saith the Lord concerning the prophets that prophesy in my name, and I sent them not, yet they say, Sword and famine shall not be in this land; By sword and famine shall those prophets be consumed. [16] And the people to whom they prophesy shall be cast out in the streets of Jerusalem because of the famine and the sword; and they shall have none to bury them, them, their wives, nor their sons, nor their daughters: for I will pour their wickedness upon them.

30. Jeremiah 15:1-4:

[1] Then said the Lord unto me, Though Moses and Samuel stood before me, yet my mind could not be toward this people: cast them out of my sight, and let them go forth. [2] And it shall come to pass, if they say unto thee, Whither shall we go forth? then thou shalt tell them, Thus saith the Lord; Such as are for death, to death; and such as are for the sword, to the sword; and such as are for the famine, to the famine; and such as are for the captivity, to the captivity. [3] And I will appoint over them four kinds, saith the Lord: the sword to slay, and the dogs to tear, and the fowls of the heaven, and the beasts of the earth, to devour and destroy. [4] And I will cause them to be removed into all kingdoms of the earth, because of Manasseh the son of Hezekiah king of Judah, for that which he did in Jerusalem.

31. Jeremiah 15:19-21:

[19] Therefore thus saith the Lord, If thou return, then will I bring thee again, and thou shalt stand before me: and if thou take forth the precious from the vile, thou shalt be as my mouth: let them return unto thee; but return not thou unto them. [20] And I will make thee unto this people a fenced brasen wall: and they shall fight against thee, but they shall not prevail against thee: for I am with thee to save thee and to deliver thee, saith the Lord. [21] And I will deliver thee out of the hand of the wicked, and I will redeem thee out of the hand of the terrible.

32. Jeremiah 16:1-4:

[1] The word of the Lord came also unto me, saying, [2] Thou shalt not take thee a wife, neither shalt thou have sons or daughters in this place. [3] For thus saith the Lord concerning the sons and concerning the daughters that are born in this place, and concerning their mothers that bare them, and concerning their fathers that begat them in this land; [4] They shall die of grievous deaths; they shall not be lamented; neither shall they be buried; but they shall be as dung upon the face of the earth: and they shall be consumed by the sword, and by famine; and their carcases shall be meat for the fowls of heaven, and for the beasts of the earth.

33. Jeremiah 16:14-15:

[14] Therefore, behold, the days come, saith the Lord, that it shall no more be said, The Lord liveth, that brought up the children of Israel out of the land of Egypt; [15] But, The Lord liveth, that brought up the children of Israel from the land of the north, and from all the lands whither he had driven them: and I will bring them again into their land that I gave unto their fathers.

34. Jeremiah 17:27:

[27] But if ye will not hearken unto me to hallow the sabbath day, and not to bear a burden, even entering in at the gates of Jerusalem on the sabbath day; then will I kindle a fire in the gates thereof, and it shall devour the

palaces of Jerusalem, and it shall not be quenched.

35. Jeremiah 18:1-10:

[1] The word which came to Jeremiah from the Lord, saying, [2] Arise, and go down to the potter's house, and there I will cause thee to hear my words. [3] Then I went down to the potter's house, and, behold, he wrought a work on the wheels. [4] And the vessel that he made of clay was marred in the hand of the potter: so he made it again another vessel, as seemed good to the potter to make it. [5] Then the word of the Lord came to me, saying, [6] O house of Israel, cannot I do with you as this potter? saith the Lord. Behold, as the clay is in the potter's hand, so are ye in mine hand, O house of Israel. [7] At what instant I shall speak concerning a nation, and concerning a kingdom, to pluck up, and to pull down, and to destroy it; [8] If that nation, against whom I have pronounced, turn from their evil, I will repent of the evil that I thought to do unto them. [9] And at what instant I shall speak concerning a nation, and concerning a kingdom, to build and to plant it; [10] If it do evil in my sight, that it obey not my voice, then I will repent of the good, wherewith I said I would benefit them.

36. Jeremiah 18:15-17:

[15] Because my people hath forgotten me, they have burned incense to vanity, and they have caused them to stumble in their ways from the ancient paths, to walk in paths, in a way not cast up; [16] To make their land

*desolate, and a perpetual hissing; every one that passeth
thereby shall be astonished, and wag his head. [17] I will
scatter them as with an east wind before the enemy; I will
shew them the back, and not the face, in the day of their
calamity.*

37. Jeremiah 19:1:

*[1] Thus saith the Lord, Go and get a potter's earthen
bottle, and take of the ancients of the people, and of the
ancients of the priests.*

38. Jeremiah 19:7-9:

*[7] And I will make void the counsel of Judah and
Jerusalem in this place; and I will cause them to fall by
the sword before their enemies, and by the hands of them
that seek their lives: and their carcases will I give to be
meat for the fowls of the heaven, and for the beasts of the
earth. [8] And I will make this city desolate, and an hissing; every one that passeth thereby shall be astonished
and hiss because of all the plagues thereof. [9] And I will
cause them to eat the flesh of their sons and the flesh of
their daughters, and they shall eat every one the flesh of
his friend in the siege and straitness, wherewith their enemies, and they that seek their lives, shall straiten them.*

39. Jeremiah 20:3-6:

*[3] And it came to pass on the morrow, that Pashur
brought forth Jeremiah out of the stocks. Then said
Jeremiah unto him, The Lord hath not called thy name*

Pashur, but Magor-missabib. [4] For thus saith the Lord, Behold, I will make thee a terror to thyself, and to all thy friends: and they shall fall by the sword of their enemies, and thine eyes shall behold it: and I will give all Judah into the hand of the king of Babylon, and he shall carry them captive into Babylon, and shall slay them with the sword. [5] Moreover I will deliver all the strength of this city, and all the labours thereof, and all the precious things thereof, and all the treasures of the kings of Judah will I give into the hand of their enemies, which shall spoil them, and take them, and carry them to Babylon. [6] And thou, Pashur, and all that dwell in thine house shall go into captivity: and thou shalt come to Babylon, and there thou shalt die, and shalt be buried there, thou, and all thy friends, to whom thou hast prophesied lies.

40. Jeremiah 21:3-7:

[3] Then said Jeremiah unto them, Thus shall ye say to Zedekiah: [4] Thus saith the Lord God of Israel; Behold, I will turn back the weapons of war that are in your hands, wherewith ye fight against the king of Babylon, and against the Chaldeans, which besiege you without the walls, and I will assemble them into the midst of this city. [5] And I myself will fight against you with an outstretched hand and with a strong arm, even in anger, and in fury, and in great wrath. [6] And I will smite the inhabitants of this city, both man and beast: they shall die of a great pestilence. [7] And afterward, saith the Lord, I will deliver Zedekiah king of Judah, and his servants,

and the people, and such as are left in this city from the pestilence, from the sword, and from the famine, into the hand of Nebuchadrezzar king of Babylon, and into the hand of their enemies, and into the hand of those that seek their life: and he shall smite them with the edge of the sword; he shall not spare them, neither have pity, nor have mercy.

41. Jeremiah 22:1:

[1] Thus saith the Lord; Go down to the house of the king of Judah, and speak there this word.

42. Jeremiah 22:4-5:

[4] For if ye do this thing indeed, then shall there enter in by the gates of this house kings sitting upon the throne of David, riding in chariots and on horses, he, and his servants, and his people. [5] But if ye will not hear these words, I swear by myself, saith the Lord, that this house shall become a desolation.

43. Jeremiah 23:1-4:

[1] Woe be unto the pastors that destroy and scatter the sheep of my pasture! saith the Lord. [2] Therefore thus saith the Lord God of Israel against the pastors that feed my people; Ye have scattered my flock, and driven them away, and have not visited them: behold, I will visit upon you the evil of your doings, saith the Lord. [3] And I will gather the remnant of my flock out of all countries whith-

er I have driven them, and will bring them again to their folds; and they shall be fruitful and increase. [4] And I will set up shepherds over them which shall feed them: and they shall fear no more, nor be dismayed, neither shall they be lacking, saith the Lord.

44. Jeremiah 23:12:

[12] Wherefore their way shall be unto them as slippery ways in the darkness: they shall be driven on, and fall therein: for I will bring evil upon them, even the year of their visitation, saith the Lord.

45. Jeremiah 23:15:

[15] Therefore thus saith the Lord of hosts concerning the prophets; Behold, I will feed them with wormwood, and make them drink the water of gall: for from the prophets of Jerusalem is profaneness gone forth into all the land.

46. Jeremiah 23:20:

[20] The anger of the Lord shall not return, until he have executed, and till he have performed the thoughts of his heart: in the latter days ye shall consider it perfectly.

47. Jeremiah 24:6-9:

[6] For I will set mine eyes upon them for good, and I will bring them again to this land: and I will build them,

and not pull them down; and I will plant them, and not pluck them up. [7] And I will give them an heart to know me, that I am the Lord: and they shall be my people, and I will be their God: for they shall return unto me with their whole heart. [8] And as the evil figs, which cannot be eaten, they are so evil; surely thus saith the Lord, So will I give Zedekiah the king of Judah, and his princes, and the residue of Jerusalem, that remain in this land, and them that dwell in the land of Egypt: [9] And I will deliver them to be removed into all the kingdoms of the earth for their hurt, to be a reproach and a proverb, a taunt and a curse, in all places whither I shall drive them.

48. Jeremiah 25:8-14:

[8] Therefore thus saith the Lord of hosts; Because ye have not heard my words, [9] Behold, I will send and take all the families of the north, saith the Lord, and Nebuchadrezzar the king of Babylon, my servant, and will bring them against this land, and against the inhabitants thereof, and against all these nations round about, and will utterly destroy them, and make them an astonishment, and an hissing, and perpetual desolations. [10] Moreover I will take from them the voice of mirth, and the voice of gladness, the voice of the bridegroom, and the voice of the bride, the sound of the millstones, and the light of the candle. [11] And this whole land shall be a desolation, and an astonishment; and these nations shall serve the king of Babylon seventy years. [12] And it shall come to pass, when seventy years are accomplished, that

I will punish the king of Babylon, and that nation, saith the Lord, for their iniquity, and the land of the Chaldeans, and will make it perpetual desolations. [13] And I will bring upon that land all my words which I have pronounced against it, even all that is written in this book, which Jeremiah hath prophesied against all the nations. [14] For many nations and great kings shall serve themselves of them also: and I will recompense them according to their deeds, and according to the works of their own hands.

49. Jeremiah 25:30-33:

[30] Therefore prophesy thou against them all these words, and say unto them, The Lord shall roar from on high, and utter his voice from his holy habitation; he shall mightily roar upon his habitation; he shall give a shout, as they that tread the grapes, against all the inhabitants of the earth. [31] A noise shall come even to the ends of the earth; for the Lord hath a controversy with the nations, he will plead with all flesh; he will give them that are wicked to the sword, saith the Lord. [32] Thus saith the Lord of hosts, Behold, evil shall go forth from nation to nation, and a great whirlwind shall be raised up from the coasts of the earth. [33] And the slain of the Lord shall be at that day from one end of the earth even unto the other end of the earth: they shall not be lamented, neither gathered, nor buried; they shall be dung upon the ground.

50. Jeremiah 26:1-6:

[1] In the beginning of the reign of Jehoiakim the son of Josiah king of Judah came this word from the Lord, saying, [2] Thus saith the Lord; Stand in the court of the Lord's house, and speak unto all the cities of Judah, which come to worship in the Lord's house, all the words that I command thee to speak unto them; diminish not a word: [3] If so be they will hearken, and turn every man from his evil way, that I may repent me of the evil, which I purpose to do unto them because of the evil of their doings. [4] And thou shalt say unto them, Thus saith the Lord; If ye will not hearken to me, to walk in my law, which I have set before you, [5] To hearken to the words of my servants the prophets, whom I sent unto you, both rising up early, and sending them, but ye have not hearkened; [6] Then will I make this house like Shiloh, and will make this city a curse to all the nations of the earth.

51. Jeremiah 26:18:

[18] Micah the Morasthite prophesied in the days of Hezekiah king of Judah, and spake to all the people of Judah, saying, Thus saith the Lord of hosts; Zion shall be plowed like a field, and Jerusalem shall become heaps, and the mountain of the house as the high places of a forest.

52. Jeremiah 27:1, 8:

[1] In the beginning of the reign of Jehoiakim the son of

Josiah king of Judah came this word unto Jeremiah from the Lord, saying, [8] And it shall come to pass, that the nation and kingdom which will not serve the same Nebuchadnezzar the king of Babylon, and that will not put their neck under the yoke of the king of Babylon, that nation will I punish, saith the Lord, with the sword, and with the famine, and with the pestilence, until I have consumed them by his hand.

53. Jeremiah 28:12,14:

[12] Then the word of the Lord came unto Jeremiah the prophet, after that Hananiah the prophet had broken the yoke from off the neck of the prophet Jeremiah, saying, [14] For thus saith the Lord of hosts, the God of Israel; I have put a yoke of iron upon the neck of all these nations, that they may serve Nebuchadnezzar king of Babylon; and they shall serve him: and I have given him the beasts of the field also.

54. Jeremiah 29:17-18:

[17] Thus saith the Lord of hosts; Behold, I will send upon them the sword, the famine, and the pestilence, and will make them like vile figs, that cannot be eaten, they are so evil. [18] And I will persecute them with the sword, with the famine, and with the pestilence, and will deliver them to be removed to all the kingdoms of the earth, to be a curse, and an astonishment, and an hissing, and a reproach, among all the nations whither I have driven them.

55. Jeremiah 29:22:

[22] And of them shall be taken up a curse by all the captivity of Judah which are in Babylon, saying, The Lord make thee like Zedekiah and like Ahab, whom the king of Babylon roasted in the fire;

56. Jeremiah 29:32:

[32] Therefore thus saith the Lord; Behold, I will punish Shemaiah the Nehelamite, and his seed: he shall not have a man to dwell among this people; neither shall he behold the good that I will do for my people, saith the Lord; because he hath taught rebellion against the Lord.

57. Jeremiah 30:1-3:

[1] The word that came to Jeremiah from the Lord, saying, [2] Thus speaketh the Lord God of Israel, saying, Write thee all the words that I have spoken unto thee in a book. [3] For, lo, the days come, saith the Lord, that I will bring again the captivity of my people Israel and Judah, saith the Lord: and I will cause them to return to the land that I gave to their fathers, and they shall possess it.

58. Jeremiah 32:3-5:

[3] For Zedekiah king of Judah had shut him up, saying, Wherefore dost thou prophesy, and say, Thus saith the Lord, Behold, I will give this city into the hand of the king of Babylon, and he shall take it; [4] And Zedekiah king of Judah shall not escape out of the hand of the Chaldeans,

but shall surely be delivered into the hand of the king of Babylon, and shall speak with him mouth to mouth, and his eyes shall behold his eyes; [5] And he shall lead Zedekiah to Babylon, and there shall he be until I visit him, saith the Lord: though ye fight with the Chaldeans, ye shall not prosper.

59. Jeremiah 32:6-7:

[6] And Jeremiah said, The word of the Lord came unto me, saying, [7] Behold, Hanameel the son of Shallum thine uncle shall come unto thee, saying, Buy thee my field that is in Anathoth: for the right of redemption is thine to buy it.

60. Jeremiah 32:15:

[15] For thus saith the Lord of hosts, the God of Israel; Houses and fields and vineyards shall be possessed again in this land.

61. Jeremiah 32:26-29:

[26] Then came the word of the Lord unto Jeremiah, saying, [27] Behold, I am the Lord, the God of all flesh: is there any thing too hard for me? [28] Therefore thus saith the Lord; Behold, I will give this city into the hand of the Chaldeans, and into the hand of Nebuchadrezzar king of Babylon, and he shall take it: [29] And the Chaldeans, that fight against this city, shall come and set fire on this city, and burn it with the houses, upon whose roofs they

*have offered incense unto Baal, and poured out drink
offerings unto other gods, to provoke me to anger.*

62. Jeremiah 32:37-41:.

*[37Behold, I will gather them out of all countries, whither
I have driven them in mine anger, and in my fury, and in
great wrath; and I will bring them again unto this place,
and I will cause them to dwell safely: [38] And they shall
be my people, and I will be their God: [39] And I will
give them one heart, and one way, that they may fear me
for ever, for the good of them, and of their children after
them: [40] And I will make an everlasting covenant with
them, that I will not turn away from them, to do them
good; but I will put my fear in their hearts, that they shall
not depart from me. [41] Yea, I will rejoice over them to
do them good, and I will plant them in this land assuredly
with my whole heart and with my whole soul.*

63. Jeremiah 33:1-3:

*[1] Moreover the word of the Lord came unto Jeremiah
the second time, while he was yet shut up in the court
of the prison, saying, [2] Thus saith the Lord the maker
thereof, the Lord that formed it, to establish it; the Lord is
his name; [3] Call unto me, and I will answer thee, and
shew thee great and mighty things, which thou knowest
not.*

64. Jeremiah 33:6-9:

[6] Behold, I will bring it health and cure, and I will cure

*them, and will reveal unto them the abundance of peace
and truth. [7] And I will cause the captivity of Judah
and the captivity of Israel to return, and will build them,
as at the first. [8] And I will cleanse them from all their
iniquity, whereby they have sinned against me; and I will
pardon all their iniquities, whereby they have sinned,
and whereby they have transgressed against me. [9] And
it shall be to me a name of joy, a praise and an honour
before all the nations of the earth, which shall hear all
the good that I do unto them: and they shall fear and
tremble for all the goodness and for all the prosperity that
I procure unto it.*

65. Jeremiah 33:19-22:

*[19] And the word of the Lord came unto Jeremiah, say-
ing, [20] Thus saith the Lord; If ye can break my covenant
of the day, and my covenant of the night, and that there
should not be day and night in their season; [21] Then
may also my covenant be broken with David my servant,
that he should not have a son to reign upon his throne; and
with the Levites the priests, my ministers. [22] As the host
of heaven cannot be numbered, neither the sand of the sea
measured: so will I multiply the seed of David my servant,
and the Levites that minister unto me.*

66. Jeremiah 33:23-26:

*[23] Moreover the word of the Lord came to Jeremi-
ah, saying, [24] Considerest thou not what this people
have spoken, saying, The two families which the Lord*

hath chosen, he hath even cast them off? thus they have despised my people, that they should be no more a nation before them. [25] Thus saith the Lord; If my covenant be not with day and night, and if I have not appointed the ordinances of heaven and earth; [26] Then will I cast away the seed of Jacob, and David my servant, so that I will not take any of his seed to be rulers over the seed of Abraham, Isaac, and Jacob: for I will cause their captivity to return, and have mercy on them.

67. Jeremiah 34:1-5:

[1] The word which came unto Jeremiah from the Lord, when Nebuchadnezzar king of Babylon, and all his army, and all the kingdoms of the earth of his dominion, and all the people, fought against Jerusalem, and against all the cities thereof, saying, [2] Thus saith the Lord, the God of Israel; Go and speak to Zedekiah king of Judah, and tell him, Thus saith the Lord; Behold, I will give this city into the hand of the king of Babylon, and he shall burn it with fire: [3] And thou shalt not escape out of his hand, but shalt surely be taken, and delivered into his hand; and thine eyes shall behold the eyes of the king of Babylon, and he shall speak with thee mouth to mouth, and thou shalt go to Babylon. [4] Yet hear the word of the Lord, O Zedekiah king of Judah; Thus saith the Lord of thee, Thou shalt not die by the sword: [5] But thou shalt die in peace: and with the burnings of thy fathers, the former kings which were before thee, so shall they burn odours for thee; and they will lament thee, saying, Ah lord! for I

have pronounced the word, saith the Lord.

68. Jeremiah 34:8-9:

[8] This is the word that came unto Jeremiah from the Lord, after that the king Zedekiah had made a covenant with all the people which were at Jerusalem, to proclaim liberty unto them; [9] That every man should let his man-servant, and every man his maidservant, being an Hebrew or an Hebrewess, go free; that none should serve himself of them, to wit, of a Jew his brother.

69. Jeremiah 35:16-17:

[16] Because the sons of Jonadab the son of Rechab have performed the commandment of their father, which he commanded them; but this people hath not hearkened unto me: [17] Therefore thus saith the Lord God of hosts, the God of Israel; Behold, I will bring upon Judah and upon all the inhabitants of Jerusalem all the evil that I have pronounced against them: because I have spoken unto them, but they have not heard; and I have called unto them, but they have not answered.

70. Jeremiah 36:30-31:

[30] Therefore thus saith the Lord of Jehoiakim king of Judah; He shall have none to sit upon the throne of Da-vid: and his dead body shall be cast out in the day to the heat, and in the night to the frost. [31] And I will punish him and his seed and his servants for their iniquity; and I

*will bring upon them, and upon the inhabitants of Jeru-
salem, and upon the men of Judah, all the evil that I have
pronounced against them; but they hearkened not.*

71. Jeremiah 37:7:

*[7] Thus saith the Lord, the God of Israel; Thus shall ye
say to the king of Judah, that sent you unto me to enquire
of me; Behold, Pharaoh's army, which is come forth to
help you, shall return to Egypt into their own land.*

72. Jeremiah 37:17:

*[17] Then Zedekiah the king sent, and took him out: and
the king asked him secretly in his house, and said, Is there
any word from the Lord? And Jeremiah said, There is:
for, said he, thou shalt be delivered into the hand of the
king of Babylon.*

73. Jeremiah 38:2-3:

*[2] Thus saith the Lord, He that remaineth in this city shall
die by the sword, by the famine, and by the pestilence: but
he that goeth forth to the Chaldeans shall live; for he shall
have his life for a prey, and shall live. [3] Thus saith the
Lord, This city shall surely be given into the hand of the
king of Babylon's army, which shall take it.*

74. Jeremiah 38:17-18:

*[17] Then said Jeremiah unto Zedekiah, Thus saith the
Lord, the God of hosts, the God of Israel; If thou wilt as-*

283

suredly go forth unto the king of Babylon's princes, then thy soul shall live, and this city shall not be burned with fire; and thou shalt live, and thine house: [18] But if thou wilt not go forth to the king of Babylon's princes, then shall this city be given into the hand of the Chaldeans, and they shall burn it with fire, and thou shalt not escape out of their hand.

75. Jeremiah 39:15-18:

[15] Now the word of the Lord came unto Jeremiah, while he was shut up in the court of the prison, saying, [16] Go and speak to Ebed-melech the Ethiopian, saying, Thus saith the Lord of hosts, the God of Israel; Behold, I will bring my words upon this city for evil, and not for good; and they shall be accomplished in that day before thee. [17] But I will deliver thee in that day, saith the Lord: and thou shalt not be given into the hand of the men of whom thou art afraid. [18] For I will surely deliver thee, and thou shalt not fall by the sword, but thy life shall be for a prey unto thee: because thou hast put thy trust in me, saith the Lord.

76. Jeremiah 42:9-10:

[9] And said unto them, Thus saith the Lord, the God of Israel, unto whom ye sent me to present your supplication before him; [10] If ye will still abide in this land, then will I build you, and not pull you down, and I will plant you, and not pluck you up: for I repent me of the evil that I have done unto you.

77. Jeremiah 43:10-12:

[10] And say unto them, Thus saith the Lord of hosts, the God of Israel; Behold, I will send and take Nebu-chadrezzar the king of Babylon, my servant, and will set his throne upon these stones that I have hid; and he shall spread his royal pavilion over them. [11] And when he cometh, he shall smite the land of Egypt, and deliver such as are for death to death; and such as are for captivity to captivity; and such as are for the sword to the sword. [12] And I will kindle a fire in the houses of the gods of Egypt; and he shall burn them, and carry them away captives: and he shall array himself with the land of Egypt, as a shepherd putteth on his garment; and he shall go forth from thence in peace.

78. Jeremiah 44:11-14:

[11] Therefore thus saith the Lord of hosts, the God of Israel; Behold, I will set my face against you for evil, and to cut off all Judah. [12] And I will take the remnant of Judah, that have set their faces to go into the land of Egypt to sojourn there, and they shall all be consumed, and fall in the land of Egypt; they shall even be consumed by the sword and by the famine: they shall die, from the least even unto the greatest, by the sword and by the famine: and they shall be an execration, and an astonishment, and a curse, and a reproach. [13] For I will punish them that dwell in the land of Egypt, as I have punished Jerusalem, by the sword, by the famine, and by the pestilence: [14] So that none of the remnant of Judah, which

are gone into the land of Egypt to sojourn there, shall
escape or remain, that they should return into the land of
Judah, to the which they have a desire to return to dwell
there: for none shall return but such as shall escape.

79. Jeremiah 44:27-28:

[27] Behold, I will watch over them for evil, and not for
good: and all the men of Judah that are in the land of
Egypt shall be consumed by the sword and by the famine,
until there be an end of them. [28] Yet a small number
that escape the sword shall return out of the land of Egypt
into the land of Judah, and all the remnant of Judah, that
are gone into the land of Egypt to sojourn there, shall
know whose words shall stand, mine, or theirs.

80. Jeremiah 45:4:

[4] Thus shalt thou say unto him, The Lord saith thus;
Behold, that which I have built will I break down, and
that which I have planted I will pluck up, even this whole
land.

81. Jeremiah 47:1-4:

[1] The word of the Lord that came to Jeremiah the
prophet against the Philistines, before that Pharaoh
smote Gaza. [2] Thus saith the Lord; Behold, waters rise
up out of the north, and shall be an overflowing flood, and
shall overflow the land, and all that is therein; the city,
and them that dwell therein: then the men shall cry, and

all the inhabitants of the land shall howl. [3] At the noise of the stamping of the hoofs of his strong horses, at the rushing of his chariots, and at the rumbling of his wheels, the fathers shall not look back to their children for feebleness of hands; [4] Because of the day that cometh to spoil all the Philistines, and to cut off from Tyrus and Zidon every helper that remaineth: for the Lord will spoil the Philistines, the remnant of the country of Caphtor.

82. Jeremiah 48:1-3:

[1] Against Moab thus saith the Lord of hosts, the God of Israel; Woe unto Nebo! for it is spoiled: Kiriathaim is confounded and taken: Misgab is confounded and dismayed. [2] There shall be no more praise of Moab: in Heshbon they have devised evil against it; come, and let us cut it off from being a nation. Also thou shalt be cut down, O Madmen; the sword shall pursue thee. [3] A voice of crying shall be from Horonaim, spoiling and great destruction.

83. Jeremiah 48:47:

[47] Yet will I bring again the captivity of Moab in the latter days, saith the Lord. Thus far is the judgment of Moab.

84. Jeremiah 49:1-2:

[1] Concerning the Ammonites, thus saith the Lord; Hath Israel no sons? hath he no heir? why then doth their

king inherit Gad, and his people dwell in his cities? [2]
Therefore, behold, the days come, saith the Lord, that
I will cause an alarm of war to be heard in Rabbah of
the Ammonites; and it shall be a desolate heap, and her
daughters shall be burned with fire: then shall Israel be
heir unto them that were his heirs, saith the Lord.

85. Jeremiah 49:7-8:

[7] Concerning Edom, thus saith the Lord of hosts; Is
wisdom no more in Teman? is counsel perished from the
prudent? is their wisdom vanished? [8] Flee ye, turn
back, dwell deep, O inhabitants of Dedan; for I will bring
the calamity of Esau upon him, the time that I will visit
him.

86. Jeremiah 49:28-29:

[28] Concerning Kedar, and concerning the kingdoms
of Hazor, which Nebuchadrezzar king of Babylon shall
smite, thus saith the Lord; Arise ye, go up to Kedar, and
spoil the men of the east. [29] Their tents and their flocks
shall they take away: they shall take to themselves their
curtains, and all their vessels, and their camels; and they
shall cry unto them, Fear is on every side.

87. Jeremiah 49:34-39:

[34] The word of the Lord that came to Jeremiah the
prophet against Elam in the beginning of the reign of
Zedekiah king of Judah, saying, [35] Thus saith the Lord

of hosts; Behold, I will break the bow of Elam, the chief of their might. [36] And upon Elam will I bring the four winds from the four quarters of heaven, and will scatter them toward all those winds; and there shall be no nation whither the outcasts of Elam shall not come. [37] For I will cause Elam to be dismayed before their enemies, and before them that seek their life: and I will bring evil upon them, even my fierce anger, saith the Lord; and I will send the sword after them, till I have consumed them: [38] And I will set my throne in Elam, and will destroy from thence the king and the princes, saith the Lord. [39] But it shall come to pass in the latter days, that I will bring again the captivity of Elam, saith the Lord.

88. Jeremiah 50:1-5:

[1] The word that the Lord spake against Babylon and against the land of the Chaldeans by Jeremiah the prophet. [2] Declare ye among the nations, and publish, and set up a standard; publish, and conceal not: say, Babylon is taken, Bel is confounded, Merodach is broken in pieces; her idols are confounded, her images are broken in pieces. [3] For out of the north there cometh up a nation against her, which shall make her land desolate, and none shall dwell therein: they shall remove, they shall depart, both man and beast. [4] In those days, and in that time, saith the Lord, the children of Israel shall come, they and the children of Judah together, going and weeping: they shall go, and seek the Lord their God. [5] They shall ask the way to Zion with their faces thitherward, saying,

Come, and let us join ourselves to the Lord in a perpetual covenant that shall not be forgotten.

89. Jeremiah 50:13:

[13] Because of the wrath of the Lord it shall not be inhabited, but it shall be wholly desolate: every one that goeth by Babylon shall be astonished, and hiss at all her plagues.

90. Jeremiah 50:18-20:

[18] Therefore thus saith the Lord of hosts, the God of Israel; Behold, I will punish the king of Babylon and his land, as I have punished the king of Assyria. [19] And I will bring Israel again to his habitation, and he shall feed on Carmel and Bashan, and his soul shall be satisfied upon mount Ephraim and Gilead. [20] In those days, and in that time, saith the Lord, the iniquity of Israel shall be sought for, and there shall be none; and the sins of Judah, and they shall not be found: for I will pardon them whom I reserve.

91. Jeremiah 50:39:

[39] Therefore the wild beasts of the desert with the wild beasts of the islands shall dwell there, and the owls shall dwell therein: and it shall be no more inhabited for ever; neither shall it be dwelt in from generation to generation.

92. Jeremiah 50:41-42:

[41] Behold, a people shall come from the north, and a great nation, and many kings shall be raised up from the coasts of the earth[42] . They shall hold the bow and the lance: they are cruel, and will not shew mercy: their voice shall roar like the sea, and they shall ride upon horses, every one put in array, like a man to the battle, against thee, O daughter of Babylon.

93. Jeremiah 51:1-2:

[1] Thus saith the Lord; Behold, I will raise up against Babylon, and against them that dwell in the midst of them that rise up against me, a destroying wind; [2] And will send unto Babylon fanners, that shall fan her, and shall empty her land: for in the day of trouble they shall be against her round about.

94. Jeremiah 51:25-27:

[25] Behold, I am against thee, O destroying mountain, saith the Lord, which destroyest all the earth: and I will stretch out mine hand upon thee, and roll thee down from the rocks, and will make thee a burnt mountain. [26] And they shall not take of thee a stone for a corner, nor a stone for foundations; but thou shalt be desolate for ever, saith the Lord. [27] Set ye up a standard in the land, blow the trumpet among the nations, prepare the nations against her, call together against her the kingdoms of Ararat, Minni, and Ashchenaz; appoint a captain against her;

cause the horses to come up as the rough caterpillers.

95. Jeremiah 51:36-38:

[36] Therefore thus saith the Lord; Behold, I will plead thy cause, and take vengeance for thee; and I will dry up her sea, and make her springs dry. [37] And Babylon shall become heaps, a dwellingplace for dragons, an astonishment, and an hissing, without an inhabitant. [38] They shall roar together like lions: they shall yell as lions' whelps.

96. Jeremiah 51:62:

[62] Then shalt thou say, O Lord, thou hast spoken against this place, to cut it off, that none shall remain in it, neither man nor beast, but that it shall be desolate for ever.

PROPHECIES IN LAMENTATION: 1

Lamentations 4:21:

[21] Rejoice and be glad, O daughter of Edom, that dwellest in the land of Uz; the cup also shall pass through unto thee: thou shalt be drunken, and shalt make thyself naked.

PROPHECIES IN EZEKIEL: 58

1. Ezekiel 3:7:

   [7] But the house of Israel will not hearken unto thee; for they will not hearken unto me: for all the house of Israel are impudent and hardhearted.

2. Ezekiel 3:25-26:

   [25] But thou, O son of man, behold, they shall put bands upon thee, and shall bind thee with them, and thou shalt not go out among them: [26] And I will make thy tongue cleave to the roof of thy mouth, that thou shalt be dumb, and shalt not be to them a reprover: for they are a rebellious house.

3. Ezekiel 4:1-2:

   [1] Thou also, son of man, take thee a tile, and lay it before thee, and pourtray upon it the city, even Jerusalem: [2] And lay siege against it, and build a fort against it, and cast a mount against it; set the camp also against it, and set battering rams against it round about.

4. Ezekiel 5:1-3:

   [1] And thou, son of man, take thee a sharp knife, take thee a barber's razor, and cause it to pass upon thine

head and upon thy beard: then take thee balances to weigh, and divide the hair. [2] Thou shalt burn with fire a third part in the midst of the city, when the days of the siege are fulfilled: and thou shalt take a third part, and smite about it with a knife: and a third part thou shalt scatter in the wind; and I will draw out a sword after them. [3] Thou shalt also take thereof a few in number, and bind them in thy skirts.

5. Ezekiel 6:1-7:

[1] And the word of the Lord came unto me, saying, [2] Son of man, set thy face toward the mountains of Israel, and prophesy against them, [3] And say, Ye mountains of Israel, hear the word of the Lord God; Thus saith the Lord God to the mountains, and to the hills, to the rivers, and to the valleys; Behold, I, even I, will bring a sword upon you, and I will destroy your high places. [4] And your altars shall be desolate, and your images shall be broken: and I will cast down your slain men before your idols. [5] And I will lay the dead carcases of the children of Israel before their idols; and I will scatter your bones round about your altars. [6] In all your dwellingplaces the cities shall be laid waste, and the high places shall be desolate; that your altars may be laid waste and made desolate, and your idols may be broken and cease, and your images may be cut down, and your works may be abolished. [7] And the slain shall fall in the midst of you, and ye shall know that I am the Lord.

6. Ezekiel 6:11-14:

[11] Thus saith the Lord God; Smite with thine hand, and stamp with thy foot, and say, Alas for all the evil abominations of the house of Israel! for they shall fall by the sword, by the famine, and by the pestilence. [12] He that is far off shall die of the pestilence; and he that is near shall fall by the sword; and he that remaineth and is besieged shall die by the famine: thus will I accomplish my fury upon them. [13] Then shall ye know that I am the Lord, when their slain men shall be among their idols round about their altars, upon every high hill, in all the tops of the mountains, and under every green tree, and under every thick oak, the place where they did offer sweet savour to all their idols. [14] So will I stretch out my hand upon them, and make the land desolate, yea, more desolate than the wilderness toward Diblath, in all their habitations: and they shall know that I am the Lord.

7. Ezekiel 7:1-4:

[1] Moreover the word of the Lord came unto me, saying, [2] Also, thou son of man, thus saith the Lord God unto the land of Israel; An end, the end is come upon the four corners of the land. [3] Now is the end come upon thee, and I will send mine anger upon thee, and will judge thee according to thy ways, and will recompense upon thee all thine abominations. [4] And mine eye shall not spare thee, neither will I have pity: but I will recompense thy ways upon thee, and thine abominations shall be in the midst of thee: and ye shall know that I am the Lord.

8. Ezekiel 7:24:

[24] Wherefore I will bring the worst of the heathen, and they shall possess their houses: I will also make the pomp of the strong to cease; and their holy places shall be defiled.

9. Ezekiel 8:18:

[18] Therefore will I also deal in fury: mine eye shall not spare, neither will I have pity: and though they cry in mine ears with a loud voice, yet will I not hear them.

10. Ezekiel 9:1-11:

[1] He cried also in mine ears with a loud voice, saying, Cause them that have charge over the city to draw near, even every man with his destroying weapon in his hand. [2] And, behold, six men came from the way of the higher gate, which lieth toward the north, and every man a slaughter weapon in his hand; and one man among them was clothed with linen, with a writer's inkhorn by his side: and they went in, and stood beside the brasen altar. [3] And the glory of the God of Israel was gone up from the cherub, whereupon he was, to the threshold of the house. And he called to the man clothed with linen, which had the writer's inkhorn by his side; [4] And the Lord said unto him, Go through the midst of the city, through the midst of Jerusalem, and set a mark upon the foreheads of the men that sigh and that cry for all the abominations that be done in the midst thereof. [5] And

to the others he said in mine hearing, Go ye after him through the city, and smite: let not your eye spare, neither have ye pity: [6] Slay utterly old and young, both maids, and little children, and women: but come not near any man upon whom is the mark; and begin at my sanctuary. Then they began at the ancient men which were before the house. [7] And he said unto them, Defile the house, and fill the courts with the slain: go ye forth. And they went forth, and slew in the city. [8] And it came to pass, while they were slaying them, and I was left, that I fell upon my face, and cried, and said, Ah Lord God ! wilt thou destroy all the residue of Israel in thy pouring out of thy fury upon Jerusalem. [9] Then said he unto me, The iniquity of the house of Israel and Judah is exceeding great, and the land is full of blood, and the city full of perverseness: for they say, The Lord hath forsaken the earth, and the Lord seeth not. [10] And as for me also, mine eye shall not spare, neither will I have pity, but I will recompense their way upon their head. [11] And, behold, the man clothed with linen, which had the inkhorn by his side, reported the matter, saying, I have done as thou hast commanded me.

11. Ezekiel 11:4-12:

[4] Therefore prophesy against them, prophesy, O son of man. [5] And the Spirit of the Lord fell upon me, and said unto me, Speak; Thus saith the Lord; Thus have ye said, O house of Israel: for I know the things that come into your mind, every one of them. [6] Ye have multiplied your slain in this city, and ye have filled the streets thereof

with the slain. [7] Therefore thus saith the Lord God;
Your slain whom ye have laid in the midst of it, they are
the flesh, and this city is the caldron: but I will bring you
forth out of the midst of it. [8] Ye have feared the sword;
and I will bring a sword upon you, saith the Lord God.
And [9] I will bring you out of the midst thereof, and
deliver you into the hands of strangers, and will execute
judgments among you. [10] Ye shall fall by the sword; I
will judge you in the border of Israel; and ye shall know
that I am the Lord. [11] This city shall not be your cal-
dron, neither shall ye be the flesh in the midst thereof; but
I will judge you in the border of Israel: [12] And ye shall
know that I am the Lord: for ye have not walked in my
statutes, neither executed my judgments, but have done
after the manners of the heathen that are round about
you.

12. Ezekiel 11:14-15:

[14] Again the word of the Lord came unto me, saying,
[15] Son of man, thy brethren, even thy brethren, the men
of thy kindred, and all the house of Israel wholly, are
they unto whom the inhabitants of Jerusalem have said,
Get you far from the Lord: unto us is this land given in
possession.

13. Ezekiel 11:17-21:

[17] Therefore say, Thus saith the Lord God; I will even
gather you from the people, and assemble you out of the
countries where ye have been scattered, and I will give

300

you the land of Israel. [18] And they shall come thither, and they shall take away all the detestable things thereof and all the abominations thereof from thence. [19] And I will give them one heart, and I will put a new spirit within you; and I will take the stony heart out of their flesh, and will give them an heart of flesh: [20] That they may walk in my statutes, and keep mine ordinances, and do them: and they shall be my people, and I will be their God. [21] But as for them whose heart walketh after the heart of their detestable things and their abominations, I will recompense their way upon their own heads, saith the Lord God.

14. Ezekiel 12:1-4:

[1] The word of the Lord also came unto me, saying, [2] Son of man, thou dwellest in the midst of a rebellious house, which have eyes to see, and see not; they have ears to hear, and hear not: for they are a rebellious house. [3] Therefore, thou son of man, prepare thee stuff for re-moving, and remove by day in their sight; and thou shalt remove from thy place to another place in their sight: it may be they will consider, though they be a rebellious house. [4] Then shalt thou bring forth thy stuff by day in their sight, as stuff for removing: and thou shalt go forth at even in their sight, as they that go forth into captivity.

15. Ezekiel 12:8-11:

[8] And in the morning came the word of the Lord unto me, saying, [9] Son of man, hath not the house of Israel,

the rebellious house, said unto thee, What doest thou? [10] Say thou unto them, Thus saith the Lord God; This burden concerneth the prince in Jerusalem, and all the house of Israel that are among them. [11] Say, I am your sign: like as I have done, so shall it be done unto them: they shall remove and go into captivity.

16. Ezekiel 12:17-20:

[17] Moreover the word of the Lord came to me, saying, [18] Son of man, eat thy bread with quaking, and drink thy water with trembling and with carefulness; [19] And say unto the people of the land, Thus saith the Lord God of the inhabitants of Jerusalem, and of the land of Israel; They shall eat their bread with carefulness, and drink their water with astonishment, that her land may be desolate from all that is therein, because of the violence of all them that dwell therein. [20] And the cities that are inhabited shall be laid waste, and the land shall be desolate; and ye shall know that I am the Lord.

17. Ezekiel 12:21-25:

[21] And the word of the Lord came unto me, saying, [22] Son of man, what is that proverb that ye have in the land of Israel, saying, The days are prolonged, and every vision faileth? [23] Tell them therefore, Thus saith the Lord God; I will make this proverb to cease, and they shall no more use it as a proverb in Israel; but say unto them, The days are at hand, and the effect of every vision. [24] For there shall be no more any vain vision nor

flattering divination within the house of Israel. [25] For I am the Lord: I will speak, and the word that I shall speak shall come to pass; it shall be no more prolonged: for in your days, O rebellious house, will I say the word, and will perform it, saith the Lord God.

18. Ezekiel 12:26-28:

[26] Again the word of the Lord came to me, saying, [26] Son of man, behold, they of the house of Israel say, The vision that he seeth is for many days to come, and he prophesieth of the times that are far off. [28] Therefore say unto them, Thus saith the Lord God; There shall none of my words be prolonged any more, but the word which I have spoken shall be done, saith the Lord God.

19. Ezekiel 13:1-4:

[1] And the word of the Lord came unto me, saying, [2] Son of man, prophesy against the prophets of Israel that prophesy, and say thou unto them that prophesy out of their own hearts, Hear ye the word of the Lord; [3] Thus saith the Lord God; Woe unto the foolish prophets, that follow their own spirit, and have seen nothing! [4] O Israel, thy prophets are like the foxes in the deserts.

20. Ezekiel 14:2-5:

[2] And the word of the Lord came unto me, saying, [3] Son of man, these men have set up their idols in their heart, and put the stumblingblock of their iniquity be-

fore their face: should I be enquired of at all by them?
[4] Therefore speak unto them, and say unto them, Thus
saith the Lord God; Every man of the house of Israel that
setteth up his idols in his heart, and putteth the stum-
blingblock of his iniquity before his face, and cometh
to the prophet; I the Lord will answer him that cometh
according to the multitude of his idols; [5] That I may
take the house of Israel in their own heart, because they
are all estranged from me through their idols.

21. Ezekiel 14:12-14:

[12] The word of the Lord came again to me, saying,
[13] Son of man, when the land sinneth against me by
trespassing grievously, then will I stretch out mine hand
upon it, and will break the staff of the bread thereof, and
will send famine upon it, and will cut off man and beast
from it: [14] Though these three men, Noah, Daniel, and
Job, were in it, they should deliver but their own souls by
their righteousness, saith the Lord God.

22. Ezekiel 15:1-2,7,8-8:

[1] And the word of the Lord came unto me, saying, [2]
Son of man, What is the vine tree more than any tree, or
than a branch which is among the trees of the forest?
[7] And I will set my face against them; they shall go out
from one fire, and another fire shall devour them; and ye
shall know that I am the Lord, when I set my face against
them. [8] And I will make the land desolate, because they
have committed a trespass, saith the Lord God.

23. Ezekiel 16:35-41:

*[35] Wherefore, O harlot, hear the word of the Lord:
[36] Thus saith the Lord God; Because thy filthiness was
poured out, and thy nakedness discovered through thy
whoredoms with thy lovers, and with all the idols of thy
abominations, and by the blood of thy children, which
thou didst give unto them; [37] Behold, therefore I will
gather all thy lovers, with whom thou hast taken pleasure,
and all them that thou hast loved, with all them that thou
hast hated; I will even gather them round about against
thee, and will discover thy nakedness unto them, that they
may see all thy nakedness. [38] And I will judge thee, as
women that break wedlock and shed blood are judged;
and I will give thee blood in fury and jealousy. [39] And
I will also give thee into their hand, and they shall throw
down thine eminent place, and shall break down thy high
places: they shall strip thee also of thy clothes, and shall
take thy fair jewels, and leave thee naked and bare[40]
. They shall also bring up a company against thee, and
they shall stone thee with stones, and thrust thee through
with their swords[41] . And they shall burn thine houses
with fire, and execute judgments upon thee in the sight of
many women: and I will cause thee to cease from playing
the harlot, and thou also shalt give no hire any more.*

24. Ezekiel 16:53-54:

*[53] When I shall bring again their captivity, the captivity
of Sodom and her daughters, and the captivity of Samaria
and her daughters, then will I bring again the captivity of*

thy captives in the midst of them: [54] That thou mayest bear thine own shame, and mayest be confounded in all that thou hast done, in that thou art a comfort unto them.

25. Ezekiel 16:59-60:

[59] For thus saith the Lord God; I will even deal with thee as thou hast done, which hast despised the oath in breaking the covenant. [60] Nevertheless I will remember my covenant with thee in the days of thy youth, and I will establish unto thee an everlasting covenant.

26. Ezekiel 17:11-14:

[11] Moreover the word of the Lord came unto me, saying, [12] Say now to the rebellious house, Know ye not what these things mean ? tell them, Behold, the king of Babylon is come to Jerusalem, and hath taken the king thereof, and the princes thereof, and led them with him to Babylon; [13] And hath taken of the king's seed, and made a covenant with him, and hath taken an oath of him: he hath also taken the mighty of the land: [14] That the kingdom might be base, that it might not lift itself up, but that by keeping of his covenant it might stand.

27. Ezekiel 17:22-23:

[22] Thus saith the Lord God; I will also take of the highest branch of the high cedar, and will set it; I will crop off from the top of his young twigs a tender one, and will plant it upon an high mountain and eminent:

[23] In the mountain of the height of Israel will I plant it: and it shall bring forth boughs, and bear fruit, and be a goodly cedar: and under it shall dwell all fowl of every wing; in the shadow of the branches thereof shall they dwell.

28. Ezekiel 20:33-35:

[33] As I live, saith the Lord God, surely with a mighty hand, and with a stretched out arm, and with fury poured out, will I rule over you: [34] And I will bring you out from the people, and will gather you out of the countries wherein ye are scattered, with a mighty hand, and with a stretched out arm, and with fury poured out. [35] And I will bring you into the wilderness of the people, and there will I plead with you face to face.

29. Ezekiel 20:45-48:

[45] Moreover the word of the Lord came unto me, saying, [46] Son of man, set thy face toward the south, and drop thy word toward the south, and prophesy against the forest of the south field; [47] And say to the forest of the south, Hear the word of the Lord; Thus saith the Lord God; Behold, I will kindle a fire in thee, and it shall devour every green tree in thee, and every dry tree: the flaming flame shall not be quenched, and all faces from the south to the north shall be burned therein. [48] And all flesh shall see that I the Lord have kindled it: it shall not be quenched.

30. Ezekiel 21:1-5:

[1] And the word of the Lord came unto me, saying, [2] Son of man, set thy face toward Jerusalem, and drop thy word toward the holy places, and prophesy against the land of Israel, [3] And say to the land of Israel, Thus saith the Lord; Behold, I am against thee, and will draw forth my sword out of his sheath, and will cut off from thee the righteous and the wicked. [4] Seeing then that I will cut off from thee the righteous and the wicked, therefore shall my sword go forth out of his sheath against all flesh from the south to the north: [5] That all flesh may know that I the Lord have drawn forth my sword out of his sheath: it shall not return any more.

31. Ezekiel 21:8-10:

[8] Again the word of the Lord came unto me, saying, [9] Son of man, prophesy, and say, Thus saith the Lord; Say, A sword, a sword is sharpened, and also furbished: [10] It is sharpened to make a sore slaughter; it is furbished that it may glitter: should we then make mirth? it contemneth the rod of my son, as every tree.

32. Ezekiel 22:17-19:

[17] And the word of the Lord came unto me, saying, [18] Son of man, the house of Israel is to me become dross: all they are brass, and tin, and iron, and lead, in the midst of the furnace; they are even the dross of silver. [19] Therefore thus saith the Lord God; Because ye are all become

dross, behold, therefore I will gather you into the midst of Jerusalem.

33. Ezekiel 23:22-27:

[22] Therefore, O Aholibah, thus saith the Lord God; Behold, I will raise up thy lovers against thee, from whom thy mind is alienated, and I will bring them against thee on every side; [23] The Babylonians, and all the Chaldeans, Pekod, and Shoa, and Koa, and all the Assyrians with them: all of them desirable young men, captains and rulers, great lords and renowned, all of them riding upon horses. [24] And they shall come against thee with chariots, wagons, and wheels, and with an assembly of people, which shall set against thee buckler and shield and helmet round about: and I will set judgment before them, and they shall judge thee according to their judgments. [25] And I will set my jealousy against thee, and they shall deal furiously with thee: they shall take away thy nose and thine ears; and thy remnant shall fall by the sword: they shall take thy sons and thy daughters; and thy residue shall be devoured by the fire. [26] They shall also strip thee out of thy clothes, and take away thy fair jewels. 9270 Thus will I make thy lewdness to cease from thee, and thy whoredom brought from the land of Egypt: so that thou shalt not lift up thine eyes unto them, nor remember Egypt any more.

34. Ezekiel 23:46:

[46] And the righteous men, they shall judge them after

the manner of adulteresses, and after the manner of women that shed blood; because they are adulteresses, and blood is in their hands. For thus saith the Lord God; I will bring up a company upon them, and will give them to be removed and spoiled.

35. Ezekiel 24:1-2:

[1] Again in the ninth year, in the tenth month, in the tenth day of the month, the word of the Lord came unto me, saying, [2] Son of man, write thee the name of the day, even of this same day: the king of Babylon set himself against Jerusalem this same day.

36. Ezekiel 25:1-5:

[1] The word of the Lord came again unto me, saying, [2] Son of man, set thy face against the Ammonites, and prophesy against them; [3] And say unto the Ammonites, Hear the word of the Lord God; Thus saith the Lord God; Because thou saidst, Aha, against my sanctuary, when it was profaned; and against the land of Israel, when it was desolate; and against the house of Judah, when they went into captivity; [4] Behold, therefore I will deliver thee to the men of the east for a possession, and they shall set their palaces in thee, and make their dwellings in thee: they shall eat thy fruit, and they shall drink thy milk. [5] And I will make Rabbah a stable for camels, and the Ammonites a couchingplace for flocks: and ye shall know that I am the Lord.

36. Ezekiel 25:8-10:

[8] Thus saith the Lord God; Because that Moab and Seir do say, Behold, the house of Judah is like unto all the heathen; [9] Therefore, behold, I will open the side of Moab from the cities, from his cities which are on his frontiers, the glory of the country, Beth-jeshimoth, Baal-meon, and Kiriathaim, [10] Unto the men of the east with the Ammonites, and will give them in possession, that the Ammonites may not be remembered among the nations.

37. Ezekiel 25:12-13:

[12] Thus saith the Lord God; Because that Edom hath dealt against the house of Judah by taking vengeance, and hath greatly offended, and revenged himself upon them; [13] Therefore thus saith the Lord God; I will also stretch out mine hand upon Edom, and will cut off man and beast from it; and I will make it desolate from Teman; and they of Dedan shall fall by the sword.

38. Ezekiel 25:15-16:

[15] Thus saith the Lord God; Because the Philistines have dealt by revenge, and have taken vengeance with a despiteful heart, to destroy it for the old hatred; [16] Therefore thus saith the Lord God; Behold, I will stretch out mine hand upon the Philistines, and I will cut off the Cherethims, and destroy the remnant of the sea coast.

39. Ezekiel 26:1-4:

[1] And it came to pass in the eleventh year, in the first day of the month, that the word of the Lord came unto me, saying, [2] Son of man, because that Tyrus hath said against Jerusalem, Aha, she is broken that was the gates of the people: she is turned unto me: I shall be replenished, now she is laid waste: [3] Therefore thus saith the Lord God; Behold, I am against thee, O Tyrus, and will cause many nations to come up against thee, as the sea causeth his waves to come up. [4] And they shall destroy the walls of Tyrus, and break down her towers: I will also scrape her dust from her, and make her like the top of a rock.

40. Ezekiel 26:15-16:

[15] Thus saith the Lord God to Tyrus; Shall not the isles shake at the sound of thy fall, when the wounded cry, when the slaughter is made in the midst of thee? [16] Then all the princes of the sea shall come down from their thrones, and lay away their robes, and put off their broidered garments: they shall clothe themselves with trembling; they shall sit upon the ground, and shall tremble at every moment, and be astonished at thee.

41. Ezekiel 28:6-8:

[6] Therefore thus saith the Lord God; Because thou hast set thine heart as the heart of God; [7] Behold, therefore I will bring strangers upon thee, the terrible of the na-

tions: and they shall draw their swords against the beauty
of thy wisdom, and they shall defile thy brightness. [8]
They shall bring thee down to the pit, and thou shalt die
the deaths of them that are slain in the midst of the seas.

42. Ezekiel 28:16-17:

[16] By the multitude of thy merchandise they have filled
the midst of thee with violence, and thou hast sinned:
therefore I will cast thee as profane out of the mountain of
God: and I will destroy thee, O covering cherub, from the
midst of the stones of fire. [17] Thine heart was lifted up
because of thy beauty, thou hast corrupted thy wisdom by
reason of thy brightness: I will cast thee to the ground, I
will lay thee before kings, that they may behold thee.

43. Ezekiel 28:23:

[23] For I will send into her pestilence, and blood into
her streets; and the wounded shall be judged in the midst
of her by the sword upon her on every side; and they shall
know that I am the Lord.

44. Ezekiel 28:24:

[24] And there shall be no more a pricking brier unto
the house of Israel, nor any grieving thorn of all that are
round about them, that despised them; and they shall
know that I am the Lord God.

45. Ezekiel 29:3-5:

[3] Speak, and say, Thus saith the Lord God; Behold, I am against thee, Pharaoh king of Egypt, the great dragon that lieth in the midst of his rivers, which hath said, My river is mine own, and I have made it for myself. [4] But I will put hooks in thy jaws, and I will cause the fish of thy rivers to stick unto thy scales, and I will bring thee up out of the midst of thy rivers, and all the fish of thy rivers shall stick unto thy scales. [5] And I will leave thee thrown into the wilderness, thee and all the fish of thy rivers: thou shalt fall upon the open fields; thou shalt not be brought together, nor gathered: I have given thee for meat to the beasts of the field and to the fowls of the heaven.

46. Ezekiel 29:17-19:

[19] And it came to pass in the seven and twentieth year, in the first month, in the first day of the month, the word of the Lord came unto me, saying, [18] Son of man, Nebuchadrezzar king of Babylon caused his army to serve a great service against Tyrus: every head was made bald, and every shoulder was peeled: yet had he no wages, nor his army, for Tyrus, for the service that he had served against it: [19] Therefore thus saith the Lord God; Behold, I will give the land of Egypt unto Nebuchadrezzar king of Babylon; and he shall take her multitude, and take her spoil, and take her prey; and it shall be the wages for his army.

47. Ezekiel 30:4-8:

[4] And the sword shall come upon Egypt, and great pain shall be in Ethiopia, when the slain shall fall in Egypt, and they shall take away her multitude, and her foundations shall be broken down. [5] Ethiopia, and Libya, and Lydia, and all the mingled people, and Chub, and the men of the land that is in league, shall fall with them by the sword. [6] Thus saith the Lord; They also that uphold Egypt shall fall; and the pride of her power shall come down: from the tower of Syene shall they fall in it by the sword, saith the Lord God.

[7] And they shall be desolate in the midst of the countries that are desolate, and her cities shall be in the midst of the cities that are wasted. [8] And they shall know that I am the Lord, when I have set a fire in Egypt, and when all her helpers shall be destroyed.

48. Ezekiel 30:11-18:

[11] He and his people with him, the terrible of the nations, shall be brought to destroy the land: and they shall draw their swords against Egypt, and fill the land with the slain. [12] And I will make the rivers dry, and sell the land into the hand of the wicked: and I will make the land waste, and all that is therein, by the hand of strangers: I the Lord have spoken it. [13] Thus saith the Lord God; I will also destroy the idols, and I will cause their images to cease out of Noph; and there shall be no more a prince of the land of Egypt: and I will put a fear in the land of Egypt. [14] And I will make Pathros desolate, and will

*set fire in Zoan, and will execute judgments in No. [15]
And I will pour my fury upon Sin, the strength of Egypt;
and I will cut off the multitude of No. [16] And I will set
fire in Egypt: Sin shall have great pain, and No shall be
rent asunder, and Noph shall have distresses daily. [17]
The young men of Aven and of Pi-beseth shall fall by
the sword: and these cities shall go into captivity. [18]
At Tehaphnehes also the day shall be darkened, when I
shall break there the yokes of Egypt: and the pomp of her
strength shall cease in her: as for her, a cloud shall cover
her, and her daughters shall go into captivity.*

49. Ezekiel 30:23-25:

*[23] And I will scatter the Egyptians among the nations,
and will disperse them through the countries. [24] And I
will strengthen the arms of the king of Babylon, and put
my sword in his hand: but I will break Pharaoh's arms,
and he shall groan before him with the groanings of a
deadly wounded man. [25] But I will strengthen the arms
of the king of Babylon, and the arms of Pharaoh shall
fall down; and they shall know that I am the Lord, when
I shall put my sword into the hand of the king of Babylon,
and he shall stretch it out upon the land of Egypt.*

50. Ezekiel 31:18:

*[18] To whom art thou thus like in glory and in great-
ness among the trees of Eden? yet shalt thou be brought
down with the trees of Eden unto the nether parts of the
earth: thou shalt lie in the midst of the uncircumcised*

with them that be slain by the sword. This is Pharaoh and all his multitude, saith the Lord God.

51. Ezekiel 32:2:

[2] Son of man, take up a lamentation for Pharaoh king of Egypt, and say unto him, Thou art like a young lion of the nations, and thou art as a whale in the seas: and thou camest forth with thy rivers, and troubledst the waters with thy feet, and fouledst their rivers.

52. Ezekiel 32:17-20:

[17] It came to pass also in the twelfth year, in the fifteenth day of the month, that the word of the Lord came unto me, saying, [18] Son of man, wail for the multitude of Egypt, and cast them down, even her, and the daughters of the famous nations, unto the nether parts of the earth, with them that go down into the pit. [18] Whom dost thou pass in beauty? go down, and be thou laid with the uncircumcised. [20] They shall fall in the midst of them that are slain by the sword: she is delivered to the sword: draw her and all her multitudes.

53. Ezekiel 33:27-28:

[27] Say thou thus unto them, Thus saith the Lord God; As I live, surely they that are in the wastes shall fall by the sword, and him that is in the open field will I give to the beasts to be devoured, and they that be in the forts and in the caves shall die of the pestilence. [28] For I will

lay the land most desolate, and the pomp of her strength shall cease; and the mountains of Israel shall be desolate, that none shall pass through.

54. Ezekiel 34:10:

[10] Thus saith the Lord God; Behold, I am against the shepherds; and I will require my flock at their hand, and cause them to cease from feeding the flock; neither shall the shepherds feed themselves any more; for I will deliver my flock from their mouth, that they may not be meat for them.

55. Ezekiel 35:3-4:

[3] And say unto it, Thus saith the Lord God; Behold, O mount Seir, I am against thee, and I will stretch out mine hand against thee, and I will make thee most desolate. [4] I will lay thy cities waste, and thou shalt be desolate, and thou shalt know that I am the Lord.

56. Ezekiel 37:19:

[19] Say unto them, Thus saith the Lord God; Behold, I will take the stick of Joseph, which is in the hand of Ephraim, and the tribes of Israel his fellows, and will put them with him, even with the stick of Judah, and make them one stick, and they shall be one in mine hand.

57. Ezekiel 38:4-6:

[4] And I will turn thee back, and put hooks into thy

jaws, and I will bring thee forth, and all thine army, horses and horsemen, all of them clothed with all sorts of armour, even a great company with bucklers and shields, all of them handling swords: [5] Persia, Ethiopia, and Libya with them; all of them with shield and helmet: [6] Gomer, and all his bands; the house of Togarmah of the north quarters, and all his bands: and many people with thee.

58. Ezekiel 40:5:

[5] And behold a wall on the outside of the house round about, and in the man's hand a measuring reed of six cubits long by the cubit and an hand breadth: so he measured the breadth of the building, one reed; and the height, one reed.

PROPHECIES IN
DANIEL:17

1. Daniel 2:31-35:

*[31] Thou, O king, sawest, and behold a great image.
This great image, whose brightness was excellent, stood
before thee; and the form thereof was terrible. [32] This
image's head was of fine gold, his breast and his arms
of silver, his belly and his thighs of brass, [33] His legs
of iron, his feet part of iron and part of clay. [34] Thou
sawest till that a stone was cut out without hands, which
smote the image upon his feet that were of iron and clay,
and brake them to pieces. [35] Then was the iron, the
clay, the brass, the silver, and the gold, broken to pieces
together, and became like the chaff of the summer thresh-
ingfloors; and the wind carried them away, that no place
was found for them: and the stone that smote the image
became a great mountain, and filled the whole earth.*

2. Daniel 2:38-45:

*[38] And wheresoever the children of men dwell, the
beasts of the field and the fowls of the heaven hath he
given into thine hand, and hath made thee ruler over
them all. Thou art this head of gold. [39] And after thee
shall arise another kingdom inferior to thee, and another
third kingdom of brass, which shall bear rule over all
the earth. [40] And the fourth kingdom shall be strong as
iron: forasmuch as iron breaketh in pieces and subdueth*

all things: and as iron that breaketh all these, shall it break in pieces and bruise. [41] And whereas thou sawest the feet and toes, part of potters' clay, and part of iron, the kingdom shall be divided; but there shall be in it of the strength of the iron, forasmuch as thou sawest the iron mixed with miry clay. [42] And as the toes of the feet were part of iron, and part of clay, so the kingdom shall be partly strong, and partly broken. [43] And whereas thou sawest iron mixed with miry clay, they shall mingle themselves with the seed of men: but they shall not cleave one to another, even as iron is not mixed with clay. [44] And in the days of these kings shall the God of heaven set up a kingdom, which shall never be destroyed: and the kingdom shall not be left to other people, but it shall break in pieces and consume all these kingdoms, and it shall stand for ever. [45] Forasmuch as thou sawest that the stone was cut out of the mountain without hands, and that it brake in pieces the iron, the brass, the clay, the silver, and the gold; the great God hath made known to the king what shall come to pass hereafter: and the dream is certain, and the interpretation thereof sure.

3. Daniel 3:17

[17] If it be so, our God whom we serve is able to deliver us from the burning fiery furnace, and he will deliver us out of thine hand, O king.

4. Daniel 4:10-16

[10] Thus were the visions of mine head in my bed; I saw,

and behold a tree in the midst of the earth, and the height thereof was great[11] . The tree grew, and was strong, and the height thereof reached unto heaven, and the sight thereof to the end of all the earth: [12] The leaves thereof were fair, and the fruit thereof much, and in it was meat for all: the beasts of the field had shadow under it, and the fowls of the heaven dwelt in the boughs thereof, and all flesh was fed of it. [13] I saw in the visions of my head upon my bed, and, behold, a watcher and an holy one came down from heaven; [14] He cried aloud, and said thus, Hew down the tree, and cut off his branches, shake off his leaves, and scatter his fruit: let the beasts get away from under it, and the fowls from his branches: [15] Nevertheless leave the stump of his roots in the earth, even with a band of iron and brass, in the tender grass of the field; and let it be wet with the dew of heaven, and let his portion be with the beasts in the grass of the earth: [16] Let his heart be changed from man's, and let a beast's heart be given unto him; and let seven times pass over him.

5. Daniel 4:20-23:

[20] The tree that thou sawest, which grew, and was strong, whose height reached unto the heaven, and the sight thereof to all the earth; [21] Whose leaves were fair, and the fruit thereof much, and in it was meat for all; under which the beasts of the field dwelt, and upon whose branches the fowls of the heaven had their habitation: [22] It is thou, O king, that art grown and become strong:

for thy greatness is grown, and reacheth unto heaven, and thy dominion to the end of the earth. [23] And whereas the king saw a watcher and an holy one coming down from heaven, and saying, Hew the tree down, and destroy it; yet leave the stump of the roots thereof in the earth, even with a band of iron and brass, in the tender grass of the field; and let it be wet with the dew of heaven, and let his portion be with the beasts of the field, till seven times pass over him.

6. Daniel 4:25-26:

[25] That they shall drive thee from men, and thy dwelling shall be with the beasts of the field, and they shall make thee to eat grass as oxen, and they shall wet thee with the dew of heaven, and seven times shall pass over thee, till thou know that the most High ruleth in the kingdom of men, and giveth it to whomsoever he will. [26] And whereas they commanded to leave the stump of the tree roots; thy kingdom shall be sure unto thee, after that thou shalt have known that the heavens do rule.

7. Daniel 4:31-32:

[31] While the word was in the king's mouth, there fell a voice from heaven, saying, O king Nebuchadnezzar, to thee it is spoken; The kingdom is departed from thee. [32] And they shall drive thee from men, and thy dwelling shall be with the beasts of the field: they shall make thee to eat grass as oxen, and seven times shall pass over thee,

until thou know that the most High ruleth in the kingdom of men, and giveth it to whomsoever he will.

8. Daniel 5:25-26:

[25] And this is the writing that was written, MENE, MENE, TEKEL, UPHARSIN. [26] This is the interpretation of the thing: MENE; God hath numbered thy kingdom, and finished it. TEKEL; Thou art weighed in the balances, and art found wanting. PERES; Thy kingdom is divided, and given to the Medes and Persians.

9. Daniel 6:16:

[16] Then the king commanded, and they brought Daniel, and cast him into the den of lions. Now the king spake and said unto Daniel, Thy God whom thou servest continually, he will deliver thee.

10. Daniel 7:2-14:

[2] Daniel spake and said, I saw in my vision by night, and, behold, the four winds of the heaven strove upon the great sea. [3] And four great beasts came up from the sea, diverse one from another. [4] The first was like a lion, and had eagle's wings: I beheld till the wings thereof were plucked, and it was lifted up from the earth, and made stand upon the feet as a man, and a man's heart was given to it. [5] And behold another beast, a second, like to a bear, and it raised up itself on one side, and it had three ribs in the mouth of it between the teeth

of it: and they said thus unto it, Arise, devour much flesh. [6] After this I beheld, and lo another, like a leopard, which had upon the back of it four wings of a fowl; the beast had also four heads; and dominion was given to it. [7] After this I saw in the night visions, and behold a fourth beast, dreadful and terrible, and strong exceedingly; and it had great iron teeth: it devoured and brake in pieces, and stamped the residue with the feet of it: and it was diverse from all the beasts that were before it; and it had ten horns. [8] I considered the horns, and, behold, there came up among them another little horn, before whom there were three of the first horns plucked up by the roots: and, behold, in this horn were eyes like the eyes of man, and a mouth speaking great things. [9] I beheld till the thrones were cast down, and the Ancient of days did sit, whose garment was white as snow, and the hair of his head like the pure wool: his throne was like the fiery flame, and his wheels as burning fire. [10] A fiery stream issued and came forth from before him: thousand thousands ministered unto him, and ten thousand times ten thousand stood before him: the judgment was set, and the books were opened. [11] I beheld then because of the voice of the great words which the horn spake: I beheld even till the beast was slain, and his body destroyed, and given to the burning flame. [12] As concerning the rest of the beasts, they had their dominion taken away: yet their lives were prolonged for a season and time. [13] I saw in the night visions, and, behold, one like the Son of man came with the clouds of heaven, and came to the Ancient of days, and they brought him near before him. [14] And

there was given him dominion, and glory, and a kingdom,
that all people, nations, and languages, should serve him:
his dominion is an everlasting dominion, which shall
not pass away, and his kingdom that which shall not be
destroyed.

11. Daniel 7:17-27:

[17] These great beasts, which are four, are four kings,
which shall arise out of the earth. [18] But the saints
of the most High shall take the kingdom, and possess
the kingdom for ever, even for ever and ever. [19] Then
I would know the truth of the fourth beast, which was
diverse from all the others, exceeding dreadful, whose
teeth were of iron, and his nails of brass; which devoured,
brake in pieces, and stamped the residue with his feet;
[20] And of the ten horns that were in his head, and of the
other which came up, and before whom three fell; even
of that horn that had eyes, and a mouth that spake very
great things, whose look was more stout than his fellows.
[21] I beheld, and the same horn made war with the
saints, and prevailed against them; [22] Until the Ancient
of days came, and judgment was given to the saints of the
most High; and the time came that the saints possessed
the kingdom. [23] Thus he said, The fourth beast shall
be the fourth kingdom upon earth, which shall be diverse
from all kingdoms, and shall devour the whole earth,
and shall tread it down, and break it in pieces. [24] And
the ten horns out of this kingdom are ten kings that shall
arise: and another shall rise after them; and he shall be

diverse from the first, and he shall subdue three kings. [25] And he shall speak great words against the most High, and shall wear out the saints of the most High, and think to change times and laws: and they shall be given into his hand until a time and times and the dividing of time. [26] But the judgment shall sit, and they shall take away his dominion, to consume and to destroy it unto the end. [27] And the kingdom and dominion, and the greatness of the kingdom under the whole heaven, shall be given to the people of the saints of the most High, whose kingdom is an everlasting kingdom, and all dominions shall serve and obey him.

12. Daniel 8:3-14:

[3] Then I lifted up mine eyes, and saw, and, behold, there stood before the river a ram which had two horns: and the two horns were high; but one was higher than the other, and the higher came up last. [4] I saw the ram pushing westward, and northward, and southward; so that no beasts might stand before him, neither was there any that could deliver out of his hand; but he did according to his will, and became great.

[5] And as I was considering, behold, an he goat came from the west on the face of the whole earth, and touched not the ground: and the goat had a notable horn between his eyes. [6] And he came to the ram that had two horns, which I had seen standing before the river, and ran unto him in the fury of his power. [7] And I saw him come close unto the ram, and he was moved with choler against

him, and smote the ram, and brake his two horns: and there was no power in the ram to stand before him, but he cast him down to the ground, and stamped upon him: and there was none that could deliver the ram out of his hand. [8] Therefore the he goat waxed very great: and when he was strong, the great horn was broken; and for it came up four notable ones toward the four winds of heaven.

[9] And out of one of them came forth a little horn, which waxed exceeding great, toward the south, and toward the east, and toward the pleasant land. [10] And it waxed great, even to the host of heaven; and it cast down some of the host and of the stars to the ground, and stamped upon them. [11] Yea, he magnified himself even to the prince of the host, and by him the daily sacrifice was taken away, and the place of his sanctuary was cast down. [12] And an host was given him against the daily sacrifice by reason of transgression, and it cast down the truth to the ground; and it practised, and prospered. [13] Then I heard one saint speaking, and another saint said unto that certain saint which spake, How long shall be the vision concerning the daily sacrifice, and the transgression of desolation, to give both the sanctuary and the host to be trodden under foot?

[14] And he said unto me, Unto two thousand and three hundred days; then shall the sanctuary be cleansed.

13. Daniel 8:17:

[17] Understand, O son of man: for at the time of the end shall be the vision.

14. Daniel 8:20-25:

[20] The ram which thou sawest having two horns are the kings of Media and Persia. [21] And the rough goat is the king of Grecia: and the great horn that is between his eyes is the first king. [22] Now that being broken, whereas four stood up for it, four kingdoms shall stand up out of the nation, but not in his power. [23] And in the latter time of their kingdom, when the transgressors are come to the full, a king of fierce countenance, and understanding dark sentences, shall stand up.

[24] And his power shall be mighty, but not by his own power: and he shall destroy wonderfully, and shall prosper, and practise, and shall destroy the mighty and the holy people. [25] And through his policy also he shall cause craft to prosper in his hand; and he shall magnify himself in his heart, and by peace shall destroy many: he shall also stand up against the Prince of princes; but he shall be broken without hand.

15. Daniel 9:24-27:

[24] Seventy weeks are determined upon thy people and upon thy holy city, to finish the transgression, and to make an end of sins, and to make reconciliation for iniquity, and to bring in everlasting righteousness, and to seal up the vision and prophecy, and to anoint the most Holy. [25] Know therefore and understand, that from the going forth of the commandment to restore and to build Jerusalem unto the Messiah the Prince shall be seven weeks, and threescore and two weeks: the street shall be built

again, and the wall, even in troublous times. [26] And after threescore and two weeks shall Messiah be cut off, but not for himself: and the people of the prince that shall come shall destroy the city and the sanctuary; and the end thereof shall be with a flood, and unto the end of the war desolations are determined.

[27] And he shall confirm the covenant with many for one week: and in the midst of the week he shall cause the sacrifice and the oblation to cease, and for the overspreading of abominations he shall make it desolate, even until the consummation, and that determined shall be poured upon the desolate.

16. Daniel 10:14:

[14] Now I am come to make thee understand what shall befall thy people in the latter days: for yet the vision is for many days.

17. Daniel 11:2-45:

[2] And now will I shew thee the truth. Behold, there shall stand up yet three kings in Persia; and the fourth shall be far richer than they all: and by his strength through his riches he shall stir up all against the realm of Grecia. [3] And a mighty king shall stand up, that shall rule with great dominion, and do according to his will. [4] And when he shall stand up, his kingdom shall be broken, and shall be divided toward the four winds of heaven; and not to his posterity, nor according to his dominion which he ruled: for his kingdom shall be plucked up, even for

others beside those. [5] And the king of the south shall
be strong, and one of his princes; and he shall be strong
above him, and have dominion; his dominion shall be a
great dominion. [6] And in the end of years they shall join
themselves together; for the king's daughter of the south
shall come to the king of the north to make an agreement:
but she shall not retain the power of the arm; neither
shall he stand, nor his arm: but she shall be given up, and
they that brought her, and he that begat her, and he that
strengthened her in these times. [7] But out of a branch
of her roots shall one stand up in his estate, which shall
come with an army, and shall enter into the fortress of the
king of the north, and shall deal against them, and shall
prevail: [8] And shall also carry captives into Egypt their
gods, with their princes, and with their precious vessels of
silver and of gold; and he shall continue more years than
the king of the north.
[9] So the king of the south shall come into his kingdom,
and shall return into his own land. [10] But his sons shall
be stirred up, and shall assemble a multitude of great
forces: and one shall certainly come, and overflow, and
pass through: then shall he return, and be stirred up,
even to his fortress. [11] And the king of the south shall
be moved with choler, and shall come forth and fight with
him, even with the king of the north: and he shall set forth
a great multitude; but the multitude shall be given into his
hand. [12] And when he hath taken away the multitude,
his heart shall be lifted up; and he shall cast down many
ten thousands: but he shall not be strengthened by it.
[13] For the king of the north shall return, and shall

*set forth a multitude greater than the former, and shall
certainly come after certain years with a great army and
with much riches. [14] And in those times there shall
many stand up against the king of the south: also the rob-
bers of thy people shall exalt themselves to establish the
vision; but they shall fall. [15] So the king of the north
shall come, and cast up a mount, and take the most fenced
cities: and the arms of the south shall not withstand, neither his chosen people, neither shall there be any strength
to withstand. [16] But he that cometh against him shall
do according to his own will, and none shall stand before
him: and he shall stand in the glorious land, which by his
hand shall be consumed.*

*[17] He shall also set his face to enter with the strength
of his whole kingdom, and upright ones with him; thus
shall he do: and he shall give him the daughter of wom-
en, corrupting her: but she shall not stand on his side,
neither be for him. [18] After this shall he turn his face
unto the isles, and shall take many: but a prince for his
own behalf shall cause the reproach offered by him to
cease; without his own reproach he shall cause it to turn
upon him. [19] Then he shall turn his face toward the fort
of his own land: but he shall stumble and fall, and not be
found. [20] Then shall stand up in his estate a raiser of
taxes in the glory of the kingdom: but within few days he
shall be destroyed, neither in anger, nor in battle.*

*[21] And in his estate shall stand up a vile person, to
whom they shall not give the honour of the kingdom: but
he shall come in peaceably, and obtain the kingdom by
flatteries. [22] And with the arms of a flood shall they*

be overflown from before him, and shall be broken; yea, also the prince of the covenant. [24] And after the league made with him he shall work deceitfully: for he shall come up, and shall become strong with a small people. He shall enter peaceably even upon the fattest places of the province; and he shall do that which his fathers have not done, nor his fathers' fathers; he shall scatter among them the prey, and spoil, and riches: yea, and he shall forecast his devices against the strong holds, even for a time.

[25] And he shall stir up his power and his courage against the king of the south with a great army; and the king of the south shall be stirred up to battle with a very great and mighty army; but he shall not stand: for they shall forecast devices against him. [26] Yea, they that feed of the portion of his meat shall destroy him, and his army shall overflow: and many shall fall down slain. [27] And both these kings' hearts shall be to do mischief, and they shall speak lies at one table; but it shall not prosper: for yet the end shall be at the time appointed. [28] Then shall he return into his land with great riches; and his heart shall be against the holy covenant; and he shall do exploits, and return to his own land.

[29] At the time appointed he shall return, and come toward the south; but it shall not be as the former, or as the latter. [30] For the ships of Chittim shall come against him: therefore he shall be grieved, and return, and have indignation against the holy covenant: so shall he do; he shall even return, and have intelligence with them that forsake the holy covenant. [31] And arms shall stand on

his part, and they shall pollute the sanctuary of strength, and shall take away the daily sacrifice, and they shall place the abomination that maketh desolate. [32] And such as do wickedly against the covenant shall he corrupt by flatteries: but the people that do know their God shall be strong, and do exploits.

[33] And they that understand among the people shall instruct many: yet they shall fall by the sword, and by flame, by captivity, and by spoil, many days. [34] Now when they shall fall, they shall be holpen with a little help: but many shall cleave to them with flatteries. [35] And some of them of understanding shall fall, to try them, and to purge, and to make them white, even to the time of the end: because it is yet for a time appointed. [36] And the king shall do according to his will; and he shall exalt himself, and magnify himself above every god, and shall speak marvellous things against the God of gods, and shall prosper till the indignation be accomplished: for that that is determined shall be done.

[37] Neither shall he regard the God of his fathers, nor the desire of women, nor regard any god: for he shall magnify himself above all. [38] But in his estate shall he honour the God of forces: and a god whom his fathers knew not shall he honour with gold, and silver, and with precious stones, and pleasant things. [39] Thus shall he do in the most strong holds with a strange god, whom he shall acknowledge and increase with glory: and he shall cause them to rule over many, and shall divide the land for gain. [40] And at the time of the end shall the king of the south push at him: and the king of the north shall

come against him like a whirlwind, with chariots, and with horsemen, and with many ships; and he shall enter into the countries, and shall overflow and pass over.
[41] He shall enter also into the glorious land, and many countries shall be overthrown: but these shall escape out of his hand, even Edom, and Moab, and the chief of the children of Ammon. [42] He shall stretch forth his hand also upon the countries: and the land of Egypt shall not escape. [43] But he shall have power over the treasures of gold and of silver, and over all the precious things of Egypt: and the Libyans and the Ethiopians shall be at his steps. [44] But tidings out of the east and out of the north shall trouble him: therefore he shall go forth with great fury to destroy, and utterly to make away many. [45 And he shall plant the tabernacles of his palace between the seas in the glorious holy mountain; yet he shall come to his end, and none shall help him.

PROPHECIES IN HOSEA: 19

1. Hosea 1:4:

[4] And the Lord said unto him, Call his name Jezreel; for yet a little while, and I will avenge the blood of Jezreel upon the house of Jehu, and will cause to cease the kingdom of the house of Israel.

2. Hosea 1:6:

[6] And she conceived again, and bare a daughter. And God said unto him, Call her name Lo-ruhamah: for I will no more have mercy upon the house of Israel; but I will utterly take them away.

3. Hosea 1:9:

[9] Then said God, Call his name Lo-ammi: for ye are not my people, and I will not be your God.

4. Hosea 1:10-11:

[10] Yet the number of the children of Israel shall be as the sand of the sea, which cannot be measured nor numbered; and it shall come to pass, that in the place where it was said unto them, Ye are not my people, there it shall be said unto them, Ye are the sons of the living God. [11] Then shall the children of Judah and the children of Israel be gathered together, and appoint themselves one head,

and they shall come up out of the land: for great shall be the day of Jezreel.

5. Hosea 3:5:

[5] Afterward shall the children of Israel return, and seek the Lord their God, and David their king; and shall fear the Lord and his goodness in the latter days.

6. Hosea 4:3-5:

[3] Therefore shall the land mourn, and every one that dwelleth therein shall languish, with the beasts of the field, and with the fowls of heaven; yea, the fishes of the sea also shall be taken away. [4] Yet let no man strive, nor reprove another: for thy people are as they that strive with the priest. [5] Therefore shalt thou fall in the day, and the prophet also shall fall with thee in the night, and I will destroy thy mother.

7. Hosea 5:6-7:

[6] They shall go with their flocks and with their herds to seek the Lord; but they shall not find him; he hath withdrawn himself from them. [7] They have dealt treacherously against the Lord: for they have begotten strange children: now shall a month devour them with their portions.

8. Hosea 5:9:

[9] Ephraim shall be desolate in the day of rebuke:

among the tribes of Israel have I made known that which
shall surely be.

9. Hosea 7:12:

[12] When they shall go, I will spread my net upon them;
I will bring them down as the fowls of the heaven; I will
chastise them, as their congregation hath heard.

10. Hosea 8:1-3):

[1] Set the trumpet to thy mouth. He shall come as an
eagle against the house of the Lord, because they have
transgressed my covenant, and trespassed against my law.
[2] Israel shall cry unto me, My God, we know thee. [3]
Israel hath cast off the thing that is good: the enemy shall
pursue him.

12. Hosea 9:3-4:

[3] They shall not dwell in the Lord's land; but Ephraim
shall return to Egypt, and they shall eat unclean things
in Assyria. [4] They shall not offer wine offerings to the
Lord, neither shall they be pleasing unto him: their sacri-
fices shall be unto them as the bread of mourners; all that
eat thereof shall be polluted: for their bread for their soul
shall not come into the house of the Lord.

13. Hosea 11:5-6):

[5] He shall not return into the land of Egypt, but the
Assyrian shall be his king, because they refused to return.

[6] And the sword shall abide on his cities, and shall consume his branches, and devour them, because of their own counsels.

14. Hosea 11:9-10:

[9] I will not execute the fierceness of mine anger, I will not return to destroy Ephraim: for I am God, and not man; the Holy One in the midst of thee: and I will not enter into the city. [10] They shall walk after the Lord: he shall roar like a lion: when he shall roar, then the children shall tremble from the west.

15. Hosea 12:2:

[2] The Lord hath also a controversy with Judah, and will punish Jacob according to his ways; according to his doings will he recompense him.

16. Hosea 12:14:

[14] Ephraim provoked him to anger most bitterly: therefore shall he leave his blood upon him, and his reproach shall his Lord return unto him.

17. Hosea 13:3:

[3] Therefore they shall be as the morning cloud, and as the early dew that passeth away, as the chaff that is driven with the whirlwind out of the floor, and as the smoke out of the chimney.

18. Hosea 13:7-10:

[7] Therefore I will be unto them as a lion: as a leopard by the way will I observe them: [8] I will meet them as a bear that is bereaved of her whelps, and will rend the caul of their heart, and there will I devour them like a lion: the wild beast shall tear them. [9] O Israel, thou hast destroyed thyself; but in me is thine help. [10] I will be thy king: where is any other that may save thee in all thy cities? and thy judges of whom thou saidst, Give me a king and princes?

19. Hosea 13:14:

[14] I will ransom them from the power of the grave; I will redeem them from death: O death, I will be thy plagues; O grave, I will be thy destruction: repentance shall be hid from mine eyes.

PROPHECIES IN JOEL: 5

1 Joel 1:4:

[4] That which the palmerworm hath left hath the locust eaten; and that which the locust hath left hath the cankerworm eaten; and that which the cankerworm hath left hath the caterpiller eaten.

2 Joel 1:15:

[15] Alas for the day! for the day of the Lord is at hand, and as a destruction from the Almighty shall it come.

3. Joel 2:32:

[32] And it shall come to pass, that whosoever shall call on the name of the Lord shall be delivered: for in mount Zion and in Jerusalem shall be deliverance, as the Lord hath said, and in the remnant whom the Lord shall call.

4. Joel 3:1-2:

[1] For, behold, in those days, and in that time, when I shall bring again the captivity of Judah and Jerusalem, [2] I will also gather all nations, and will bring them down into the valley of Jehoshaphat, and will plead with them there for my people and for my heritage Israel, whom they have scattered among the nations, and parted my land.

5. Joel 3:17-21:

[17] So shall ye know that I am the Lord your God dwelling in Zion, my holy mountain: then shall Jerusalem be holy, and there shall no strangers pass through her any more. [18] And it shall come to pass in that day, that the mountains shall drop down new wine, and the hills shall flow with milk, and all the rivers of Judah shall flow with waters, and a fountain shall come forth of the house of the Lord, and shall water the valley of Shittim. [19] Egypt shall be a desolation, and Edom shall be a desolate wilderness, for the violence against the children of Judah, because they have shed innocent blood in their land. [20] But Judah shall dwell for ever, and Jerusalem from generation to generation. [21] For I will cleanse their blood that I have not cleansed: for the Lord dwelleth in Zion.

PROPHECIES IN AMOS: 14

1 Amos 1:2:

[2] And he said, The Lord will roar from Zion, and utter his voice from Jerusalem; and the habitations of the shepherds shall mourn, and the top of Carmel shall wither.

2. Amos 3:11-12:

[11] Therefore thus saith the Lord God; An adversary there shall be even round about the land; and he shall bring down thy strength from thee, and thy palaces shall be spoiled.
[12] Thus saith the Lord; As the shepherd taketh out of the mouth of the lion two legs, or a piece of an ear; so shall the children of Israel be taken out that dwell in Samaria in the corner of a bed, and in Damascus in a couch.

3. Amos 4:2-3:

[2] The Lord God hath sworn by his holiness, that, lo, the days shall come upon you, that he will take you away with hooks, and your posterity with fishhooks. [3] And ye shall go out at the breaches, every cow at that which is before her; and ye shall cast them into the palace, saith the Lord.

4. Amos 5:1-6:

[1] Hear ye this word which I take up against you, even a lamentation, O house of Israel. [2] The virgin of Israel is fallen; she shall no more rise: she is forsaken upon her land; there is none to raise her up. [3] For thus saith the Lord God; The city that went out by a thousand shall leave an hundred, and that which went forth by an hundred shall leave ten, to the house of Israel. [4] For thus saith the Lord unto the house of Israel, Seek ye me, and ye shall live: [5] But seek not Beth-el, nor enter into Gilgal, and pass not to Beer-sheba: for Gilgal shall surely go into captivity, and Beth-el shall come to nought. [6] Seek the Lord, and ye shall live; lest he break out like fire in the house of Joseph, and devour it, and there be none to quench it in Beth-el.

5. Amos 5:11-13:

[11] Forasmuch therefore as your treading is upon the poor, and ye take from him burdens of wheat: ye have built houses of hewn stone, but ye shall not dwell in them; ye have planted pleasant vineyards, but ye shall not drink wine of them. [12] For I know your manifold transgressions and your mighty sins: they afflict the just, they take a bribe, and they turn aside the poor in the gate from their right. [13] Therefore the prudent shall keep silence in that time; for it is an evil time.

6. Amos 5:16-17:

[16] Therefore the Lord, the God of hosts, the Lord, saith thus; Wailing shall be in all streets; and they shall say in all the highways, Alas! alas! and they shall call the husbandman to mourning, and such as are skilful of lamentation to wailing. [17] And in all vineyards shall be wailing: for I will pass through thee, saith the Lord.

7. Amos 5:27:

[27] Therefore will I cause you to go into captivity beyond Damascus, saith the Lord, whose name is The God of hosts.

8. Amos 7:1:

[1] Thus hath the Lord God shewed unto me; and, behold, he formed grasshoppers in the beginning of the shooting up of the latter growth; and, lo, it was the latter growth after the king's mowings.

9. Amos 7:11:

[11] For thus Amos saith, Jeroboam shall die by the sword, and Israel shall surely be led away captive out of their own land.

10. Amos 7:16-17:

[16] Now therefore hear thou the word of the Lord: Thou sayest, Prophesy not against Israel, and drop not

thy word against the house of Isaac. [17] Therefore thus saith the Lord; Thy wife shall be an harlot in the city, and thy sons and thy daughters shall fall by the sword, and thy land shall be divided by line; and thou shalt die in a polluted land: and Israel shall surely go into captivity forth of his land.

11. Amos 8:7-10:

[7] The Lord hath sworn by the excellency of Jacob, Surely I will never forget any of their works. [8] Shall not the land tremble for this, and every one mourn that dwelleth therein? and it shall rise up wholly as a flood; and it shall be cast out and drowned, as by the flood of Egypt.
[9] And it shall come to pass in that day, saith the Lord God, that I will cause the sun to go down at noon, and I will darken the earth in the clear day:
[10] And I will turn your feasts into mourning, and all your songs into lamentation; and I will bring up sackcloth upon all loins, and baldness upon every head; and I will make it as the mourning of an only son, and the end thereof as a bitter day.

13. Amos 9:1:

[1] I saw the Lord standing upon the altar: and he said, Smite the lintel of the door, that the posts may shake: and cut them in the head, all of them; and I will slay the last of them with the sword: he that fleeth of them shall not flee away, and he that escapeth of them shall not be delivered.

14. Amos 9:8-9:

[8] Behold, the eyes of the Lord God are upon the sinful kingdom, and I will destroy it from off the face of the earth; saving that I will not utterly destroy the house of Jacob, saith the Lord.

[9] For, lo, I will command, and I will sift the house of Israel among all nations, like as corn is sifted in a sieve, yet shall not the least grain fall upon the earth.

PROPHECIES IN OBADIAH: 3

1. Obadiah 1:4:

[4] Though thou exalt thyself as the eagle, and though thou set thy nest among the stars, thence will I bring thee down, saith the Lord.

2. Obadiah 1:7:

[7] All the men of thy confederacy have brought thee even to the border: the men that were at peace with thee have deceived thee, and prevailed against thee; they that eat thy bread have laid a wound under thee: there is none understanding in him.

3. Obadiah 1:15-21:

[15] For the day of the Lord is near upon all the heathen: as thou hast done, it shall be done unto thee: thy reward shall return upon thine own head. [16] For as ye have drunk upon my holy mountain, so shall all the heathen drink continually, yea, they shall drink, and they shall swallow down, and they shall be as though they had not been. [17] But upon mount Zion shall be deliverance, and there shall be holiness; and the house of Jacob shall possess their possessions.
[18] And the house of Jacob shall be a fire, and the house of Joseph a flame, and the house of Esau for stubble,

and they shall kindle in them, and devour them; and there shall not be any remaining of the house of Esau; for the Lord hath spoken it. [19] And they of the south shall possess the mount of Esau; and they of the plain the Philistines: and they shall possess the fields of Ephraim, and the fields of Samaria: and Benjamin shall possess Gilead. [20] And the captivity of this host of the children of Israel shall possess that of the Canaanites, even unto Zarephath; and the captivity of Jerusalem, which is in Sepharad, shall possess the cities of the south. [21] And saviours shall come up on mount Zion to judge the mount of Esau; and the kingdom shall be the Lord's.

PROPHECIES IN JONAH: 1

Jonah 3:4:

[4] And Jonah began to enter into the city a day's journey, and he cried, and said, Yet forty days, and Nineveh shall be overthrown.

PROPHECIES IN MICAH: 9

1. Micah 1:2-4:

[2] Hear, all ye people; hearken, O earth, and all that therein is: and let the Lord God be witness against you, the Lord from his holy temple. [3] For, behold, the Lord cometh forth out of his place, and will come down, and tread upon the high places of the earth. [4] And the mountains shall be molten under him, and the valleys shall be cleft, as wax before the fire, and as the waters that are poured down a steep place.

2. Micah 1:6-8:

[6] Therefore I will make Samaria as an heap of the field, and as plantings of a vineyard: and I will pour down the stones thereof into the valley, and I will discover the foundations thereof. [7] And all the graven images thereof shall be beaten to pieces, and all the hires thereof shall be burned with the fire, and all the idols thereof will I lay desolate: for she gathered it of the hire of an harlot, and they shall return to the hire of an harlot. [8] Therefore I will wail and howl, I will go stripped and naked: I will make a wailing like the dragons, and mourning as the owls.

3. Micah. 2:3-4:

[3] Behold, against this family do I devise an evil, from which ye shall not remove your necks; neither shall ye go haughtily: for this time is evil. [4] In that day shall one take up a parable against you, and lament with a doleful lamentation, and say, We be utterly spoiled: he hath changed the portion of my people: how hath he removed it from me! turning away he hath divided our fields.

4. Micah 2:10:

[10] Arise ye, and depart; for this is not your rest: because it is polluted, it shall destroy you, even with a sore destruction.

5. Micah 3:6-7:

[6] Therefore night shall be unto you, that ye shall not have a vision; and it shall be dark unto you, that ye shall not divine; and the sun shall go down over the prophets, and the day shall be dark over them.
[7] Then shall the seers be ashamed, and the diviners confounded: yea, they shall all cover their lips; for there is no answer of God.

6. Micah 3:12:

[12] Therefore shall Zion for your sake be plowed as a field, and Jerusalem shall become heaps, and the mountain of the house as the high places of the forest.

7. Micah 4:1-12:

[1] But in the last days it shall come to pass, that the mountain of the house of the Lord shall be established in the top of the mountains, and it shall be exalted above the hills; and people shall flow unto it. [2] And many nations shall come, and say, Come, and let us go up to the mountain of the Lord, and to the house of the God of Jacob; and he will teach us of his ways, and we will walk in his paths: for the law shall go forth of Zion, and the word of the Lord from Jerusalem. [3] And he shall judge among many people, and rebuke strong nations afar off; and they shall beat their swords into plowshares, and their spears into pruninghooks: nation shall not lift up a sword against nation, neither shall they learn war any more. [4] But they shall sit every man under his vine and under his fig tree; and none shall make them afraid: for the mouth of the Lord of hosts hath spoken it.

[5] For all people will walk every one in the name of his god, and we will walk in the name of the Lord our God for ever and ever. [6] In that day, saith the Lord, will I assemble her that halteth, and I will gather her that is driven out, and her that I have afflicted; [7] And I will make her that halted a remnant, and her that was cast far off a strong nation: and the Lord shall reign over them in mount Zion from henceforth, even for ever. [8] And thou, O tower of the flock, the strong hold of the daughter of Zion, unto thee shall it come, even the first dominion; the kingdom shall come to the daughter of Jerusalem. [9] Now why dost thou cry out aloud? is there no king in thee? is thy counsellor perished? for pangs have taken

thee as a woman in travail. [10] Be in pain, and labour to
bring forth, O daughter of Zion, like a woman in travail:
for now shalt thou go forth out of the city, and thou shalt
dwell in the field, and thou shalt go even to Babylon;
there shalt thou be delivered; there the Lord shall redeem
thee from the hand of thine enemies.
[11] Now also many nations are gathered against thee,
that say, Let her be defiled, and let our eye look upon
Zion. [12] But they know not the thoughts of the Lord,
neither understand they his counsel: for he shall gather
them as the sheaves into the floor.

8. Micah 5:1-15:

[1] Now gather thyself in troops, O daughter of troops: he
hath laid siege against us: they shall smite the judge of Is-
rael with a rod upon the cheek. [2] But thou, Beth-lehem
Ephratah, though thou be little among the thousands of
Judah, yet out of thee shall he come forth unto me that is
to be ruler in Israel; whose goings forth have been from
of old, from everlasting. [3] Therefore will he give them
up, until the time that she which travaileth hath brought
forth: then the remnant of his brethren shall return unto
the children of Israel. [4] And he shall stand and feed in
the strength of the Lord, in the majesty of the name of the
Lord his God; and they shall abide: for now shall he be
great unto the ends of the earth. [5] And this man shall
be the peace, when the Assyrian shall come into our land:
and when he shall tread in our palaces, then shall we
raise against him seven shepherds, and eight principal

men.

[6] And they shall waste the land of Assyria with the sword, and the land of Nimrod in the entrances thereof: thus shall he deliver us from the Assyrian, when he cometh into our land, and when he treadeth within our borders. [7] And the remnant of Jacob shall be in the midst of many people as a dew from the Lord, as the showers upon the grass, that tarrieth not for man, nor waiteth for the sons of men. [8] And the remnant of Jacob shall be among the Gentiles in the midst of many people as a lion among the beasts of the forest, as a young lion among the flocks of sheep: who, if he go through, both treadeth down, and teareth in pieces, and none can deliver. [9] Thine hand shall be lifted up upon thine adversaries, and all thine enemies shall be cut off. [10] And it shall come to pass in that day, saith the Lord, that I will cut off thy horses out of the midst of thee, and I will destroy thy chariots:

[11] And I will cut off the cities of thy land, and throw down all thy strong holds: [12] And I will cut off witchcrafts out of thine hand; and thou shalt have no more soothsayers: [13] Thy graven images also will I cut off, and thy standing images out of the midst of thee; and thou shalt no more worship the work of thine hands. [14] And I will pluck up thy groves out of the midst of thee: so will I destroy thy cities. [15] And I will execute vengeance in anger and fury upon the heathen, such as they have not heard.

9. Micah 6:13-15:

[13] Therefore also will I make thee sick in smiting thee, in making thee desolate because of thy sins. [14] Thou shalt eat, but not be satisfied; and thy casting down shall be in the midst of thee; and thou shalt take hold, but shalt not deliver; and that which thou deliverest will I give up to the sword. [15] Thou shalt sow, but thou shalt not reap; thou shalt tread the olives, but thou shalt not anoint thee with oil; and sweet wine, but shalt not drink wine.

PROPHECIES IN NAHUM: 3

1. Nahum 1:2:

> *[2] God is jealous, and the Lord revengeth; the Lord revengeth, and is furious; the Lord will take vengeance on his adversaries, and he reserveth wrath for his enemies.*

2 Nahum 1:10:

> *[10] For while they be folden together as thorns, and while they are drunken as drunkards, they shall be devoured as stubble fully dry.*

3. Nahum 1:15:

> *[15] Behold upon the mountains the feet of him that bringeth good tidings, that publisheth peace! O Judah, keep thy solemn feasts, perform thy vows: for the wicked shall no more pass through thee; he is utterly cut off.*

PROPHECIES IN HABAKKUK: 3

1 Habakkuk 1:5-11:

[5] Behold ye among the heathen, and regard, and wonder marvellously: for I will work a work in your days, which ye will not believe, though it be told you. [6] For, lo, I raise up the Chaldeans, that bitter and hasty nation, which shall march through the breadth of the land, to possess the dwelling places that are not theirs.

[7] They are terrible and dreadful: their judgment and their dignity shall proceed of themselves. [8] Their horses also are swifter than the leopards, and are more fierce than the evening wolves: and their horsemen shall spread themselves, and their horsemen shall come from far; they shall fly as the eagle that hasteth to eat. [9] They shall come all for violence: their faces shall sup up as the east wind, and they shall gather the captivity as the sand. [10] And they shall scoff at the kings, and the princes shall be a scorn unto them: they shall deride every strong hold; for they shall heap dust, and take it. [11] Then shall his mind change, and he shall pass over, and offend, imputing this his power unto his god.

2. Habakkuk 2:2-3:

[2] And the Lord answered me, and said, Write the vision, and make it plain upon tables, that he may run that

readeth it. [3] For the vision is yet for an appointed time, but at the end it shall speak, and not lie: though it tarry, wait for it; because it will surely come, it will not tarry.

3. Habakkuk 2:14:

[14] For the earth shall be filled with the knowledge of the glory of the Lord, as the waters cover the sea.

PROPHECIES IN ZEPHANIAH: 4

1. Zephaniah 1:2-6:

[2] I will utterly consume all things from off the land, saith the Lord. [3] I will consume man and beast; I will consume the fowls of the heaven, and the fishes of the sea, and the stumblingblocks with the wicked; and I will cut off man from off the land, saith the Lord. [4] I will also stretch out mine hand upon Judah, and upon all the inhabitants of Jerusalem; and I will cut off the remnant of Baal from this place, and the name of the Chemarims with the priests; [5] And them that worship the host of heaven upon the housetops; and them that worship and that swear by the Lord, and that swear by Malcham; [6] And them that are turned back from the Lord; and those that have not sought the Lord, nor enquired for him.

2. Zephaniah 2:6-7:

[6] And the sea coast shall be dwellings and cottages for shepherds, and folds for flocks. [7] And the coast shall be for the remnant of the house of Judah; they shall feed thereupon: in the houses of Ashkelon shall they lie down in the evening: for the Lord their God shall visit them, and turn away their captivity.

3. Zephaniah 2:9-14:

> *[9] Therefore as I live, saith the Lord of hosts, the God of Israel, Surely Moab shall be as Sodom, and the children of Ammon as Gomorrah, even the breeding of nettles, and saltpits, and a perpetual desolation: the residue of my people shall spoil them, and the remnant of my people shall possess them. [10] This shall they have for their pride, because they have reproached and magnified themselves against the people of the Lord of hosts.*
> *[11] The Lord will be terrible unto them: for he will famish all the gods of the earth; and men shall worship him, every one from his place, even all the isles of the heathen. [12] Ye Ethiopians also, ye shall be slain by my sword. [13] And he will stretch out his hand against the north, and destroy Assyria; and will make Nineveh a desolation, and dry like a wilderness. [14] And flocks shall lie down in the midst of her, all the beasts of the nations: both the cormorant and the bittern shall lodge in the upper lintels of it; their voice shall sing in the windows; desolation shall be in the thresholds: for he shall uncover the cedar work.*

4. Zephaniah 3:8- 12

> *[8] Therefore wait ye upon me, saith the Lord, until the day that I rise up to the prey: for my determination is to gather the nations, that I may assemble the kingdoms, to pour upon them mine indignation, even all my fierce anger: for all the earth shall be devoured with the fire of my jealousy. [9] For then will I turn to the people a pure lan-*

guage, that they may all call upon the name of the Lord, to serve him with one consent. [10] From beyond the rivers of Ethiopia my suppliants, even the daughter of my dispersed, shall bring mine offering. [11] In that day shalt thou not be ashamed for all thy doings, wherein thou hast transgressed against me: for then I will take away out of the midst of thee them that rejoice in thy pride, and thou shalt no more be haughty because of my holy mountain. [12] I will also leave in the midst of thee an afflicted and poor people, and they shall trust in the name of the Lord. The remnant of Israel shall not do iniquity, nor speak lies; neither shall a deceitful tongue be found in their mouth: for they shall feed and lie down, and none shall make them afraid.

PROPHECIES IN HAGGAI: 3

1. Haggai 2:6-9:

[6] For thus saith the Lord of hosts; Yet once, it is a little while, and I will shake the heavens, and the earth, and the sea, and the dry land; [7] And I will shake all nations, and the desire of all nations shall come: and I will fill this house with glory, saith the Lord of hosts. [8] The silver is mine, and the gold is mine, saith the Lord of hosts. [9] The glory of this latter house shall be greater than of the former, saith the Lord of hosts: and in this place will I give peace, saith the Lord of hosts.

2. Haggai 2:18:

[18] Consider now from this day and upward, from the four and twentieth day of the ninth month, even from the day that the foundation of the Lord's temple was laid, consider it..

3. Haggai 2:21-23:

[21] Speak to Zerubbabel, governor of Judah, saying, I will shake the heavens and the earth; [22] And I will overthrow the throne of kingdoms, and I will destroy the strength of the kingdoms of the heathen; and I will overthrow the chariots, and those that ride in them; and the horses and their riders shall come down, every one by

the sword of his brother. [23] In that day, saith the Lord of hosts, will I take thee, O Zerubbabel, my servant, the son of Shealtiel, saith the Lord, and will make thee as a signet: for I have chosen thee, saith the Lord of hosts.

PROPHECIES IN ZECHARIAH: 16

1. Zechariah 1:16:

[16] Therefore thus saith the Lord; I am returned to Jerusalem with mercies: my house shall be built in it, saith the Lord of hosts, and a line shall be stretched forth upon Jerusalem.

2. Zechariah 1:18-19:

[18] Then lifted I up mine eyes, and saw, and behold four horns. [19] And I said unto the angel that talked with me, What be these? And he answered me, These are the horns which have scattered Judah, Israel, and Jerusalem.

3. Zechariah 1:20-21:

[20] And the Lord shewed me four carpenters. [21] Then said I, What come these to do? And he spake, saying, These are the horns which have scattered Judah, so that no man did lift up his head: but these are come to fray them, to cast out the horns of the Gentiles, which lifted up their horn over the land of Judah to scatter it.

4. Zechariah 2:1-5:

[1] I lifted up mine eyes again, and looked, and behold a man with a measuring line in his hand. [2] Then said

I, Whither goest thou? And he said unto me, To measure Jerusalem, to see what is the breadth thereof, and what is the length thereof. [3] And, behold, the angel that talked with me went forth, and another angel went out to meet him, [4] And said unto him, Run, speak to this young man, saying, Jerusalem shall be inhabited as towns without walls for the multitude of men and cattle therein: [5] For I, saith the Lord, will be unto her a wall of fire round about, and will be the glory in the midst of her.

5. Zechariah 2:11-12:

[11] And many nations shall be joined to the Lord in that day, and shall be my people: and I will dwell in the midst of thee, and thou shalt know that the Lord of hosts hath sent me unto thee. [12] And the Lord shall inherit Judah his portion in the holy land, and shall choose Jerusalem again.

6. Zechariah 3:9-10:

[9] For behold the stone that I have laid before Joshua; upon one stone shall be seven eyes: behold, I will engrave the graving thereof, saith the Lord of hosts, and I will remove the iniquity of that land in one day. [10] In that day, saith the Lord of hosts, shall ye call every man his neighbour under the vine and under the fig tree.

7. Zechariah 4:7:

[7] Who art thou, O great mountain? before Zerubbabel

thou shalt become a plain: and he shall bring forth the headstone thereof with shoutings, crying, Grace, grace unto it.

8. Zechariah 6:12-15:

[12] And speak unto him, saying, Thus speaketh the Lord of hosts, saying, Behold the man whose name is The BRANCH; and he shall grow up out of his place, and he shall build the temple of the Lord: [13] Even he shall build the temple of the Lord; and he shall bear the glory, and shall sit and rule upon his throne; and he shall be a priest upon his throne: and the counsel of peace shall be between them both. [14] And the crowns shall be to Helem, and to Tobijah, and to Jedaiah, and to Hen the son of Zephaniah, for a memorial in the temple of the Lord. [15] And they that are far off shall come and build in the temple of the Lord, and ye shall know that the Lord of hosts hath sent me unto you. And this shall come to pass, if ye will diligently obey the voice of the Lord your God.

9. Zechariah 8:3-5:

[3] Thus saith the Lord; I am returned unto Zion, and will dwell in the midst of Jerusalem: and Jerusalem shall be called a city of truth; and the mountain of the Lord of hosts the holy mountain. [4] Thus saith the Lord of hosts; There shall yet old men and old women dwell in the streets of Jerusalem, and every man with his staff in his hand for very age. [5] And the streets of the city shall be

373

full of boys and girls playing in the streets thereof.

10. Zechariah 8:11-13:

[11] But now I will not be unto the residue of this people as in the former days, saith the Lord of hosts. [12] For the seed shall be prosperous; the vine shall give her fruit, and the ground shall give her increase, and the heavens shall give their dew; and I will cause the remnant of this people to possess all these things.

[13] And it shall come to pass, that as ye were a curse among the heathen, O house of Judah, and house of Israel; so will I save you, and ye shall be a blessing: fear not, but let your hands be strong.

11. Zechariah 8:19-23:

[19] Thus saith the Lord of hosts; The fast of the fourth month, and the fast of the fifth, and the fast of the seventh, and the fast of the tenth, shall be to the house of Judah joy and gladness, and cheerful feasts; therefore love the truth and peace. [20] Thus saith the Lord of hosts; It shall yet come to pass, that there shall come people, and the inhabitants of many cities: [21] And the inhabitants of one city shall go to another, saying, Let us go speedily to pray before the Lord, and to seek the Lord of hosts: I will go also. [22] Yea, many people and strong nations shall come to seek the Lord of hosts in Jerusalem, and to pray before the Lord. [23] Thus saith the Lord of hosts; In those days it shall come to pass, that ten men shall take hold out of all languages of the nations, even shall take

hold of the skirt of him that is a Jew, saying, We will go with you: for we have heard that God is with you.

12. Zechariah 9:1:

[1] The burden of the word of the Lord in the land of Hadrach, and Damascus shall be the rest thereof: when the eyes of man, as of all the tribes of Israel, shall be toward the Lord.

14. Zechariah 10:1:

[1] Ask ye of the Lord rain in the time of the latter rain; so the Lord shall make bright clouds, and give them showers of rain, to every one grass in the field.

15. Zechariah 12:1-14:

[1] The burden of the word of the Lord for Israel, saith the Lord, which stretcheth forth the heavens, and lay-eth the foundation of the earth, and formeth the spirit of man within him. [2] Behold, I will make Jerusalem a cup of trembling unto all the people round about, when they shall be in the siege both against Judah and against Jerusalem. [3] And in that day will I make Jerusalem a burdensome stone for all people: all that burden them-selves with it shall be cut in pieces, though all the people of the earth be gathered together against it. [4] In that day, saith the Lord, I will smite every horse with astonish-ment, and his rider with madness: and I will open mine eyes upon the house of Judah, and will smite every horse

of the people with blindness. [5] And the governors of Judah shall say in their heart, The inhabitants of Jerusalem shall be my strength in the Lord of hosts their God. [6] In that day will I make the governors of Judah like an hearth of fire among the wood, and like a torch of fire in a sheaf; and they shall devour all the people round about, on the right hand and on the left: and Jerusalem shall be inhabited again in her own place, even in Jerusalem. [7] The Lord also shall save the tents of Judah first, that the glory of the house of David and the glory of the inhabitants of Jerusalem do not magnify themselves against Judah. [8] In that day shall the Lord defend the inhabitants of Jerusalem; and he that is feeble among them at that day shall be as David; and the house of David shall be as God, as the angel of the Lord before them. [9] And it shall come to pass in that day, that I will seek to destroy all the nations that come against Jerusalem. [10] And I will pour upon the house of David, and upon the inhabitants of Jerusalem, the spirit of grace and of supplications: and they shall look upon me whom they have pierced, and they shall mourn for him, as one mourneth for his only son, and shall be in bitterness for him, as one that is in bitterness for his firstborn. [11] In that day shall there be a great mourning in Jerusalem, as the mourning of Hadadrimmon in the valley of Megiddon. [12] And the land shall mourn, every family apart; the family of the house of David apart, and their wives apart; the family of the house of Nathan apart, and their wives apart; [13] The family of the house of Levi apart, and their wives apart; the family of Shimei apart, and their wives apart;

[14] All the families that remain, every family apart, and their wives apart.

16. Zechariah 13:7-9:

[7] Awake, O sword, against my shepherd, and against the man that is my fellow, saith the Lord of hosts: smite the shepherd, and the sheep shall be scattered: and I will turn mine hand upon the little ones. [8] And it shall come to pass, that in all the land, saith the Lord, two parts therein shall be cut off and die; but the third shall be left therein. [9] And I will bring the third part through the fire, and will refine them as silver is refined, and will try them as gold is tried: they shall call on my name, and I will hear them: I will say, It is my people: and they shall say, The Lord is my God.

PROPHECIES IN MALACHI: 5

1. Malachi 1:4-5:

[4] Whereas Edom saith, We are impoverished, but we will return and build the desolate places; thus saith the Lord of hosts, They shall build, but I will throw down; and they shall call them, The border of wickedness, and, The people against whom the Lord hath indignation for ever. [5] And your eyes shall see, and ye shall say, The Lord will be magnified from the border of Israel.

2. Malachi 1:11:

[11] For from the rising of the sun even unto the going down of the same my name shall be great among the Gentiles; and in every place incense shall be offered unto my name, and a pure offering: for my name shall be great among the heathen, saith the Lord of hosts.

3. Malachi 2:2-3:

[2] If ye will not hear, and if ye will not lay it to heart, to give glory unto my name, saith the Lord of hosts, I will even send a curse upon you, and I will curse your blessings: yea, I have cursed them already, because ye do not lay it to heart. [3] Behold, I will corrupt your seed, and spread dung upon your faces, even the dung of your solemn feasts; and one shall take you away with it.

4. Malachi 3:1:

[1] Behold, I will send my messenger, and he shall prepare the way before me: and the Lord, whom ye seek, shall suddenly come to his temple, even the messenger of the covenant, whom ye delight in: behold, he shall come, saith the Lord of hosts.

5. Malachi 3:17-18:

[17] And they shall be mine, saith the Lord of hosts, in that day when I make up my jewels; and I will spare them, as a man spareth his own son that serveth him. [18] Then shall ye return, and discern between the righteous and the wicked, between him that serveth God and him that serveth him not.

PROPHECIES IN NEW TESTAMENT

PROPHECIES IN SAINT MATTHEW: 44

1. Matthew 1:21-23:

[21] And she shall bring forth a son, and thou shalt call his name JESUS: for he shall save his people from their sins. [22] Now all this was done, that it might be fulfilled which was spoken of the Lord by the prophet, saying, [23] Behold, a virgin shall be with child, and shall bring forth a son, and they shall call his name Emmanuel, which being interpreted is, God with us.

2. Matthew 2:6:

[6] And thou Bethlehem, in the land of Juda, art not the least among the princes of Juda: for out of thee shall come a Governor, that shall rule my people Israel.

3. Matthew 2:13:

[13] And when they were departed, behold, the angel of the Lord appeareth to Joseph in a dream, saying, Arise, and take the young child and his mother, and flee into Egypt, and be thou there until I bring thee word: for Herod will seek the young child to destroy him.

4. Matthew 2:15:

[15] And was there until the death of Herod: that it might

be fulfilled which was spoken of the Lord by the prophet, saying, Out of Egypt have I called my son.

5. Matthew 2:18:

[18] In Rama was there a voice heard, lamentation, and weeping, and great mourning, Rachel weeping for her children, and would not be comforted, because they are not.

6. Matthew 2:23:

[23] And he came and dwelt in a city called Nazareth: that it might be fulfilled which was spoken by the prophets, He shall be called a Nazarene.

7. Matthew 3:3:

[3] For this is he that was spoken of by the prophet Esaias, saying, The voice of one crying in the wilderness, Prepare ye the way of the Lord, make his paths straight.

8. Matthew 4:14-16:

[14] That it might be fulfilled which was spoken by Esaias the prophet, saying,
[15] The land of Zabulon, and the land of Nephthalim, by the way of the sea, beyond Jordan, Galilee of the Gentiles; [16] The people which sat in darkness saw great light; and to them which sat in the region and shadow of death light is sprung up.

9. Matthew 8:17:

[17] That it might be fulfilled which was spoken by Esaias the prophet, saying, Himself took our infirmities, and bare our sicknesses.

10. Matthew 9:15:

[15] And Jesus said unto them, Can the children of the bridechamber mourn, as long as the bridegroom is with them? but the days will come, when the bridegroom shall be taken from them, and then shall they fast.

11. Matthew 10:15-26:

[15] Verily I say unto you, It shall be more tolerable for the land of Sodom and Gomorrha in the day of judgment, than for that city. [16] Behold, I send you forth as sheep in the midst of wolves: be ye therefore wise as serpents, and harmless as doves. [17] But beware of men: for they will deliver you up to the councils, and they will scourge you in their synagogues; [18] And ye shall be brought before governors and kings for my sake, for a testimony against them and the Gentiles. [19] But when they deliver you up, take no thought how or what ye shall speak: for it shall be given you in that same hour what ye shall speak. [20] For it is not ye that speak, but the Spirit of your Father which speaketh in you. [21] And the brother shall deliver up the brother to death, and the father the child: and the children shall rise up against their parents, and cause them to be put to death. [22] And ye shall be hated

of all men for my name's sake: but he that endureth to the end shall be saved. [23] But when they persecute you in this city, flee ye into another: for verily I say unto you, Ye shall not have gone over the cities of Israel, till the Son of man be come. [24] The disciple is not above his master, nor the servant above his lord. [25] It is enough for the disciple that he be as his master, and the servant as his lord. If they have called the master of the house Beelzebub, how much more shall they call them of his household? [26] Fear them not therefore: for there is nothing covered, that shall not be revealed; and hid, that shall not be known.

12. Matthew 10:32-33:

[32] Whosoever therefore shall confess me before men, him will I confess also before my Father which is in heaven. [33] But whosoever shall deny me before men, him will I also deny before my Father which is in heaven.

13. Matthew 12:17-18:

[17] That it might be fulfilled which was spoken by Esaias the prophet, saying, [18] Behold my servant, whom I have chosen; my beloved, in whom my soul is well pleased: I will put my spirit upon him, and he shall shew judgment to the Gentiles.

14. Matthew 12:36-37:

[36] But I say unto you, That every idle word that men

shall speak, they shall give account thereof in the day of judgment. [37] For by thy words thou shalt be justified, and by thy words thou shalt be condemned.

15. Matthew 12:39-40:

[39] But he answered and said unto them, An evil and adulterous generation seeketh after a sign; and there shall no sign be given to it, but the sign of the prophet Jonas: [40] For as Jonas was three days and three nights in the whale's belly; so shall the Son of man be three days and three nights in the heart of the earth.

16. Matthew 13:14-15:

[14] And in them is fulfilled the prophecy of Esaias, which saith, By hearing ye shall hear, and shall not understand; and seeing ye shall see, and shall not perceive: [15] For this people's heart is waxed gross, and their ears are dull of hearing, and their eyes they have closed; lest at any time they should see with their eyes, and hear with their ears, and should understand with their heart, and should be converted, and I should heal them.

17. Matthew 13:35:

[35] That it might be fulfilled which was spoken by the prophet, saying, I will open my mouth in parables; I will utter things which have been kept secret from the foundation of the world.

18. Matthew 16:18-19:

[18] And I say also unto thee, That thou art Peter, and upon this rock I will build my church; and the gates of hell shall not prevail against it. [19] And I will give unto thee the keys of the kingdom of heaven: and whatsoever thou shalt bind on earth shall be bound in heaven: and whatsoever thou shalt loose on earth shall be loosed in heaven.

19. Matthew 16:21:

[21] From that time forth began Jesus to shew unto his disciples, how that he must go unto Jerusalem, and suffer many things of the elders and chief priests and scribes, and be killed, and be raised again the third day.

20. Matthew 16:27:

[27] For the Son of man shall come in the glory of his Father with his angels; and then he shall reward every man according to his works.

21. Matthew 17:11:

[11] And Jesus answered and said unto them, Elias truly shall first come, and restore all things.

22. Matthew 17:22-23:

[22] And while they abode in Galilee, Jesus said unto them, The Son of man shall be betrayed into the hands of

men: [23] And they shall kill him, and the third day he shall be raised again. And they were exceeding sorry.

23. Matthew 19:28-30:

[28] And Jesus said unto them, Verily I say unto you, That ye which have followed me, in the regeneration when the Son of man shall sit in the throne of his glory, ye also shall sit upon twelve thrones, judging the twelve tribes of Israel. [29] And every one that hath forsaken houses, or brethren, or sisters, or father, or mother, or wife, or children, or lands, for my name's sake, shall receive an hundredfold, and shall inherit everlasting life. [30] But many that are first shall be last; and the last shall be first.

24. Matthew 20:18-19:

[18] Behold, we go up to Jerusalem; and the Son of man shall be betrayed unto the chief priests and unto the scribes, and they shall condemn him to death, [19] And shall deliver him to the Gentiles to mock, and to scourge, and to crucify him: and the third day he shall rise again.

25. Matthew 20:23:

[23] And he saith unto them, Ye shall drink indeed of my cup, and be baptized with the baptism that I am baptized with: but to sit on my right hand, and on my left, is not mine to give, but it shall be given to them for whom it is prepared of my Father.

26. Matthew 21:2-3:

[2] Saying unto them, Go into the village over against you, and straightway ye shall find an ass tied, and a colt with her: loose them, and bring them unto me. [3] And if any man say ought unto you, ye shall say, The Lord hath need of them; and straightway he will send them.

27. Matthew 21:4-5:

[4] All this was done, that it might be fulfilled which was spoken by the prophet, saying, [5] Tell ye the daughter of Sion, Behold, thy King cometh unto thee, meek, and sitting upon an ass, and a colt the foal of an ass.

29. Matthew 21:9:

[9] And the multitudes that went before, and that followed, cried, saying, Hosanna to the Son of David: Blessed is he that cometh in the name of the Lord; Hosanna in the highest.

30. Matthew 21:42-43:

[42] Jesus saith unto them, Did ye never read in the scriptures, The stone which the builders rejected, the same is become the head of the corner: this is the Lord's doing, and it is marvellous in our eyes[43] ? Therefore say I unto you, The kingdom of God shall be taken from you, and given to a nation bringing forth the fruits thereof.

31. Matthew 22:44:

[44] The Lord said unto my Lord, Sit thou on my right hand, till I make thine enemies thy footstool?

32. Matthew 23:34-36:

[34] Wherefore, behold, I send unto you prophets, and wise men, and scribes: and some of them ye shall kill and crucify; and some of them shall ye scourge in your synagogues, and persecute them from city to city: [35] That upon you may come all the righteous blood shed upon the earth, from the blood of righteous Abel unto the blood of Zacharias son of Barachias, whom ye slew between the temple and the altar. [36] Verily I say unto you, All these things shall come upon this generation.

33. Matthew 24:2:

[2] And Jesus said unto them, See ye not all these things? verily I say unto you, There shall not be left here one stone upon another, that shall not be thrown down.

34. Matthew 24:4-14:

[4] And Jesus answered and said unto them, Take heed that no man deceive you. [5] For many shall come in my name, saying, I am Christ; and shall deceive many. [6] And ye shall hear of wars and rumours of wars: see that ye be not troubled: for all these things must come to pass, but the end is not yet.
[7] For nation shall rise against nation, and kingdom

*against kingdom: and there shall be famines, and pesti-
lences, and earthquakes, in divers places. [8] All these
are the beginning of sorrows. [9] Then shall they deliver
you up to be afflicted, and shall kill you: and ye shall be
hated of all nations for my name's sake. [10] And then
shall many be offended, and shall betray one another,
and shall hate one another. [11] And many false prophets shall rise, and shall deceive many. [12] And because
iniquity shall abound, the love of many shall wax cold.
[13] But he that shall endure unto the end, the same shall
be saved. [14] And this gospel of the kingdom shall be
preached in all the world for a witness unto all nations;
and then shall the end come.*

35. Matthew 26:2:

*[2] Ye know that after two days is the feast of the pass-
over, and the Son of man is betrayed to be crucified.*

36. Matthew 26:12-13:

*[12] For in that she hath poured this ointment on my
body, she did it for my burial. [13] Verily I say unto you,
Wheresoever this gospel shall be preached in the whole
world, there shall also this, that this woman hath done, be
told for a memorial of her.*

37. Matthew 26:21:

*[21] And as they did eat, he said, Verily I say unto you,
that one of you shall betray me.*

38. Matthew 26:26-29:

[26] And as they were eating, Jesus took bread, and blessed it, and brake it, and gave it to the disciples, and said, Take, eat; this is my body. [27] And he took the cup, and gave thanks, and gave it to them, saying, Drink ye all of it; [28] For this is my blood of the new testament, which is shed for many for the remission of sins. [29] But I say unto you, I will not drink henceforth of this fruit of the vine, until that day when I drink it new with you in my Father's kingdom.

39. Matthew 26:31-32:

[31] Then saith Jesus unto them, All ye shall be offended because of me this night: for it is written, I will smite the shepherd, and the sheep of the flock shall be scattered abroad. [32] But after I am risen again, I will go before you into Galilee.

40. Matthew 26:34:

[34] Jesus said unto him, Verily I say unto thee, That this night, before the cock crow, thou shalt deny me thrice.

41. Matthew 26:45-46:

[45] Then cometh he to his disciples, and saith unto them, Sleep on now, and take your rest: behold, the hour is at hand, and the Son of man is betrayed into the hands of sinners. [46] Rise, let us be going: behold, he is at hand that doth betray me.

42. Matthew 26:64:

[64] Jesus saith unto him, Thou hast said: nevertheless I say unto you, Hereafter shall ye see the Son of man sitting on the right hand of power, and coming in the clouds of heaven.

43. Matthew 27:9-10:

[9] Then was fulfilled that which was spoken by Jeremy the prophet, saying, And they took the thirty pieces of silver, the price of him that was valued, whom they of the children of Israel did value; [10] And gave them for the potter's field, as the Lord appointed me.

44. Matthew 27:34:

[34] They gave him vinegar to drink mingled with gall: and when he had tasted thereof, he would not drink.

PROPHECIES IN SAINT MARK: 37

1 Mark 1:2:

[2] As it is written in the prophets, Behold, I send my messenger before thy face, which shall prepare thy way before thee.

2. Mark 1:3:

[3] The voice of one crying in the wilderness, Prepare ye the way of the Lord, make his paths straight.

3. Mark 1:7:

[7] And preached, saying, There cometh one mightier than I after me, the latchet of whose shoes I am not worthy to stoop down and unloose.

4. Mark 2:20:

[20] But the days will come, when the bridegroom shall be taken away from them, and then shall they fast in those days.

5. Mark 4:12:

[12] That seeing they may see, and not perceive; and hearing they may hear, and not understand; lest at any

time they should be converted, and their sins should be forgiven them.

6. Mark 6:11:

[11] And whosoever shall not receive you, nor hear you, when ye depart thence, shake off the dust under your feet for a testimony against them. Verily I say unto you, It shall be more tolerable for Sodom and Gomorrha in the day of judgment, than for that city.

7. Mark 8:31.

[31] And he began to teach them, that the Son of man must suffer many things, and be rejected of the elders, and of the chief priests, and scribes, and be killed, and after three days rise again.

8. Mark 9:1:

[1] And he said unto them, Verily I say unto you, That there be some of them that stand here, which shall not taste of death, till they have seen the kingdom of God come with power.

9. Mark 9:9:

[9] And as they came down from the mountain, he charged them that they should tell no man what things they had seen, till the Son of man were risen from the dead.

10. Mark 9:12:

[12] And he answered and told them, Elias verily cometh first, and restoreth all things; and how it is written of the Son of man, that he must suffer many things, and be set at nought.

11. Mark 9:31:

[31] For he taught his disciples, and said unto them, The Son of man is delivered into the hands of men, and they shall kill him; and after that he is killed, he shall rise the third day.

12. Mark 9:43-48:

[43] And if thy hand offend thee, cut it off: it is better for thee to enter into life maimed, than having two hands to go into hell, into the fire that never shall be quenched: [44] Where their worm dieth not, and the fire is not quenched. [45] And if thy foot offend thee, cut it off: it is better for thee to enter halt into life, than having two feet to be cast into hell, into the fire that never shall be quenched: [46] Where their worm dieth not, and the fire is not quenched. [47] And if thine eye offend thee, pluck it out: it is better for thee to enter into the kingdom of God with one eye, than having two eyes to be cast into hell fire: [48] Where their worm dieth not, and the fire is not quenched.

13. Mark 10:29-30:

[29] And Jesus answered and said, Verily I say unto you, There is no man that hath left house, or brethren, or sisters, or father, or mother, or wife, or children, or lands, for my sake, and the gospel's, [30] But he shall receive an hundredfold now in this time, houses, and brethren, and sisters, and mothers, and children, and lands, with persecutions; and in the world to come eternal life.

14. Mark 10:33-34:

[33] Saying, Behold, we go up to Jerusalem; and the Son of man shall be delivered unto the chief priests, and unto the scribes; and they shall condemn him to death, and shall deliver him to the Gentiles: [34] And they shall mock him, and shall scourge him, and shall spit upon him, and shall kill him: and the third day he shall rise again.

15. Mark 10:39-40:

[39] And they said unto him, We can. And Jesus said unto them, Ye shall indeed drink of the cup that I drink of; and with the baptism that I am baptized withal shall ye be baptized: [40] But to sit on my right hand and on my left hand is not mine to give; but it shall be given to them for whom it is prepared.

16. Mark 10:45:

[45] For even the Son of man came not to be ministered unto, but to minister, and to give his life a ransom for many.

17. Mark 11:2-3:

[2] And saith unto them, Go your way into the village over against you: and as soon as ye be entered into it, ye shall find a colt tied, whereon never man sat; loose him, and bring him. [3] And if any man say unto you, Why do ye this? say ye that the Lord hath need of him; and straightway he will send him hither.

18. Mark 11:17:

[17] And he taught, saying unto them, Is it not written, My house shall be called of all nations the house of prayer? but ye have made it a den of thieves.

19. Mark 11:23:

[23] For verily I say unto you, That whosoever shall say unto this mountain, Be thou removed, and be thou cast into the sea; and shall not doubt in his heart, but shall believe that those things which he saith shall come to pass; he shall have whatsoever he saith.

20. Mark 12:10-11:

[10] And have ye not read this scripture; The stone which the builders rejected is become the head of the corner: [11] This was the Lord's doing, and it is marvellous in our eyes?

21. Mark 12:24-27:

[24] And Jesus answering said unto them, Do ye not therefore err, because ye know not the scriptures, neither the power of God? [25] For when they shall rise from the dead, they neither marry, nor are given in marriage; but are as the angels which are in heaven. [26] And as touching the dead, that they rise: have ye not read in the book of Moses, how in the bush God spake unto him, saying, I am the God of Abraham, and the God of Isaac, and the God of Jacob? [27] He is not the God of the dead, but the God of the living: ye therefore do greatly err.

23. Mark 12:36-37:

[36] For David himself said by the Holy Ghost, The Lord said to my Lord, Sit thou on my right hand, till I make thine enemies thy footstool. [37] David therefore himself calleth him Lord; and whence is he then his son? And the common people heard him gladly.

24. Mark 12:40:

[40] Which devour widows' houses, and for a pretence make long prayers: these shall receive greater damnation.

25. Mark 13:2:

[2] And Jesus answering said unto him, Seest thou these great buildings? there shall not be left one stone upon another, that shall not be thrown down.

26. Mark 13:5-13:

[5] And Jesus answering them began to say, Take heed lest any man deceive you: [6] For many shall come in my name, saying, I am Christ; and shall deceive many. [7] And when ye shall hear of wars and rumours of wars, be ye not troubled: for such things must needs be; but the end shall not be yet. [8] For nation shall rise against nation, and kingdom against kingdom: and there shall be earthquakes in divers places, and there shall be famines and troubles: these are the beginnings of sorrows. [9] But take heed to yourselves: for they shall deliver you up to councils; and in the synagogues ye shall be beaten: and ye shall be brought before rulers and kings for my sake, for a testimony against them. [10] And the gospel must first be published among all nations. [11] But when they shall lead you, and deliver you up, take no thought beforehand what ye shall speak, neither do ye premeditate: but whatsoever shall be given you in that hour, that speak

*ye: for it is not ye that speak, but the Holy Ghost. [12]
Now the brother shall betray the brother to death, and
the father the son; and children shall rise up against their
parents, and shall cause them to be put to death. [13] And
ye shall be hated of all men for my name's sake: but he
that shall endure unto the end, the same shall be saved.*

27. Mark 14:8-9:

*[8] She hath done what she could: she is come aforehand
to anoint my body to the burying. [9] Verily I say unto
you, Wheresoever this gospel shall be preached throughout the whole world, this also that she hath done shall be
spoken of for a memorial of her.*

28. Mark 14:13-14:

*[13] And he sendeth forth two of his disciples, and saith
unto them, Go ye into the city, and there shall meet you
a man bearing a pitcher of water: follow him. [14] And
wheresoever he shall go in, say ye to the goodman of
the house, The Master saith, Where is the guestchamber,
where I shall eat the passover with my disciples?*

29. Mark 14:18:

*[18] And as they sat and did eat, Jesus said, Verily I say
unto you, One of you which eateth with me shall betray
me.*

30. Mark 14:20:

   [20] And he answered and said unto them, It is one of the twelve, that dippeth with me in the dish.

31. Mark 14:22-25:

   [22] And as they did eat, Jesus took bread, and blessed, and brake it, and gave to them, and said, Take, eat: this is my body. [23] And he took the cup, and when he had given thanks, he gave it to them: and they all drank of it. [24] And he said unto them, This is my blood of the new testament, which is shed for many. [25] Verily I say unto you, I will drink no more of the fruit of the vine, until that day that I drink it new in the kingdom of God.

32. Mark 14:27-28:

   [27] And Jesus saith unto them, All ye shall be offended because of me this night: for it is written, I will smite the shepherd, and the sheep shall be scattered. [28] But after that I am risen, I will go before you into Galilee.

33. Mark 14:30:

   [30] And Jesus saith unto him, Verily I say unto thee, That this day, even in this night, before the cock crow twice, thou shalt deny me thrice.

34. Mark 14:40-42:

   [40] And when he returned, he found them asleep again,

*(for their eyes were heavy,) neither wist they what to
answer him. [41] And he cometh the third time, and saith
unto them, Sleep on now, and take your rest: it is enough,
the hour is come; behold, the Son of man is betrayed into
the hands of sinners. [42] Rise up, let us go; lo, he that
betrayeth me is at hand.*

35. Mark 14:62:

*[62] And Jesus said, I am: and ye shall see the Son of
man sitting on the right hand of power, and coming in the
clouds of heaven.*

36. Mark 15:28:

*[28] And the scripture was fulfilled, which saith, And he
was numbered with the transgressors.*

37. Mark 15:34-36:

*[34] And at the ninth hour Jesus cried with a loud voice,
saying, Eloi, Eloi, lama sabachthani? which is, being interpreted, My God, my God, why hast thou forsaken me?
[35] And some of them that stood by, when they heard it,
said, Behold, he calleth Elias. [36] And one ran and filled
a spunge full of vinegar, and put it on a reed, and gave
him to drink, saying, Let alone; let us see whether Elias
will come to take him down.*

PROPHECIES IN SAINT LUKE: 50

1. Luke 1:13-17:

[13] But the angel said unto him, Fear not, Zacharias: for thy prayer is heard; and thy wife Elisabeth shall bear thee a son, and thou shalt call his name John. [14] And thou shalt have joy and gladness; and many shall rejoice at his birth. [15] For he shall be great in the sight of the Lord, and shall drink neither wine nor strong drink; and he shall be filled with the Holy Ghost, even from his mother's womb. [16] And many of the children of Israel shall he turn to the Lord their God. [17] And he shall go before him in the spirit and power of Elias, to turn the hearts of the fathers to the children, and the disobedient to the wisdom of the just; to make ready a people prepared for the Lord.

2. Luke 1:20:

[20] And, behold, thou shalt be dumb, and not able to speak, until the day that these things shall be performed, because thou believest not my words, which shall be fulfilled in their season.

3. Luke 1:28:

[28] And the angel came in unto her, and said, Hail, thou that art highly favoured, the Lord is with thee: blessed art

thou among women.

4. Luke 1:30-33:

[30] And the angel said unto her, Fear not, Mary: for thou hast found favour with God. [31] And, behold, thou shalt conceive in thy womb, and bring forth a son, and shalt call his name JESUS. [32] He shall be great, and shall be called the Son of the Highest: and the Lord God shall give unto him the throne of his father David: [33] And he shall reign over the house of Jacob for ever; and of his kingdom there shall be no end.

5. Luke 1:35:

[35] And the angel answered and said unto her, The Holy Ghost shall come upon thee, and the power of the Highest shall overshadow thee: therefore also that holy thing which shall be born of thee shall be called the Son of God.

6. Luke 1:42-46:

[42] And she spake out with a loud voice, and said, Blessed art thou among women, and blessed is the fruit of thy womb. [43] And whence is this to me, that the mother of my Lord should come to me? [44] For, lo, as soon as the voice of thy salutation sounded in mine ears, the babe leaped in my womb for joy. [45] And blessed is she that believed: for there shall be a performance of those things which were told her from the Lord. [46] And Mary said,

My soul doth magnify the Lord, my spirit hath rejoiced in God my Saviour.

7. Luke 1:67-75:

[67] And his father Zacharias was filled with the Holy Ghost, and prophesied, saying, [68] Blessed be the Lord God of Israel; for he hath visited and redeemed his people, [69] And hath raised up an horn of salvation for us in the house of his servant David; [70] As he spake by the mouth of his holy prophets, which have been since the world began: [71] That we should be saved from our enemies, and from the hand of all that hate us; [72] To perform the mercy promised to our fathers, and to remember his holy covenant; [73] The oath which he sware to our father Abraham, {74] That he would grant unto us, that we being delivered out of the hand of our enemies might serve him without fear, [75] In holiness and righteousness before him, all the days of our life.

8. Luke 2:10-12:

[10] And the angel said unto them, Fear not: for, behold, I bring you good tidings of great joy, which shall be to all people. [11] For unto you is born this day in the city of David a Saviour, which is Christ the Lord. [12] And this shall be a sign unto you; Ye shall find the babe wrapped in swaddling clothes, lying in a manger.

9. Luke 2:26:

> *[26] And it was revealed unto him by the Holy Ghost, that he should not see death, before he had seen the Lord' s Christ.*

10. Luke 2:28-32:

> *[28] Then took he him up in his arms, and blessed God, and said, [29] Lord, now lettest thou thy servant depart in peace, according to thy word: [30] For mine eyes have seen thy salvation, [31] Which thou hast prepared before the face of all people; [32] A light to lighten the Gentiles, and the glory of thy people Israel.*

11. Luke 2:34-35:

> *[34] And Simeon blessed them, and said unto Mary his mother, Behold, this child is set for the fall and rising again of many in Israel; and for a sign which shall be spoken against; [35] Yea, a sword shall pierce through thy own soul also, that the thoughts of many hearts may be revealed.*

12. Luke 3:4-6:

> *[4] As it is written in the book of the words of Esaias the prophet, saying, The voice of one crying in the wilderness, Prepare ye the way of the Lord, make his paths straight. [5] Every valley shall be filled, and every mountain and hill shall be brought low; and the crooked shall be made straight, and the rough ways shall be made*

smooth; [6] And all flesh shall see the salvation of God.

13. Luke 3:9:

[9] And now also the axe is laid unto the root of the trees: every tree therefore which bringeth not forth good fruit is hewn down, and cast into the fire.

14. Luke 3:16-17:

[16] John answered, saying unto them all, I indeed baptize you with water; but one mightier than I cometh, the latchet of whose shoes I am not worthy to unloose: he shall baptize you with the Holy Ghost and with fire: [17] Whose fan is in his hand, and he will throughly purge his floor, and will gather the wheat into his garner; but the chaff he will burn with fire unquenchable.

15. Luke 4:17-19:

[17] And there was delivered unto him the book of the prophet Esaias. And when he had opened the book, he found the place where it was written, [18] The Spirit of the Lord is upon me, because he hath anointed me to preach the gospel to the poor; he hath sent me to heal the brokenhearted, to preach deliverance to the captives, and recovering of sight to the blind, to set at liberty them that are bruised, [19] To preach the acceptable year of the Lord.

16. Luke 5:10:

*[10] And so was also James, and John, the sons of Zebe-
dee, which were partners with Simon. And Jesus said unto
Simon, Fear not; from henceforth thou shalt catch men.*

17. Luke 6:20-26:

*[20] And he lifted up his eyes on his disciples, and said,
Blessed be ye poor: for yours is the kingdom of God. [21]
Blessed are ye that hunger now: for ye shall be filled.
Blessed are ye that weep now: for ye shall laugh. [22]
Blessed are ye, when men shall hate you, and when they
shall separate you from their company, and shall reproach you, and cast out your name as evil, for the Son of
man's sake. [23] Rejoice ye in that day, and leap for joy:
for, behold, your reward is great in heaven: for in the like
manner did their fathers unto the prophets. [24] But woe
unto you that are rich! for ye have received your consola-
tion. [25] Woe unto you that are full! for ye shall hunger.
Woe unto you that laugh now! for ye shall mourn and
weep. [26] Woe unto you, when all men shall speak well
of you! for so did their fathers to the false prophets.*

18. Luke 7:27:

*[27] This is he, of whom it is written, Behold, I send my
messenger before thy face, which shall prepare thy way
before thee.*

19. Luke 9:22:

*[22] Saying, The Son of man must suffer many things,
and be rejected of the elders and chief priests and scribes,
and be slain, and be raised the third day.*

20. Luke 9:24:

*[24] For whosoever will save his life shall lose it: but
whosoever will lose his life for my sake, the same shall
save it.*

21. Luke 9:44:

*[44] Let these sayings sink down into your ears: for the
Son of man shall be delivered into the hands of men.*

22. Luke 10:12:

*[10] But I say unto you, that it shall be more tolerable in
that day for Sodom, than for that city.*

23. Luke 11:29-30:

*[29] And when the people were gathered thick together,
he began to say, This is an evil generation: they seek a
sign; and there shall no sign be given it, but the sign of
Jonas the prophet. [30] For as Jonas was a sign unto the
Ninevites, so shall also the Son of man be to this generation.*

24. Luke 11:48-49:

[48] Truly ye bear witness that ye allow the deeds of your fathers: for they indeed killed them, and ye build their sepulchres. [49] Therefore also said the wisdom of God, I will send them prophets and apostles, and some of them they shall slay and persecute.

25. Luke 12:8-10:

[8] Also I say unto you, Whosoever shall confess me before men, him shall the Son of man also confess before the angels of God: [9] But he that denieth me before men shall be denied before the angels of God. [10] And whosoever shall speak a word against the Son of man, it shall be forgiven him: but unto him that blasphemeth against the Holy Ghost it shall not be forgiven.

26. Luke 13:3:

[3] I tell you, Nay: but, except ye repent, ye shall all likewise perish.

27. Luke 13:5:

[5] I tell you, Nay: but, except ye repent, ye shall all likewise perish.

28. Luke 13:24:

[24] Strive to enter in at the strait gate: for many, I say unto you, will seek to enter in, and shall not be able.

29. Luke 13:32:

[32] And he said unto them, Go ye, and tell that fox, Behold, I cast out devils, and I do cures to day and to morrow, and the third day I shall be perfected.

30. Luke 14:14:

[14] And thou shalt be blessed; for they cannot recompense thee: for thou shalt be recompensed at the resurrection of the just.

31. Luke 17:22:

[22] And he said unto the disciples, The days will come, when ye shall desire to see one of the days of the Son of man, and ye shall not see it.

32. Luke 18:29:

[29] And he said unto them, Verily I say unto you, There is no man that hath left house, or parents, or brethren, or wife, or children, for the kingdom of God's sake,

33. Luke 19:30-31:

[30] Saying, Go ye into the village over against you; in the which at your entering ye shall find a colt tied, whereon yet never man sat: loose him, and bring him hither. [31] And if any man ask you, Why do ye loose him ? thus shall ye say unto him, Because the Lord hath need of him.

34. Luke 19:38:

[38] Saying, Blessed be the King that cometh in the name of the Lord: peace in heaven, and glory in the highest.

35. Luke 19:46:

[46] Saying unto them, It is written, My house is the house of prayer: but ye have made it a den of thieves.

36. Luke 20:17-18:

[17] And he beheld them, and said, What is this then that is written, The stone which the builders rejected, the same is become the head of the corner? [18] Whosoever shall fall upon that stone shall be broken; but on whomsoever it shall fall, it will grind him to powder.

37. Luke 20:42:

[42] And David himself saith in the book of Psalms, The Lord said unto my Lord, Sit thou on my right hand,

38. Luke 20:47:

[47] Which devour widows' houses, and for a shew make long prayers: the same shall receive greater damnation.

39 Luke 21:6:

[6] As for these things which ye behold, the days will come, in the which there shall not be left one stone upon another, that shall not be thrown down.

40 Luke 21:8-11:

[8] And he said, Take heed that ye be not deceived: for many shall come in my name, saying, I am Christ; and the time draweth near: go ye not therefore after them. [9] But when ye shall hear of wars and commotions, be not terrified: for these things must first come to pass; but the end is not by and by. [10] Then said he unto them, Nation shall rise against nation, and kingdom against kingdom: [11] And great earthquakes shall be in divers places, and famines, and pestilences; and fearful sights and great signs shall there be from heaven.

41. Luke 22:10:

[10] And he said unto them, Behold, when ye are entered into the city, there shall a man meet you, bearing a pitcher of water; follow him into the house where he entereth in.

42. Luke 22:15-16:

[15] And he said unto them, With desire I have desired to eat this passover with you before I suffer: [16] For I say unto you, I will not any more eat thereof, until it be fulfilled in the kingdom of God.

43. Luke 22:29-30:

[29] And I appoint unto you a kingdom, as my Father hath appointed unto me; [30] That ye may eat and drink at my table in my kingdom, and sit on thrones judging the

twelve tribes of Israel.

44. Luke 22:31-32:

[31] And the Lord said, Simon, Simon, behold, Satan hath desired to have you, that he may sift you as wheat: [32] But I have prayed for thee, that thy faith fail not: and when thou art converted, strengthen thy brethren.

45. Luke 22:34:

[34] And he said, I tell thee, Peter, the cock shall not crow this day, before that thou shalt thrice deny that thou knowest me.

46. Luke 22:37:

[37] For I say unto you, that this that is written must yet be accomplished in me, And he was reckoned among the transgressors: for the things concerning me have an end.

47. Luke 23:28-30:

[28] But Jesus turning unto them said, Daughters of Jerusalem, weep not for me, but weep for yourselves, and for your children. [29] For, behold, the days are coming, in the which they shall say, Blessed are the barren, and the wombs that never bare, and the paps which never gave suck. [30] Then shall they begin to say to the mountains, Fall on us; and to the hills, Cover us.

48. Luke 23:43:

[43] And Jesus said unto him, Verily I say unto thee, To day shalt thou be with me in paradise.

49. Luke 24:7:

[7] Saying, The Son of man must be delivered into the hands of sinful men, and be crucified, and the third day rise again.

50. Luke 24:49:

[49] And, behold, I send the promise of my Father upon you: but tarry ye in the city of Jerusalem, until ye be endued with power from on high.

PROPHECIES IN SAINT JOHN: 55

1. John 1:23:

*[23] He said, I am the voice of one crying in the wil-
derness, Make straight the way of the Lord, as said the
prophet Esaias.*

2. John 1:29-33:

*[29] The next day John seeth Jesus coming unto him, and
saith, Behold the Lamb of God, which taketh away the
sin of the world. [30] This is he of whom I said, After me
cometh a man which is preferred before me: for he was
before me. [31] And I knew him not: but that he should
be made manifest to Israel, therefore am I come baptizing
with water. [32] And John bare record, saying, I saw the
Spirit descending from heaven like a dove, and it abode
upon him. [33] And I knew him not: but he that sent me
to baptize with water, the same said unto me, Upon whom
thou shalt see the Spirit descending, and remaining on
him, the same is he which baptizeth with the Holy Ghost.*

3. John 1:50-51:

*[50] Jesus answered and said unto him, Because I said
unto thee, I saw thee under the fig tree, believest thou?
thou shalt see greater things than these. [51] And he saith
unto him, Verily, verily, I say unto you, Hereafter ye shall*

see heaven open, and the angels of God ascending and descending upon the Son of man.

4. John 2:17:

[17] And his disciples remembered that it was written, The zeal of thine house hath eaten me up.

5. John 2:19:

[19] Jesus answered and said unto them, Destroy this temple, and in three days I will raise it up.

6. John 3:14-15:

[14] And as Moses lifted up the serpent in the wilderness, even so must the Son of man be lifted up: [15] That whosoever believeth in him should not perish, but have eternal life.

7. John 3:30-31:

[30] He must increase, but I must decrease. [31] He that cometh from above is above all: he that is of the earth is earthly, and speaketh of the earth: he that cometh from heaven is above all.

8. John 4:21-24:

[21] Jesus saith unto her, Woman, believe me, the hour cometh, when ye shall neither in this mountain, nor yet at Jerusalem, worship the Father. [22] Ye worship ye know

not what: we know what we worship: for salvation is of the Jews. [23] But the hour cometh, and now is, when the true worshippers shall worship the Father in spirit and in truth: for the Father seeketh such to worship him. [24] God is a Spirit: and they that worship him must worship him in spirit and in truth.

9. John 4:50:

[50] Jesus saith unto him, Go thy way; thy son liveth. And the man believed the word that Jesus had spoken unto him, and he went his way.

10. John 5:20:

[20] For the Father loveth the Son, and sheweth him all things that himself doeth: and he will shew him greater works than these, that ye may marvel.

11. John 5:25:

[25] Verily, verily, I say unto you, The hour is coming, and now is, when the dead shall hear the voice of the Son of God: and they that hear shall live.

12. John 5:28-29:

[28] Marvel not at this: for the hour is coming, in the which all that are in the graves shall hear his voice, [29] And shall come forth; they that have done good, unto the resurrection of life; and they that have done evil, unto the resurrection of damnation.

13. John 5:43:

[43] I am come in my Father's name, and ye receive me not: if another shall come in his own name, him ye will receive.

14. John 6:35:

[35] And Jesus said unto them, I am the bread of life: he that cometh to me shall never hunger; and he that believeth on me shall never thirst.

15. John 6:37:

[37] All that the Father giveth me shall come to me; and him that cometh to me I will in no wise cast out.

16. John 6:39-40:

[39] And this is the Father's will which hath sent me, that of all which he hath given me I should lose nothing, but should raise it up again at the last day. [40] And this is the will of him that sent me, that every one which seeth the Son, and believeth on him, may have everlasting life: and I will raise him up at the last day.

17. John 6:44-45:

[44] No man can come to me, except the Father which hath sent me draw him: and I will raise him up at the last day. [45] It is written in the prophets, And they shall be all taught of God. Every man therefore that hath heard,

and hath learned of the Father, cometh unto me.

18. John 6:50-51:

This is the bread which cometh down from heaven, that a man may eat thereof, and not die. I am the living bread which came down from heaven: if any man eat of this bread, he shall live for ever: and the bread that I will give is my flesh, which I will give for the life of the world.

19. John 6:53-54:

[53] Then Jesus said unto them, Verily, verily, I say unto you, Except ye eat the flesh of the Son of man, and drink his blood, ye have no life in you[54] . Whoso eateth my flesh, and drinketh my blood, hath eternal life; and I will raise him up at the last day.

20. John 6:62:

[62] What and if ye shall see the Son of man ascend up where he was before?

21. John 7:33-34:

[33] Then said Jesus unto them, Yet a little while am I with you, and then I go unto him that sent me. [34] Ye shall seek me, and shall not find me: and where I am, thither ye cannot come.

22. John 7:42:

[42] Hath not the scripture said, That Christ cometh of the seed of David, and out of the town of Bethlehem, where David was?

23. John 8:21:

[21] Then said Jesus again unto them, I go my way, and ye shall seek me, and shall die in your sins: whither I go, ye cannot come.

24 John 10:14-18:

[14] I am the good shepherd, and know my sheep, and am known of mine. [15] As the Father knoweth me, even so know I the Father: and I lay down my life for the sheep. [16] And other sheep I have, which are not of this fold: them also I must bring, and they shall hear my voice; and there shall be one fold, and one shepherd. [17] Therefore doth my Father love me, because I lay down my life, that I might take it again. [18] No man taketh it from me, but I lay it down of myself. I have power to lay it down, and I have power to take it again. This commandment have I received of my Father.

25. John 11:51-52:

[51] And this spake he not of himself: but being high priest that year, he prophesied that Jesus should die for that nation; [52] And not for that nation only, but that also he should gather together in one the children of God

that were scattered abroad.

26. John 12:13:

> *[13] Took branches of palm trees, and went forth to meet him, and cried, Hosanna: Blessed is the King of Israel that cometh in the name of the Lord.*

27. John 12:15:

> *[15] Fear not, daughter of Sion: behold, thy King cometh, sitting on an ass's colt.*

28. John 12:23-24:

> *[23] And Jesus answered them, saying, The hour is come, that the Son of man should be glorified. [24] Verily, verily, I say unto you, Except a corn of wheat fall into the ground and die, it abideth alone: but if it die, it bringeth forth much fruit.*

29. John 12:31-32:

> *[31] Now is the judgment of this world: now shall the prince of this world be cast out. [32] And I, if I be lifted up from the earth, will draw all men unto me.*

30. John 12:38:

> *[38] That the saying of Esaias the prophet might be fulfilled, which he spake, Lord, who hath believed our report? and to whom hath the arm of the Lord been revealed?*

31. John 12:40:

[40] He hath blinded their eyes, and hardened their heart; that they should not see with their eyes, nor understand with their heart, and be converted, and I should heal them.

32. John 12:48:

[48] He that rejecteth me, and receiveth not my words, hath one that judgeth him: the word that I have spoken, the same shall judge him in the last day.

33 John 13:18.

[18] I speak not of you all: I know whom I have chosen: but that the scripture may be fulfilled, He that eateth bread with me hath lifted up his heel against me.

34. John 13:21:

[21] When Jesus had thus said, he was troubled in spirit, and testified, and said, Verily, verily, I say unto you, that one of you shall betray me.

35. John 13:26:

[26] Jesus answered, He it is, to whom I shall give a sop, when I have dipped it. And when he had dipped the sop, he gave it to Judas Iscariot, the son of Simon.

36. John 13:31-33:

> *[31] Therefore, when he was gone out, Jesus said, Now is the Son of man glorified, and God is glorified in him. [32] If God be glorified in him, God shall also glorify him in himself, and shall straightway glorify him. [33] Little children, yet a little while I am with you. Ye shall seek me: and as I said unto the Jews, Whither I go, ye cannot come; so now I say to you.*

37. John 13:36:

> *[36] Simon Peter said unto him, Lord, whither goest thou? Jesus answered him, Whither I go, thou canst not follow me now; but thou shalt follow me afterwards.*

38. John 13:38:

> *[38] Jesus answered him, Wilt thou lay down thy life for my sake? Verily, verily, I say unto thee, The cock shall not crow, till thou hast denied me thrice.*

39. John 14:1-3:

> *[1] Let not your heart be troubled: ye believe in God, believe also in me. [2] In my Father's house are many mansions: if it were not so, I would have told you. I go to prepare a place for you. [3] And if I go and prepare a place for you, I will come again, and receive you unto myself; that where I am, there ye may be also.*

40. John 14:16-21:

[16] And I will pray the Father, and he shall give you another Comforter, that he may abide with you for ever; [17] Even the Spirit of truth; whom the world cannot receive, because it seeth him not, neither knoweth him: but ye know him; for he dwelleth with you, and shall be in you. [18] I will not leave you comfortless: I will come to you. [19] Yet a little while, and the world seeth me no more; but ye see me: because I live, ye shall live also. [20] At that day ye shall know that I am in my Father, and ye in me, and I in you. [21] He that hath my command-ments, and keepeth them, he it is that loveth me: and he that loveth me shall be loved of my Father, and I will love him, and will manifest myself to him.

41. John 14:23-26:

[23] Jesus answered and said unto him, If a man love me, he will keep my words: and my Father will love him, and we will come unto him, and make our abode with him. [24] He that loveth me not keepeth not my sayings: and the word which ye hear is not mine, but the Father's which sent me. [25] These things have I spoken unto you, being yet present with you. [26] But the Comforter, which is the Holy Ghost, whom the Father will send in my name, he shall teach you all things, and bring all things to your remembrance, whatsoever I have said unto you.

42. John 14:28:

[28] Ye have heard how I said unto you, I go away, and come again unto you. If ye loved me, ye would rejoice, because I said, I go unto the Father: for my Father is greater than I.

43. John 15:18:

[18] If the world hate you, ye know that it hated me before it hated you.

44. John 15:25-27:

[25] But this cometh to pass, that the word might be fulfilled that is written in their law, They hated me without a cause. [26] But when the Comforter is come, whom I will send unto you from the Father, even the Spirit of truth, which proceedeth from the Father, he shall testify of me: [27] And ye also shall bear witness, because ye have been with me from the beginning.

45. John 16:1-16:

[1] These things have I spoken unto you, that ye should not be offended. [2] They shall put you out of the synagogues: yea, the time cometh, that whosoever killeth you will think that he doeth God service. [3] And these things will they do unto you, because they have not known the Father, nor me. [4] But these things have I told you, that when the time shall come, ye may remember that I told you of them. And these things I said not unto you at the beginning, because I was with you. [5] But now I go

my way to him that sent me; and none of you asketh me, Whither goest thou? [6] But because I have said these things unto you, sorrow hath filled your heart. [7] Nevertheless I tell you the truth; It is expedient for you that I go away: for if I go not away, the Comforter will not come unto you; but if I depart, I will send him unto you. [8] And when he is come, he will reprove the world of sin, and of righteousness, and of judgment: [9] Of sin, because they believe not on me; [10] Of righteousness, because I go to my Father, and ye see me no more; [11] Of judgment, because the prince of this world is judged. [12] I have yet many things to say unto you, but ye cannot bear them now. [13] Howbeit when he, the Spirit of truth, is come, he will guide you into all truth: for he shall not speak of himself; but whatsoever he shall hear, that shall he speak: and he will shew you things to come. [14] He shall glorify me: for he shall receive of mine, and shall shew it unto you. [15] All things that the Father hath are mine: therefore said I, that he shall take of mine, and shall shew it unto you. [16] A little while, and ye shall not see me: and again, a little while, and ye shall see me, because I go to the Father.

46. John 16:19-20:

[19] Now Jesus knew that they were desirous to ask him, and said unto them, Do ye enquire among yourselves of that I said, A little while, and ye shall not see me: and again, a little while, and ye shall see me? [20] Verily, verily, I say unto you, That ye shall weep and lament, but the

*world shall rejoice: and ye shall be sorrowful, but your
sorrow shall be turned into joy.*

47. John 16:32:

*[32] Behold, the hour cometh, yea, is now come, that ye
shall be scattered, every man to his own, and shall leave
me alone: and yet I am not alone, because the Father is
with me.*

48. John 17:12:

*[12] While I was with them in the world, I kept them in
thy name: those that thou gavest me I have kept, and none
of them is lost, but the son of perdition; that the scripture
might be fulfilled.*

49. John 18:9:

*[9] That the saying might be fulfilled, which he spake, Of
them which thou gavest me have I lost none.*

50. John 19:24:

*[24] They said therefore among themselves, Let us not
rend it, but cast lots for it, whose it shall be: that the
scripture might be fulfilled, which saith, They parted my
raiment among them, and for my vesture they did cast
lots. These things therefore the soldiers did.*

51. John 19:28:

[28] After this, Jesus knowing that all things were now accomplished, that the scripture might be fulfilled, saith, I thirst.

52. John 19:36-37:

[36] For these things were done, that the scripture should be fulfilled, A bone of him shall not be broken. [37] And again another scripture saith, They shall look on him whom they pierced.

53. John 20:9:

[9] For as yet they knew not the scripture, that he must rise again from the dead.

54. John 20:17:

[17] Jesus saith unto her, Touch me not; for I am not yet ascended to my Father: but go to my brethren, and say unto them, I ascend unto my Father, and your Father; and to my God, and your God.

55. John 21:18:

[18] Verily, verily, I say unto thee, When thou wast young, thou girdedst thyself, and walkedst whither thou wouldest: but when thou shalt be old, thou shalt stretch forth thy hands, and another shall gird thee, and carry thee whither thou wouldest not.

PROPHECIES IN ACTS OF THE APOSTLES: 32

1. Acts 1:5:

[5] For John truly baptized with water; but ye shall be baptized with the Holy Ghost not many days hence.

2. Acts 1:8:

[8] But ye shall receive power, after that the Holy Ghost is come upon you: and ye shall be witnesses unto me both in Jerusalem, and in all Judaea, and in Samaria, and unto the uttermost part of the earth.

3. Acts 1:11:

[11] Which also said, Ye men of Galilee, why stand ye gazing up into heaven? This same Jesus, which is taken up from you into heaven, shall so come in like manner as ye have seen him go into heaven.

4. Acts 1:20:

[20] For it is written in the book of Psalms, Let his habitation be desolate, and let no man dwell therein: and his bishoprick let another take.

5. Acts 2:16-21:

[16] But this is that which was spoken by the prophet

Joel; [17] And it shall come to pass in the last days, saith God, I will pour out of my Spirit upon all flesh: and your sons and your daughters shall prophesy, and your young men shall see visions, and your old men shall dream dreams: [18] And on my servants and on my handmaidens I will pour out in those days of my Spirit; and they shall prophesy: [19] And I will shew wonders in heaven above, and signs in the earth beneath; blood, and fire, and vapour of smoke: [20] The sun shall be turned into darkness, and the moon into blood, before that great and notable day of the Lord come: [21] And it shall come to pass, that whosoever shall call on the name of the Lord shall be saved.

6. Acts 2:25-27:

[25] For David speaketh concerning him, I foresaw the Lord always before my face, for he is on my right hand, that I should not be moved: [26] Therefore did my heart rejoice, and my tongue was glad; moreover also my flesh shall rest in hope: [26] Because thou wilt not leave my soul in hell, neither wilt thou suffer thine Holy One to see corruption.

7. Acts 2:30-31:

[30] Therefore being a prophet, and knowing that God had sworn with an oath to him, that of the fruit of his loins, according to the flesh, he would raise up Christ to sit on his throne; [31] He seeing this before spake of the resurrection of Christ, that his soul was not left in hell,

neither his flesh did see corruption.

8. Acts 2:34-35:

[34] For David is not ascended into the heavens: but he saith himself, The Lord said unto my Lord, Sit thou on my right hand, [35] Until I make thy foes thy footstool.

9. Acts 3:22-23:

[22] For Moses truly said unto the fathers, A prophet shall the Lord your God raise up unto you of your brethren, like unto me; him shall ye hear in all things whatsoever he shall say unto you. [23] And it shall come to pass, that every soul, which will not hear that prophet, shall be destroyed from among the people.

10. Acts 3:25:

[25] Ye are the children of the prophets, and of the covenant which God made with our fathers, saying unto Abraham, And in thy seed shall all the kindreds of the earth be blessed.

11. Acts 4:11:

[11] This is the stone which was set at nought of you builders, which is become the head of the corner.

12. Acts 4:25:

[25] Who by the mouth of thy servant David hast said,

Why did the heathen rage, and the people imagine vain things?

13. Acts 7:6-7:

[6] And God spake on this wise, That his seed should sojourn in a strange land; and that they should bring them into bondage, and entreat them evil four hundred years. [7] And the nation to whom they shall be in bondage will I judge, said God: and after that shall they come forth, and serve me in this place.

14. Acts 7:37:

[37] This is that Moses, which said unto the children of Israel, A prophet shall the Lord your God raise up unto you of your brethren, like unto me; him shall ye hear.

15. Acts 8:32-3)3

[32] The place of the scripture which he read was this, He was led as a sheep to the slaughter; and like a lamb dumb before his shearer, so opened he not his mouth: [33] In his humiliation his judgment was taken away: and who shall declare his generation? for his life is taken from the earth.

16. Acts 9:15-16:

[15] But the Lord said unto him, Go thy way: for he is a chosen vessel unto me, to bear my name before the Gentiles, and kings, and the children of Israel: [16] For I will

shew him how great things he must suffer for my name's sake.

17. Acts 11:28:

[28] And there stood up one of them named Agabus, and signified by the Spirit that there should be great dearth throughout all the world: which came to pass in the days of Claudius Caesar.

18. Acts 13:33-35:

[33] God hath fulfilled the same unto us their children, in that he hath raised up Jesus again; as it is also written in the second psalm, Thou art my Son, this day have I begotten thee. [34] And as concerning that he raised him up from the dead, now no more to return to corruption, he said on this wise, I will give you the sure mercies of David. [35] Wherefore he saith also in another psalm, Thou shalt not suffer thine Holy One to see corruption.

19. Acts 13:47:

[47] For so hath the Lord commanded us, saying, I have set thee to be a light of the Gentiles, that thou shouldest be for salvation unto the ends of the earth.

20. Acts 15:16-17:

[16] After this I will return, and will build again the tabernacle of David, which is fallen down; and I will build

*again the ruins thereof, and I will set it up: [17] That the
residue of men might seek after the Lord, and all the Gentiles, upon whom my name is called, saith the Lord, who
doeth all these things.*

21. Acts 17:31:

*[31] Because he hath appointed a day, in the which he
will judge the world in righteousness by that man whom
he hath ordained; whereof he hath given assurance unto
all men, in that he hath raised him from the dead.*

22. Acts 20:29-30:

*[29] For I know this, that after my departing shall griev-
ous wolves enter in among you, not sparing the flock.
[30] Also of your own selves shall men arise, speaking
perverse things, to draw away disciples after them.*

Acts 21:11:

*[11] And when he was come unto us, he took Paul's
girdle, and bound his own hands and feet, and said, Thus
saith the Holy Ghost, So shall the Jews at Jerusalem bind
the man that owneth this girdle, and shall deliver him into
the hands of the Gentiles.*

24. Acts 22:10:

*[10] And I said, What shall I do, Lord? And the Lord said
unto me, Arise, and go into Damascus; and there it shall*

be told thee of all things which are appointed for thee to do.

25. Acts 23:3:

[3] Then said Paul unto him, God shall smite thee, thou whited wall: for sittest thou to judge me after the law, and commandest me to be smitten contrary to the law?

26. Acts 23:11:

And the night following the Lord stood by him, and said, Be of good cheer, Paul: for as thou hast testified of me in Jerusalem, so must thou bear witness also at Rome.

27. Acts 26:16-18:

[16] But rise, and stand upon thy feet: for I have appeared unto thee for this purpose, to make thee a minister and a witness both of these things which thou hast seen, and of those things in the which I will appear unto thee; [17] Delivering thee from the people, and from the Gentiles, unto whom now I send thee, [18] To open their eyes, and to turn them from darkness to light, and from the power of Satan unto God, that they may receive forgiveness of sins, and inheritance among them which are sanctified by faith that is in me.

28. Acts 26:23:

[23] That Christ should suffer, and that he should be the first that should rise from the dead, and should shew light

unto the people, and to the Gentiles.

29. Acts 27:10:

[10] And said unto them, Sirs, I perceive that this voyage will be with hurt and much damage, not only of the lading and ship, but also of our lives.

30. Acts 27:22:

[22] And now I exhort you to be of good cheer: for there shall be no loss of any man's life among you, but of the ship.

31. Acts 27:34:

[34] Wherefore I pray you to take some meat: for this is for your health: for there shall not an hair fall from the head of any of you.

32. Acts 28:26-27:

[26] Saying, Go unto this people, and say, Hearing ye shall hear, and shall not understand; and seeing ye shall see, and not perceive: [27] For the heart of this people is waxed gross, and their ears are dull of hearing, and their eyes have they closed; lest they should see with their eyes, and hear with their ears, and understand with their heart, and should be converted, and I should heal them.

PROPHECIES IN ROMANS: 17

1. Romans 8:17:

[17] And if children, then heirs; heirs of God, and joint-heirs with Christ; if so be that we suffer with him, that we may be also glorified together.

2. Romans 8:36:

[36] As it is written, For thy sake we are killed all the day long; we are accounted as sheep for the slaughter.

3. Romans 9:7:

[7] Neither, because they are the seed of Abraham, are they all children: but, In Isaac shall thy seed be called.

4. Romans 9:25-28:

[25] As he saith also in Osee, I will call them my people, which were not my people; and her beloved, which was not beloved. [26] And it shall come to pass, that in the place where it was said unto them, Ye are not my people; there shall they be called the children of the living God. [27] Esaias also crieth concerning Israel, Though the number of the children of Israel be as the sand of the sea, a remnant shall be saved: [28] For he will finish the work, and cut it short in righteousness: because a short work will the Lord make upon the earth.

5. Romans 9:33:

[33] As it is written, Behold, I lay in Sion a stumbling-stone and rock of offence: and whosoever believeth on him shall not be ashamed.

6. Romans 10:15:

[15] And how shall they preach, except they be sent? as it is written, How beautiful are the feet of them that preach the gospel of peace, and bring glad tidings of good things!

7. Romans 10:16:

[16] But they have not all obeyed the gospel. For Esaias saith, Lord, who hath believed our report?

8. Romans 10:19.

[19] But I say, Did not Israel know? First Moses saith, I will provoke you to jealousy by them that are no people, and by a foolish nation I will anger you.

9. Romans 10:20:

[20] But Esaias is very bold, and saith, I was found of them that sought me not; I was made manifest unto them that asked not after me.

10. Romans 11:8:

[8] According as it is written, God hath given them the spirit of slumber, eyes that they should not see, and ears that they should not hear; unto this day.

11. Romans 11:9-10:

[9] And David saith, Let their table be made a snare, and a trap, and a stumblingblock, and a recompence unto them: [10] Let their eyes be darkened, that they may not see, and bow down their back alway.

12. Romans 14:10-12:

[10] But why dost thou judge thy brother? or why dost thou set at nought thy brother? for we shall all stand before the judgment seat of Christ. [11] For it is written, As I live, saith the Lord, every knee shall bow to me, and every tongue shall confess to God. [12] So then every one of us shall give account of himself to God.

13. Romans 15:3:

[3] For even Christ pleased not himself; but, as it is written, The reproaches of them that reproached thee fell on me.

14. Romans 15:9:

[9] And that the Gentiles might glorify God for his mercy; as it is written, For this cause I will confess to thee among the Gentiles, and sing unto thy name.

15. Romans 15:10-12:

[10] And again he saith, Rejoice, ye Gentiles, with his people. [11] And again, Praise the Lord, all ye Gentiles; and laud him, all ye people. [12] And again, Esaias saith, There shall be a root of Jesse, and he that shall rise to reign over the Gentiles; in him shall the Gentiles trust.

16. Romans 15:21:

[21] But as it is written, To whom he was not spoken of, they shall see: and they that have not heard shall understand.

17. Romans 16:20:

[20] And the God of peace shall bruise Satan under your feet shortly. The grace of our Lord Jesus Christ be with you. Amen.

PROPHECIES IN FIRST CORINTHIANS: 12

1. 1 Corinthians 1:7-8:

> *[7] So that ye come behind in no gift; waiting for the coming of our Lord Jesus Christ: [8] Who shall also confirm you unto the end, that ye may be blameless in the day of our Lord Jesus Christ.*

2. 1 Corinthians 1:19-20:

> *[19] For it is written, I will destroy the wisdom of the wise, and will bring to nothing the understanding of the prudent. [20] Where is the wise? where is the scribe? where is the disputer of this world? hath not God made foolish the wisdom of this world?*

3. 1 Corinthians 1:31:

> *[31] That, according as it is written, He that glorieth, let him glory in the Lord.*

4. 1 Corinthians 2:9:

> *[9] But as it is written, Eye hath not seen, nor ear heard, neither have entered into the heart of man, the things which God hath prepared for them that love him.*

5. 1 Corinthians 3:12-13:

[12] Now if any man build upon this foundation gold, silver, precious stones, wood, hay, stubble; [13] Every man's work shall be made manifest: for the day shall declare it, because it shall be revealed by fire; and the fire shall try every man's work of what sort it is.

6. 1 Corinthians 4:5:

[5] Therefore judge nothing before the time, until the Lord come, who both will bring to light the hidden things of darkness, and will make manifest the counsels of the hearts: and then shall every man have praise of God.

7. 1 Corinthians 4:8:

[8] Now ye are full, now ye are rich, ye have reigned as kings without us: and I would to God ye did reign, that we also might reign with you.

8. 1 Corinthians 6:2:

[2] Do ye not know that the saints shall judge the world? and if the world shall be judged by you, are ye unworthy to judge the smallest matters?

9. 1 Corinthians 6:9-10:

[9] Know ye not that the unrighteous shall not inherit the kingdom of God? Be not deceived: neither fornicators, nor idolaters, nor adulterers, nor effeminate, nor abusers of themselves with mankind, [10] Nor thieves, nor covetous, nor drunkards, nor revilers, nor extortioners, shall

inherit the kingdom of God.

10. 1 Corinthians 13:8:

[8] Charity never faileth: but whether there be prophe-
cies, they shall fail; whether there be tongues, they shall
cease; whether there be knowledge, it shall vanish away.

11. 1 Corinthians 14:21:

[21] In the law it is written, With men of other tongues
and other lips will I speak unto this people; and yet for all
that will they not hear me, saith the Lord.

12. 1 Corinthians 15:21-22:

[21] For since by man came death, by man came also
the resurrection of the dead. [22] For as in Adam all die,
even so in Christ shall all be made alive.

PROPHECIES IN SECOND CORINTHIANS: 6

1. 2 Corinthians 1:14:

   [14] As also ye have acknowledged us in part, that we are your rejoicing, even as ye also are ours in the day of the Lord Jesus.

2. 2 Corinthians 3:16:

   [16] Nevertheless when it shall turn to the Lord, the vail shall be taken away.

3. 2 Corinthians 4:14:

   [14] Knowing that he which raised up the Lord Jesus shall raise up us also by Jesus, and shall present us with you.

4. 2 Corinthians 5:10:

   [10] For we must all appear before the judgment seat of Christ; that every one may receive the things done in his body, according to that he hath done, whether it be good or bad.

5. 2 Corinthians 6:16-17:

   [16] And what agreement hath the temple of God with

idols? For ye are the temple of the living God; as God hath said, I will dwell in them, and walk in them; and I will be their God, and they shall be my people. [17] Wherefore come out from among them, and be ye separate, saith the Lord, and touch not the unclean thing; and I will receive you, And will be a Father unto you, and ye shall be my sons and daughters, saith the Lord Almighty.

6. 2 Corinthians 9:9-10:

[9] As it is written, He hath dispersed abroad; he hath given to the poor: his righteousness remaineth for ever. [10] Now he that ministereth seed to the sower both minister bread for your food, and multiply your seed sown, and increase the fruits of your righteousness.

PROPHECIES IN GALATIANS: 6

1. Galatians 3:8-9:

[8] And the scripture, foreseeing that God would justify the heathen through faith, preached before the gospel unto Abraham, saying, In thee shall all nations be blessed. [9] So then they which be of faith are blessed with faithful Abraham.

2. Galatians 3:11-12:

[11] But that no man is justified by the law in the sight of God, it is evident: for, The just shall live by faith. [12] And the law is not of faith: but, The man that doeth them shall live in them.

3. Galatians 3:13-14:

[13] Christ hath redeemed us from the curse of the law, being made a curse for us: for it is written, Cursed is every one that hangeth on a tree: [14] That the blessing of Abraham might come on the Gentiles through Jesus Christ; that we might receive the promise of the Spirit through faith.

4. Galatians 3:16:

[16] Now to Abraham and his seed were the promises

made. He saith not, And to seeds, as of many; but as of one, And to thy seed, which is Christ.

5. Galatians 5:21:

[21] Envyings, murders, drunkenness, revellings, and such like: of the which I tell you before, as I have also told you in time past, that they which do such things shall not inherit the kingdom of God.

6. Galatians 6:7:

[7] Be not deceived; God is not mocked: for whatsoever a man soweth, that shall he also reap.

PROPHECIES IN EPHESIANS: 8

1. Ephesians 1:10-11:

[10] That in the dispensation of the fulness of times he might gather together in one all things in Christ, both which are in heaven, and which are on earth; even in him: [11] In whom also we have obtained an inheritance, being predestinated according to the purpose of him who worketh all things after the counsel of his own will: [12] That we should be to the praise of his glory, who first trusted in Christ.

2. Ephesians 1:21-23:

[21] Far above all principality, and power, and might, and dominion, and every name that is named, not only in this world, but also in that which is to come: [22] And hath put all things under his feet, and gave him to be the head over all things to the church, [23] Which is his body, the fulness of him that filleth all in all.

3. Ephesians 2:7:

[7] That in the ages to come he might shew the exceeding riches of his grace in his kindness toward us through Christ Jesus.

4. Ephesians 3:20-21:

[20] Now unto him that is able to do exceeding abundantly above all that we ask or think, according to the power that worketh in us, [21] Unto him be glory in the church by Christ Jesus throughout all ages, world without end. Amen.

5. Ephesians 4:8:

[8] Wherefore he saith, When he ascended up on high, he led captivity captive, and gave gifts unto men.

6. Ephesians 4:12-16:

[12] For the perfecting of the saints, for the work of the ministry, for the edifying of the body of Christ: [13] Till we all come in the unity of the faith, and of the knowledge of the Son of God, unto a perfect man, unto the measure of the stature of the fulness of Christ: [14] That we henceforth be no more children, tossed to and fro, and carried about with every wind of doctrine, by the sleight of men, and cunning craftiness, whereby they lie in wait to deceive; [15] But speaking the truth in love, may grow up into him in all things, which is the head, even Christ: [16] From whom the whole body fitly joined together and compacted by that which every joint supplieth, according to the effectual working in the measure of every part, maketh increase of the body unto the edifying of itself in love.

7. Ephesians 5:5:

[5] For this ye know, that no whoremonger, nor unclean person, nor covetous man, who is an idolater, hath any inheritance in the kingdom of Christ and of God.

8. Ephesians 5:27:

[27] That he might present it to himself a glorious church, not having spot, or wrinkle, or any such thing; but that it should be holy and without blemish.

PROPHECIES IN PHILIPPIANS: 3

1. Philippians 1:6-7:

[6] Being confident of this very thing, that he which hath begun a good work in you will perform it until the day of Jesus Christ: [7] Even as it is meet for me to think this of you all, because I have you in my heart; inasmuch as both in my bonds, and in the defence and confirmation of the gospel, ye all are partakers of my grace.

2. Philippians 2:10-11:

[10] That at the name of Jesus every knee should bow, of things in heaven, and things in earth, and things under the earth; [11] And that every tongue should confess that Jesus Christ is Lord, to the glory of God the Father.

3. Philippians 3:21:

[21] Who shall change our vile body, that it may be fashioned like unto his glorious body, according to the working whereby he is able even to subdue all things unto himself.

PROPHECIES IN COLOSSIANS: 2

1. Colossians 3:4:

   [4] When Christ, who is our life, shall appear, then shall ye also appear with him in glory.

2. Colossians 3:24:

   [24] Knowing that of the Lord ye shall receive the reward of the inheritance: for ye serve the Lord Christ.

PROPHECIES IN FIRST THESSALONIANS: 2

1. 1 Thes salonians 1:10:

> *[10] And to wait for his Son from heaven, whom he raised from the dead, even Jesus, which delivered us from the wrath to come.*

2. 1 Thessalonians 2:19:

> *[19] For what is our hope, or joy, or crown of rejoicing? Are not even ye in the presence of our Lord Jesus Christ at his coming?*

PROPHECIES IN SECOND THESSALONIANS: 2

1. 2 Thessalonians 1:7-10:

[7] And to you who are troubled rest with us, when the Lord Jesus shall be revealed from heaven with his mighty angels, [8] In flaming fire taking vengeance on them that know not God, and that obey not the gospel of our Lord Jesus Christ: [9] Who shall be punished with everlasting destruction from the presence of the Lord, and from the glory of his power; [10] When he shall come to be glorified in his saints, and to be admired in all them that believe (because our testimony among you was believed) in that day.

2. 2 Thessalonians 2:1-2:

[1] Now we beseech you, brethren, by the coming of our Lord Jesus Christ, and by our gathering together unto him, [2] That ye be not soon shaken in mind, or be troubled, neither by spirit, nor by word, nor by letter as from us, as that the day of Christ is at hand.

PROPHECIES IN FIRST TIMOTHY: 2

1. 1 Timothy 4:1-3:

[1] Now the Spirit speaketh expressly, that in the latter times some shall depart from the faith, giving heed to seducing spirits, and doctrines of devils; [2] Speaking lies in hypocrisy; having their conscience seared with a hot iron; [3] Forbidding to marry, and commanding to abstain from meats, which God hath created to be received with thanksgiving of them which believe and know the truth.

2. 1 Timothy 6:14-16:

[14] That thou keep this commandment without spot, unrebukeable, until the appearing of our Lord Jesus Christ: [15] Which in his times he shall shew, who is the blessed and only Potentate, the King of kings, and Lord of lords; [16] Who only hath immortality, dwelling in the light which no man can approach unto; whom no man hath seen, nor can see: to whom be honour and power everlasting. Amen.

PROPHECIES IN SECOND TIMOTHY: 7

1. 2 Timothy 2:11-13:

[11] It is a faithful saying: For if we be dead with him, we shall also live with him: [12] If we suffer, we shall also reign with him: if we deny him, he also will deny us: [13] If we believe not, yet he abideth faithful: he cannot deny himself.

2. 2 Timothy 3:1-5:

[1] This know also, that in the last days perilous times shall come. [2] For men shall be lovers of their own selves, covetous, boasters, proud, blasphemers, disobedient to parents, unthankful, unholy, [3] Without natural affection, trucebreakers, false accusers, incontinent, fierce, despisers of those that are good, [4] Traitors, heady, highminded, lovers of pleasures more than lovers of God; [5] Having a form of godliness, but denying the power thereof: from such turn away.

3. 2 Timothy 3:12:

[12] Yea, and all that will live godly in Christ Jesus shall suffer persecution.
But evil men and seducers shall wax worse and worse, deceiving, and being deceived.

4. 2 Timothy 4:1-2:

[1] I charge thee therefore before God, and the Lord Jesus Christ, who shall judge the quick and the dead at his appearing and his kingdom : [2] Preach the word; be instant in season, out of season; reprove, rebuke, exhort with all longsuffering and doctrine.

5. 2 Timothy 4:3:

[3] For the time will come when they will not endure sound doctrine; but after their own lusts shall they heap to themselves teachers, having itching ears;

6. 2 Timothy 4:8:

[8] Henceforth there is laid up for me a crown of righteousness, which the Lord, the righteous judge, shall give me at that day: and not to me only, but unto all them also that love his appearing.

7. 2 Timothy 4:18:

[18] And the Lord shall deliver me from every evil work, and will preserve me unto his heavenly kingdom: to whom be glory for ever and ever. Amen.

PROPHECIES IN TITUS: 1

Titus 2:13-14:

> *[13] Looking for that blessed hope, and the glorious appearing of the great God and our Saviour Jesus Christ; [14] Who gave himself for us, that he might redeem us from all iniquity, and purify unto himself a peculiar people, zealous of good works.*

PROPHECIES IN HEBREWS: 19

1. Hebrews 1:5-6:

*[5] For unto which of the angels said he at any time,
Thou art my Son, this day have I begotten thee? And
again, I will be to him a Father, and he shall be to me a
Son? [6] And again, when he bringeth in the firstbegot-
ten into the world, he saith, And let all the angels of God
worship him.*

2. Hebrews 1:8:

*[8] But unto the Son he saith, Thy throne, O God, is for
ever and ever: a sceptre of righteousness is the sceptre of
thy kingdom.*

3. Hebrews 1:10-11:

*[10] And, Thou, Lord, in the beginning hast laid the
foundation of the earth; and the heavens are the works
of thine hands: [11] They shall perish; but thou remainest; and they all shall wax old as doth a garment; And
as a vesture shalt thou fold them up, and they shall be
changed: but thou art the same, and thy years shall not
fail.*

4 Hebrews 1:13:

[13] But to which of the angels said he at any time, Sit on

my right hand, until I make thine enemies thy footstool?

5. Hebrews 2:6:

[6] But one in a certain place testified, saying, What is man, that thou art mindful of him? Or the son of man, that thou visitest him?

6. Hebrews 2:12-13:

[12] Saying, I will declare thy name unto my brethren, in the midst of the church will I sing praise unto thee. And again, I will put my trust in him. [13] And again, Behold I and the children which God hath given me.

7. Hebrews 3:7-11:

[7] Wherefore as the Holy Ghost saith, To day if ye will hear his voice, [8] Harden not your hearts, as in the provocation, in the day of temptation in the wilderness: [9] When your fathers tempted me, proved me, and saw my works forty years. [10] Wherefore I was grieved with that generation, and said, They do I err in their heart; and they have not known my ways[11] . So I sware in my wrath, They shall not enter into my rest.

8. Hebrews 4:7:

[7] Again, he limiteth a certain day, saying in David, To day, after so long a time; as it is said, To day if ye will hear his voice, harden not your hearts………….. Psalm95:7

9. Hebrews 5:5:

*[5] So also Christ glorified not himself to be made an
high priest; but he that said unto him, Thou art my Son, to
day have I begotten thee.*

10. Hebrews 5:6:

*[6] As he saith also in another place, Thou art a priest
for ever after the order of Melchisedec.*

11. Hebrews 6:14:

*[14] Saying, Surely blessing I will bless thee, and multi-
plying I will multiply thee……Gen 22:17*

12. Hebrews 8:8:

*[8] For finding fault with them, he saith, Behold, the days
come, saith the Lord, when I will make a new covenant
with the house of Israel and with the house of Judah:*

13. Hebrews 10:5-6:

*[5] Wherefore when he cometh into the world, he saith,
Sacrifice and offering thou wouldest not, but a body hast
thou prepared me: [6] In burnt offerings and sacrifices
for sin thou hast had no pleasure.*

14. Hebrews 10:16-17:

*[16] This is the covenant that I will make with them after
those days, saith the Lord, I will put my laws into their*

hearts, and in their minds will I write them; [17] And
their sins and iniquities will I remember no more.

15. Hebrews 10:26-27:

[26] For if we sin wilfully after that we have received
the knowledge of the truth, there remaineth no more
sacrifice for sins, [27] But a certain fearful looking for
of judgment and fiery indignation, which shall devour the
adversaries.

16. Hebrews 10:30-31:

[30] For we know him that hath said, Vengeance be-
longeth unto me, I will recompense, saith the Lord. And
again, The Lord shall judge his people. [31] It is a fearful
thing to fall into the hands of the living God.

17. Hebrews 10:37:

[37] For yet a little while, and he that shall come will
come, and will not tarry.

18. Hebrews 11:18-19:

[18] Of whom it was said, That in Isaac shall thy seed be
called: [19] Accounting that God was able to raise him
up, even from the dead; from whence also he received him
in a figure.

19. Hebrews 12:26-27:

*[26] Whose voice then shook the earth: but now he hath
promised, saying, Yet once more I shake not the earth
only, but also heaven. [27] And this word, Yet once more,
signifieth the removing of those things that are shaken, as
of things that are made, that those things which cannot be
shaken may remain.*

PROPHECIES IN JAMES: 1

James 5:1-8:

[1] Go to now, ye rich men, weep and howl for your miseries that shall come upon you. [2] Your riches are corrupted, and your garments are motheaten. [3] Your gold and silver is cankered; and the rust of them shall be a witness against you, and shall eat your flesh as it were fire. Ye have heaped treasure together for the last days. [4] Behold, the hire of the labourers who have reaped down your fields, which is of you kept back by fraud, crieth: and the cries of them which have reaped are entered into the ears of the Lord of sabaoth. [5] Ye have lived in pleasure on the earth, and been wanton; ye have nourished your hearts, as in a day of slaughter. [6] Ye have condemned and killed the just; and he doth not resist you. [7] Be patient therefore, brethren, unto the coming of the Lord. Behold, the husbandman waiteth for the precious fruit of the earth, and hath long patience for it, until he receive the early and latter rain. [8] Be ye also patient; stablish your hearts: for the coming of the Lord draweth nigh.

PROPHECIES IN FIRST PETER: 10

1. 1 Peter 1:4-5:

[4] To an inheritance incorruptible, and undefiled, and that fadeth not away, reserved in heaven for you, [5] Who are kept by the power of God through faith unto salvation ready to be revealed in the last time.

2. 1 Peter 1:7-9:

[7] That the trial of your faith, being much more precious than of gold that perisheth, though it be tried with fire, might be found unto praise and honour and glory at the appearing of Jesus Christ: [8] Whom having not seen, ye love; in whom, though now ye see him not, yet believing, ye rejoice with joy unspeakable and full of glory: [8] Receiving the end of your faith, even the salvation of your souls.

3. 1 Peter 1:13-16:

[13] Wherefore gird up the loins of your mind, be sober, and hope to the end for the grace that is to be brought unto you at the revelation of Jesus Christ; [14] As obedient children, not fashioning yourselves according to the former lusts in your ignorance: [15] But as he which hath called you is holy, so be ye holy in all manner of conversation; [16] Because it is written, Be ye holy; for I am holy.

4. 1 Peter 1:24-25:

[24] For all flesh is as grass, and all the glory of man as the flower of grass. The grass withereth, and the flower thereof falleth away: [25] But the word of the Lord endureth for ever. And this is the word which by the gospel is preached unto you.

5. 1 Peter 2:6-8:

[6] Wherefore also it is contained in the scripture, Behold, I lay in Sion a chief corner stone, elect, precious: and he that believeth on him shall not be confounded. [7] Unto you therefore which believe he is precious: but unto them which be disobedient, the stone which the builders disallowed, the same is made the head of the corner, [8] And a stone of stumbling, and a rock of offence, even to them which stumble at the word, being disobedient: whereunto also they were appointed.

7. 1 Peter 2:9-10:

[9] But ye are a chosen generation, a royal priesthood, an holy nation, a peculiar people; that ye should shew forth the praises of him who hath called you out of darkness into his marvellous light: [10] Which in time past were not a people, but are now the people of God: which had not obtained mercy, but now have obtained mercy.

8. 1 Peter 2:22-23:

[22] Who did no sin, neither was guile found in his

mouth: [23] Who, when he was reviled, reviled not again; when he suffered, he threatened not; but committed himself to him that judgeth righteously: Who his own self bare our sins in his own body on the tree, that we, being dead to sins, should live unto righteousness: by whose stripes ye were healed.

9. 1 Peter 4:5-6:

[5] Who shall give account to him that is ready to judge the quick and the dead. [6] For for this cause was the gospel preached also to them that are dead, that they might be judged according to men in the flesh, but live according to God in the spirit.

10. 1 Peter 4:13:

[13] But rejoice, inasmuch as ye are partakers of Christ's sufferings; that, when his glory shall be revealed, ye may be glad also with exceeding joy.

PROPHECIES IN SECOND PETER: 7

1. 2 Peter 1:11:

[11] For so an entrance shall be ministered unto you abundantly into the everlasting kingdom of our Lord and Saviour Jesus Christ.

2. 2 Peter 1:19-20:

[19] We have also a more sure word of prophecy; whereunto ye do well that ye take heed, as unto a light that shineth in a dark place, until the day dawn, and the day star arise in your hearts: [20] Knowing this first, that no prophecy of the scripture is of any private interpretation.

3. 2 Peter 2:1:

[1] But there were false prophets also among the people, even as there shall be false teachers among you, who privily shall bring in damnable heresies, even denying the Lord that bought them, and bring upon themselves swift destruction.

4. 2 Peter 2:9-10:

[9] The Lord knoweth how to deliver the godly out of temptations, and to reserve the unjust unto the day of judgment to be punished: [10] But chiefly them that walk after the flesh in the lust of uncleanness, and despise gov-

ernment. Presumptuous are they, selfwilled, they are not afraid to speak evil of dignities.

5. 2 Peter 3:3-4:

[3] Knowing this first, that there shall come in the last days scoffers, walking after their own lusts, [4] And saying, Where is the promise of his coming? for since the fathers fell asleep, all things continue as they were from the beginning of the creation.

6. 2 Peter 3:7:

[7] But the heavens and the earth, which are now, by the same word are kept in store, reserved unto fire against the day of judgment and perdition of ungodly men.

7. 2 Peter 3:10:

[10] But the day of the Lord will come as a thief in the night; in the which the heavens shall pass away with a great noise, and the elements shall melt with fervent heat, the earth also and the works that are therein shall be burned up.

PROPHECIES IN FIRST JOHN: 5

1. 1 John 2:17:

> *[17] And the world passeth away, and the lust thereof: but he that doeth the will of God abideth for ever.*

2. 1 John 2:18:

> *[18] Little children, it is the last time: and as ye have heard that antichrist shall come, even now are there many antichrists; whereby we know that it is the last time.*

3. 1 John 2:28:

> *[28] And now, little children, abide in him; that, when he shall appear, we may have confidence, and not be ashamed before him at his coming.*

4. 1 John 3:2:

> *[2] Beloved, now are we the sons of God, and it doth not yet appear what we shall be: but we know that, when he shall appear, we shall be like him; for we shall see him as he is.*

5. 1 John 4:17:

> *[17] Herein is our love made perfect, that we may have boldness in the day of judgment: because as he is, so are we in this world.*

PROPHECIES IN JUDE: 2

1. Jude 1:14-15:

[14] And Enoch also, the seventh from Adam, prophesied of these, saying, Behold, the Lord cometh with ten thousands of his saints, [15] To execute judgment upon all, and to convince all that are ungodly among them of all their ungodly deeds which they have ungodly committed, and of all their hard speeches which ungodly sinners have spoken against him.

2. Jude 1:18:

[18] How that they told you there should be mockers in the last time, who should walk after their own ungodly lusts.

PROPHECIES IN REVELATION: 13

1. Revelation 1:6-7:

[6] And hath made us kings and priests unto God and his Father; to him be glory and dominion for ever and ever. Amen. [7] Behold, he cometh with clouds; and every eye shall see him, and they also which pierced him: and all kindreds of the earth shall wail because of him. Even so, Amen.

2. Revelation 2:5:

[5] Remember therefore from whence thou art fallen, and repent, and do the first works; or else I will come unto thee quickly, and will remove thy candlestick out of his place, except thou repent.

3. Revelation 2:7:

[7] He that hath an ear, let him hear what the Spirit saith unto the churches; To him that overcometh will I give to eat of the tree of life, which is in the midst of the paradise of God.

4. Revelation 2:10:

[10] Fear none of those things which thou shalt suffer: behold, the devil shall cast some of you into prison, that ye may be tried; and ye shall have tribulation ten days:

*be thou faithful unto death, and I will give thee a crown
of life.*

5. Revelation 2:16-17:

*[16] Repent; or else I will come unto thee quickly, and
will fight against them with the sword of my mouth. [17]
He that hath an ear, let him hear what the Spirit saith
unto the churches; To him that overcometh will I give
to eat of the hidden manna, and will give him a white
stone, and in the stone a new name written, which no man
knoweth saving he that receiveth it.*

6. Revelation 2:22-23:

*[22] Behold, I will cast her into a bed, and them that
commit adultery with her into great tribulation, except
they repent of their deeds. [23] And I will kill her children
with death; and all the churches shall know that I am he
which searcheth the reins and hearts: and I will give unto
every one of you according to your works.*

7. Revelation 2:25:

[25] But that which ye have already hold fast till I come.

8. Revelation 3:3:

*[3] Remember therefore how thou hast received and
heard, and hold fast, and repent. If therefore thou shalt
not watch, I will come on thee as a thief, and thou shalt
not know what hour I will come upon thee.*

9. Revelation 3:9:

[9] Behold, I will make them of the synagogue of Satan, which say they are Jews, and are not, but do lie; behold, I will make them to come and worship before thy feet, and to know that I have loved thee.

10. Revelation 3:16:

[16] So then because thou art lukewarm, and neither cold nor hot, I will spue thee out of my mouth.

11. Revelation 3:20:

[20] Behold, I stand at the door, and knock: if any man hear my voice, and open the door, I will come in to him, and will sup with him, and he with me.

12. Revelation 4:1:

[1] After this I looked, and, behold, a door was opened in heaven: and the first voice which I heard was as it were of a trumpet talking with me; which said, Come up hither, and I will shew thee things which must be hereafter.

13. Revelation 22:10-12:

[10] And he saith unto me, Seal not the sayings of the prophecy of this book: for the time is at hand. [11] He that is unjust, let him be unjust still: and he which is filthy, let him be filthy still: and he that is righteous, let him be righteous still: and he that is holy, let him be holy

still. [12] And, behold, I come quickly; and my reward is with me, to give every man according as his work shall be.

13. Revelation 22:14:

[14] Blessed are they that do his commandments, that they may have right to the tree of life, and may enter in through the gates into the city.

14. Revelation 22:18-19:

[18] For I testify unto every man that heareth the words of the prophecy of this book, If any man shall add unto these things, God shall add unto him the plagues that are written in this book: [19] And if any man shall take away from the words of the book of this prophecy, God shall take away his part out of the book of life, and out of the holy city, and from the things which are written in this book.

9 781637 696347